CW00361908

The Shambles, York (see p. 142).

Discovering Yorkshire's History

A Guide to Places & People

Len Markham

Wharncliffe Books

First published in Great Britain in 2004 by
Wharncliffe Books
an imprint of
Pen & Sword Books Ltd
47 Church Street
Barnsley
South Yorkshire
S70 2AS

ISBN 1-903425-73-5

A CIP catalogue record for this book is
available from the British Library

Printed and bound in England by
CPI UK

For a complete list of Wharncliffe titles, please contact
Wharncliffe Books Limited
47 Church Street, Barnsley, South Yorkshire, S70 2AS, England
E-mail: enquiries@pen-and-sword.co.uk
Website: www.wharncliffebooks.co.uk

Contents

Introduction

Yorkshire, independent and inimitable; the biggest and the most interesting county in England. This famous land of the Tykes has helped shape our nation, over the centuries, from the Pennines in the west to the towering chalky bastion of Flamborough Head in the east, the broad acres providing a national lexicon of war, insurrection, invention, industrial expansion, political and social development and pioneering achievements in literature, art and science.

In over 50 years of exploring Yorkshire on foot, I have come across a host of places that are forever imbued by history, the smoke of glorious victories and the odours of dark deeds alike raising the pulse rate and rousing the mind to remember. The wizened old bones of history can, however, be the most unappetising of dishes, most academic annals leaving the average reader bored and listless. But I hope to change all that.

This is no conventional history book. There are no tired recitations and limp lists of dates and dynasties in these pages. In this delightfully atmospheric rampage through past times, only my inquisitive nose has been my guide. Uninhibited, free from the strictures of themes and epochs, I have wandered through the centuries, making an eclectic choice of subjects. Most of these are well known; some less so. One topic sees the light of day for the first time. All the subjects receive my own highly individual treatment. Unusual perhaps, but, I hope, never boring.

In this very personal search, a search that is regularly punctuated with humour, I will take you across the county and across the years, showing you the more obvious historical sites and a number of other secret places that have previously escaped the attention of the professors. Along the way we will meet monarchs, archbishops, generals, industrialists, scientists, inventors, authors, renegades, rogues, eccentrics, murderers and plain ordinary working men and women.

An unusual wall plaque on a house in Snaith.

For convenience, I have divided the topics geographically into the five constituent parts of the county, clustering the entries so that visitors can maximise their enjoyment. Where appropriate, at the bottom of each page, I have also shown the surprisingly common relationships between entries, numbered pointers showing the linkages.

This historical journey demands a certain amount of imagination, but in nearly every case, there is some interpretation board, plaque, ruin, mound, gravestone, commemorative cross, relic or structure on the ground to set the cerebral time machine spinning into reverse. In some cases, historical sites have been incorporated into museums and visitor centres, organisations such as the National Trust and English Heritage providing a wealth of information for visitors.

I must say again that this is no ordinary history book. It must ***not*** gather dust. Mine is a search for the tactile and the sensory and, with the book firmly in your grasp as a guide, you must accompany me in confronting the past, visiting the sites to immerse yourself in an uncommon historical experience. There can be something immensely fascinating and emotionally stimulating in seeking to empathise with people who made history, their stories making your blood race and your scalp tingle. So prepare yourself for an interesting, entertaining and sometimes nerve jangling roller-coaster ride into history … and join me … ***discovering Yorkshire's history.***

Len Markham

North Yorkshire

1 to 65

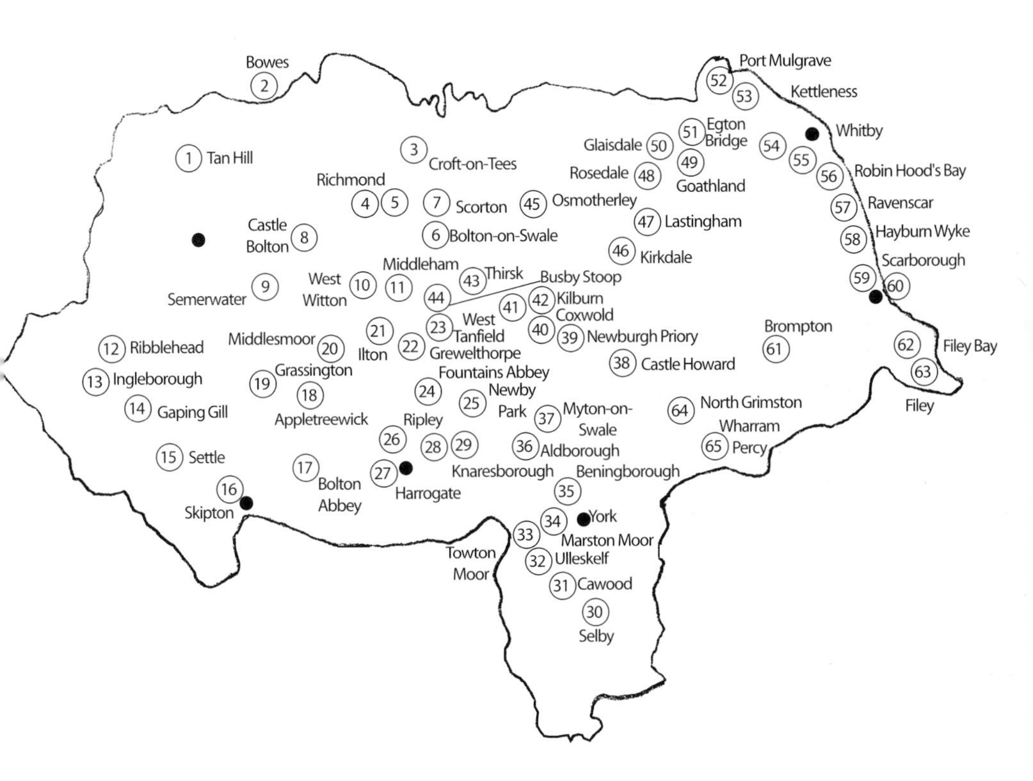

If Yorkshire has more acres than the Bible has words, most of them are in the old North Riding, its vast landmass encompassing parts of the Pennines, the limestone Dales, the Vale of York, the North York Moors and a hundred mile stretch of the East coast. Geographically diverse, the county has witnessed monumental events in English history, the clash of Brigantian, Roman and Viking swords echoing down the centuries. Other armies have also shed their life-blood here, internal strife, plunder, accidents, murders and executions adding to a gory list of events that will have you reaching for the salts! But it's not all thrust and guts. Follow me to Richmond and find a fortune in gold. Let me lead you to the most breathtaking garden in the world, and have a drink on me in the highest and most characterful pub in England.

WENSLEYDALE COURIER – 12th OCTOBER 1568

MARY STUART CAPTURED AFTER DRAMATIC ESCAPE BID

The whole dale has been alive this week to rumours of the Scottish Queen's dash for freedom. This journal can confirm that, assisted by loyal servants, she broke out from Bolton Castle on Wednesday last, making a desperate escape from her long incarceration. Happily, the fugitive was overtaken and apprehended on Leyburn Shawl.

UREDALE TRIBUNE – 5th FEBRUARY 1869

SIX DIE DURING FOXHUNT

Foxhunting has been suspended in the area following the tragic death yesterday of six members of the York and Ainsty Hunt. Sir Charles Slingsby of Scriven Park was the most prominent casualty of a tragic accident that occured while a group of huntsman and horses were attempting to cross the swollen waters of the Ure on a ferry.

1. TAN HILL: ONE FOR THE STRODE

The famous Tan Hill Inn has saved more lives than the St Bernard dog. The highest licensed premises in the country at an altitude of 1732 feet, this dot, on the line of the Pennine Way, surveys an ocean of emptiness, looking north to a wilderness, 'rock-ribbed and as ancient as the sun.'

On the route of an ancient pack-horse trail, the inn has served countless travellers over the years, customers also coming from the long defunct coalmines that once littered the surrounding moors. Being the only building for miles, the inn was also a popular meeting point. Weddings and boxing matches were also held here.

The Tan Hill Inn at Tan Hill.

Seen from afar on the all too frequent squally days that besiege this wilderness, the inn merges with the landscape, defiant smoke intermingling with cloud and dribbling on a canvas sodden with rain. Not to worry. The coal fires blaze 365 days a year at the redoubtable Tan Hill, benighted travellers thanking heaven for yard thick walls. But beware. In the past, some people marooned in the unique inn have greeted their first New Year's visitors in March!

Directions: *The Tan Hill Inn is at the far-flung northern boundary of the Yorkshire Dales National Park. All routes to this isolated inn are potentially problematical, especially in bad weather. The easiest access from the south is via the minor road from Reeth, passing through Arkengarthdale – about 14 miles. From the north, leave the A 66 at Maiden Castle and take the winding moorland road generally south –east for about eight miles. Map Landranger 92 – Grid Ref: 896067.*

2. BOWES: DOUREST DOTHEBOYS

In his search for atmosphere and authenticity, Charles Dickens braved the vilest places, opium dens, prisons, workhouses, slums and dark satanic mills, all came under his scrutiny. In writing his novel, Nicholas Nickelby, the author vowed to seek out and expose the iniquities of private schools. So where did he come? He came to Bowes in the wilds of Yorkshire, seeking out a man who had been denounced in court for routinely allowing boys in his care to go blind through lack of nutrition and medical attention.

Shivering Bowes lies at a northerly outpost of Yorkshire in an upland redoubt that is all sky and peat, the great moors of Stainmore, Cotherstone and Scargill closing in on the village like wolves. Several days' carriage ride from major centres of population, Bowes had all the assets for developing young minds, its perpetual cold, spartan diets, scouring winds that muffled the cries of despair and anguish and a number of tyrannical headmasters, marking it out as a popular choice for parents. One of the village's more typical establishments was the infamous Bowes Academy, its reputation attracting the curious Dickens in the winter of 1838.

The Ancient Unicorn at Bowes.

Renamed Dotheboys Hall in the novel ('Terms twenty guineas per annum. No extras, no vacation, and diet unparalleled ...'), the academy was run by a man called William Shaw, this inspiration for Wackford Squeers rebuffing Dickens and refusing to escort him round his school. But Dickens had met the pedagogue and had 'taken his mental portrait' scribbling down a description that still sends a shiver down the spine: 'He had but one eye, and the popular prejudice runs in favour of two. The eye he had was unquestionably useful, but decidedly not ornamental: being of a greenish grey, and in shape resembling the fan-light of a street door. The blank side of his face was much wrinkled and puckered up, which gave him a very sinister appearance, especially when he smiled, at which times his expression bordered closely on the villainous.'

Directions: *Just off the A166 between Scotch Corner and Appleby, Bowes has hardly altered since Dickens' time. You can visit the front parlour of the imposing Ancient Unicorn where he 'baited' after setting out for his confrontation with Shaw and you can walk to the end of the street to view the old academy that has since assumed the name of Dotheboys Hall. Opposite the inn is the churchyard, a careful inspection (roadside in the nave/transept corner) revealing the grave of William Shaw. Nearby is another sight that tugged at the author's pen, the grave of 19-year-old George Ashton Taylor who 'died suddenly at Mr William Shaw's Academy' prompting Dickens to write: 'I think his ghost put Smike into my mind, upon the spot.' Map Landranger 92 – Map Ref: 995136 (Ancient Unicorn – turn right 250 yards to Dotheboys Hall).*

3. CROFT-ON-TEES: WHITE RABBITS AND THE FRUMIOUS BANDERSNATCH

The author of two of the most inventive and best-loved childrens' books in the English language, was inspired by Yorkshire. As the son of a rector, Lewis Carroll, whose real name was Charles Lutwidge Dodgson, spent much of his early life in Croft, its church of St Peter's, with its remarkable tombs, carvings of animals, gargoyles (and pompous preachers!) providing a vast repository of images which later surfaced in his books *Alice's Adventures in Wonderland* and *Through the Looking Glass.*

One of 11 children, the impressionable and whimsical boy of 11 came to Croft in 1843. Shortly afterwards he attended a school in nearby Richmond, later going to Rugby and Oxford academies, teaching at the latter institution as a mathematical lecturer for 26 years. Throughout those years, he developed a remarkable rapport with children, writing his best-known fantasy for his young friend Alice Liddell. During the long years of absence, he made repeated visits back to his beloved northern home.

The rambling rectory at Croft was his playground. He constructed an ingenious toy railway in its garden and invented all sorts of strange games in its rooms, recording some of his more outlandish fantasies in home-produced magazines.

In the 1940s, Croft rectory underwent alteration, the removal of floorboards in what was believed to have been the old nursery in the attic, revealing playthings that might have belonged to the author. The discoveries included part of a child's tea –set – 'The March Hare took the watch and looked at it gloomily: then he dipped it into his cup of tea, and looked at it again …' – a small leather shoe, a pair of child's gloves and several mysterious scribbles on paper and wood. Close by, in a young hand, the scratched initials C.L.D. were found on a window-pane.

Directions: *Croft-on-Tees is south of Darlington, about six miles north-east of Scotch Corner (A1) via Middleton Tyas. Croft Rectory and St Peter's Church are in the centre of the village. Inside the church is a memorial to Carroll whose literary invention must have been inspired by the outrageously pompous and presumptuous Milbanke Pews and the earth-cracking bulk of two tomb chests. Next to the church is an ancient bridge over the Tees. On this bridge, the*

Charles Lutwidge Dodgson (Lewis Caroll), native of Croft-on-Tees.

The old rectory at Croft-on-Tees.

Bishop Prince of Durham was ceremoniously presented with a falchion (a curved sword). This weapon was supposed to have been used to slay the notorious Sockburn Worm (village to the south-east) a type of dragon that once terrorised the area:

He took his vorpal sword in hand:
Long time the manxome foe he sought-
So rested he by the Tumtum tree,
And stood awhile in thought.
And as in uffish thought he stood,
The Jabberwock, with eyes of flame,
Came whiffling through the tulgye wood,
And burbled as it came!
One, two! One two! And through and through
The vorpal blade went snicker – snack!
And left it dead, and with its head
He went galumphing back.

Directions: *Map Landranger 93 – Grid Refs: 289098 (Croft Rectory and St Peter's Church); 290098 (Croft bridge).*

4. RICHMOND: GOLD BRUSH

It's a complete fiction of course, but I defy you not to look for King Arthur's treasure. Concealed, so the legend goes, in a subterranean palace beneath the ramparts of Richmond Castle, it has been disturbed only once in all history, one Potter Thompson finding the loot but rushing home empty handed – stupid boy!

A shy and lonely child, Potter Thompson spent long hours wandering along the banks of the River Swale. One day, he noticed a recent rock fall beneath the castle walls. Intrigued, he ventured into a newly opened cave and was astonished at the sight. There before him was King Arthur and his entire knightly court – all asleep. On the famous Round Table in front of the King was a mound of gold, a magic horn and a jewel-encrusted sword. Shaking with fright and peering through the dusty light, Potter ventured out a hand and grabbed the weapon. There upon, one of the knights stretched himself and blinked, uttering the words: 'Is it time?' Panic-stricken, Potter dropped the sword and turned to run, a loud sepulchral voice booming after him:

Potter Thompson, Potter Thompson,
If thou hadst either drawn the sword or blown the horn,
Thou'd been the luckiest man that ever yet was born.

Returning home to his mother, Potter told his incredible tale, returning next day to find the cave, but it had vanished in the night.

Directions: *Richmond is about five miles south-west of Scotch Corner via the A6108. According to my own detailed research and surveys (although I could be lying to put you off the scent) King Arthur's long lost vault is on the river side of the castle mound about 75 yards below the curtain wall. English Heritage, who own the pile, dissuade all visitors from undermining its walls, strongly censoring the use of metal detectors, JCBs, boring machines and explosives. Map Landranger 92: Grid Ref: 172006 (Richmond Castle).*

5. RICHMOND: CURTAIN UP

A Tom Thumb of a building, the Georgian Theatre Royal should jump up and take a bow. Built in 1788, it is one of the oldest and best preserved theatrical gems in the country, its near perfect proscenium and ground floor boxes and upper boxes supported on Tuscan columns, giving it the intimacy and electricity of a boudoir. The ancient boards, which were strode by such distinguished actors as Shakespearian master Edmund Kean and John Philip Kemble, a tragedian who became a member of the famous York group of players in 1778, are still in use today, although for a while the theatre was threatened with oblivion.

In the intervening war years, it suffered the ignominy of becoming a warehouse and a salvage dump. Rescued in 1943 by an enthusiastic band of local people, it was re –opened on the 850th anniversary of the borough, one proud Richmond man describing it thus: 'It's a round sort of place with the stage sunk in a kind of pit, and there's a gallery on pillars, and the space below partitioned off in boxes where the big noises used to sit, some of them with coats of arms on the front panels. And in the ceiling are holes through which they used to pull up the lights – candelabra – during the acts.'

The theatre has a small museum displaying a unique collection of original playbills and the oldest and largest complete set of painted scenery in Britain.

Directions: *Richmond is about five miles south-west of Scotch Corner via the A6108. The Georgian Theatre Royal, whose museum is open between March and October, is on Victoria Road adjacent to the Fleece Hotel. Map Landranger 92 – Grid Ref: 171010.*

6. BOLTON-ON-SWALE: THE YORKSHIRE METHUSELAH

This sleepy little village in North Yorkshire should have been the spa capital of Europe, the waters of Harrogate ranking as poison compared to the remarkable elixirs of the Swale. For how else can you account for the incredible longevity of the local inhabitants, the geriatric hall of fame including several centenarians and one fellow of an astounding 169 years?

Henry Jenkins claimed to have been born in a neighbouring village in 1500, and to have lived through the reigns of eight monarchs – Henry VII, Henry VIII, Edward VI, Mary, Elizabeth I, James I and Charles I. A poor, illiterate salmon fisherman and farm labourer who regularly imbibed of the Swale, Henry exploited his phenomenal powers of memory and celebrity status by telling tall tales. As a confidant of the Abbot of Fountains Abbey, he boasted of boozy monastic sprees recounting memories of the Dissolution: 'When the order came to Yorkshire, great lamentation was made, and the country all in tumult when the monks were turned out.'

Jenkin's earliest recollection, as an eight or 10 year old boy (a touch of senility might just have crept in) was of a journey to Northallerton in charge of a horse- load of arrows intended for the Earl of Surrey. The arrows were fired at the Scots at Flodden Field in 1513! These and other details of his early life were recounted to Anne Saville in 1661 or 1662 with great historical accuracy (he couldn't read?) and passed on in a letter to the Society of Antiquities in London in 1766. Another document also

The monument to Henry Jenkins at Bolton-On-Swale.

gives some veracity to Jenkin's claims. Among a clutch of papers known as 'Depositions in Chancery', is an affidavit referring to 'Henry Jenkins of Ellerton-upon-Swale in the County of Yorke, labourer, aged one hundred and fifty seaven or theirabouts, sworne and examined.'

Jenkin's died in 1670, an obelisk being raised to his memory by public subscription in 1743.

Directions: *Bolton-on-Swale is on the B 6271 just east of Catterick and the A1. The memorial to Henry Jenkins is in St Mary's churchyard. In the church is a long epitaph composed by Dr Thomas Chapman. The Henry Jenkins Inn in Bolton-on-Swale has long since been demolished but there is another hostelry of the same name in Kirkby Malzeard. The National Portrait Gallery in London has a copy of an engraved Jenkin's portrait. Map Landranger 99 – Grid Ref: 253992 (St Mary's Church).*

7. SCORTON: AN ARROWING EXPERIENCE

It was once compulsory to practice a sport that gave the English lion its roar, the famous victories at Crécy and Agincourt owing much to the proficiency of our kinsmen with the longbow. After the heroics of 1346 and 1415, archery has always had a special place in English hearts, one of the oldest sporting competitions in the country keeping the ancient skills very much alive.

Elizabeth I gave a silver arrow to the Oxford Colleges as a trophy to be awarded to the best toxophilite each year. But a reprobate Yorkshireman – John Wastell – made off with the prize, taking it to his manor house home in Scorton. The disgraced John – there is some suggestion of a steamy liaison with a serving maid – was evicted, the silver arrow flighting its way into the possession of one Henry Calverley. On the 14th May 1673, this gentleman convened a meeting of twenty or so friends, the assembly drawing up a set of rules and deciding to hold an annual archery competition for the arrow. With breaks only for the war years the contest has been held every year since.

Originally reserved for Yorkshiremen only, the competition is now open to all comers, the rules stipulating two-way shooting at separate targets at 100 yards range. Each archer is allowed two shots at each of his chosen targets. The first archer who strikes the three inches diameter inner gold is deemed to be the competition winner. Other prizes awarded for lesser feats of accuracy

The Scorton Silver Arrow entry record book.

are a bugle, a horn spoon, a sword, silver medals, cups and various cash prizes, paid in good old English shillings. Many archers, some in traditional dress, use traditional longbows although some prefer modern carbon and kevlar weapons. All competitors are charged with adhering to a strict code of conduct and etiquette, the use of intemperate language incurring a fine of one shilling. The four hour long event is punctuated by a formal lunch, the Robin Hoods among the diners receiving over-sized wine glasses.

At the end of the competition, the trophies are awarded during a celebratory dinner, the winner being declared Captain for the forthcoming event.

Directions: *The village of Scorton is on the B1263. Cross the Swale at Catterick Bridge and leave the A1, going east on the B6271 for about two and a half miles. The annual venue for the Scorton Silver Arrow tournament, which is usually held on the Saturday nearest to the 14th May, is determined by the Captain elect, although the Scorton Grammar School Playing Field has been a popular shooting ground in recent years. The original 1673 rules governing the competition are kept by the County Archivist in Northallerton. Except on tournament day, the Scorton Silver Arrow is kept in a bank vault. Map Landranger 93 – Grid Ref: 252002 (Scorton Grammar School).*

8. CASTLE BOLTON: A PAWNED QUEEN

Mary Stuart, the star-crossed flower of Scotland, fled to England after the Battle of Langside in 1567, her rout at the hands of her fellow Scots, coming in the wake of thirteen years exile in France, the murder of her husband, an abdication in favour of her son James, and imprisonment in Lochleven Castle. Mary Queen of Scots 'never drew bit till she reached the Abbey of Dundrennan in Galloway,' embarking by sea for Workington. Seeking the protection of Queen Elizabeth I, she wrote an impassioned letter, concluding:

> *... It is my earnest request that your majesty will send for me as soon as possible, for my condition is pitiable, not to say for a queen, but even for a simple gentlewoman. I have not other dress than that in which I escaped from the field. My first day's ride was sixty miles across the country and I have not since dared travel except by night.*

But Mary had put her head on the block. Some years before, her claim to the English throne had been urged with great pertinacity against Elizabeth. Determined to stifle the claims of her rival, and anxious to prevent her escape to France to thwart a potential alliance against England, the queen, who was also jealous of Mary's superior beauty, ordered immediate incarceration, Mary arriving in Yorkshire's Bolton Castle under armed guard on 13th July 1568.

Bolton Castle.

Begun by Sir Richard Scrope in 1379, the magnificent Bolton Castle radiates an aura of shock and menace, its soaring towers and pinnacles originally looking out over the Forest of Wensleydale. Attended by a retinue of 51 knights and ladies in waiting, Mary spent six months in Bolton, occupying her time in English lessons – 'Excus my iuel writin thes furst tym,' she wrote to her tutor Sir Francis Knollyes – keeping up with her correspondence, knitting and occasional hunting. Allowed to leave the castle under escort, she visited places like Nappa Hall, taking an opportunity to plan her escape.

Assisted by her attendants, she managed to deceive her guards and was lowered from the turret by rope. But she only managed to cover four miles before she was intercepted and taken back to Bolton where she remained under even closer scrutiny until 26th January 1569. Fearing further sallies for freedom, Elizabeth ordered her removal to the ruinous Tutbury Castle. After enduring progressively worsening conditions in yet more prisons, Mary was finally found guilty of complicity in the Babington conspiracy and was beheaded at Fotheringay Castle on 8th February 1587.

Directions: *Bolton Castle (entry fee) is in the village of Castle Bolton. The easiest access is from the A684 (one mile south-west of Leyburn) going north – west for three and a half miles. Mary Queen of Scots bed-chamber is unaltered since 1569. A pane of glass, scratched 'Marie R' with a diamond ring, was preserved for some years but it was hopelessly smashed in the course of repairs. On Leyburn Shawl (marked footpath* *access from the market square in Leyburn) is the spot where Mary was apprehended. It is known to this day as the Queen's Gap. Accessed from a footpath (south, off the minor road one mile east of Askrigg near Nappa Scar) is Nappa Hall (private house). Mary Queen of Scots is said to haunt this place. Map Landranger 98 – Grid Ref: 034918 (Bolton Castle).*

9. SEMERWATER: YORKSHIRE'S ATLANTIS

Catch yourself alone on the banks of Yorkshire's most romantic lake and you too might believe in legends. Step amongst the ruins of its shoreline chapel and hear the lament of the curlews peeling off the heights of Green Scar Mire and the tale of a lost city beneath the waves seems more than a mere dream.

The origins of the legend of the inundated city of gold are lost in time. Tradition recalls a thriving metropolis under the gaze of a Roman camp on Addlebrough. Visited by an angel in the guise of an old tramp, this hedonistic place spurned the angelic emissary, refusing him food and shelter, only one lowly couple on the edge of the city offering him assistance. On the morning of his departure, the angel thanked his hosts turning on the accursed city and invoking a retribution of fire and brimstone with the words:

Semerwater rise , Semerwater sink,
And swallow all the town
But this little house
Where they gave me meat and drink.

Fables seldom smoulder on without the fires of actual events. What happened to that city beneath the waves? Was it razed to the ground by a marauding tribe of Brigantian clansmen who sought revenge on the collaborators with Rome? The answer is surely down there.

Directions: *Semerwater is in the Yorkshire Dales National Park on a minor road two miles south-west of Bainbridge (A684). A public footpath skirts the eastern bank of the lake, taking in the ruins of an abandoned chapel (built in 1603 and repaired in 1722) and a tumble of gravestones. Map Landranger 98 – Grid Ref: 920874.*

10. WEST WITTON: BURN BARTLE, BURN!

Shake a bridle over a Yorkshireman's grave and he will arise and steal a horse. It's an instinctive sort of thing, much like the burning of Old Bartle. A purloiner of sheep, this gentleman is ceremonially burnt in effigy (perhaps) every year by the villagers of West Witton in Wensleydale, on the August Saturday nearest to the 24th – St Bartholomew's Day. But why do they do it? Well, they're not rightly sure. It may be to commemorate a sheep rustler who was apprehended on nearby Penhill and summarily sent to his maker some

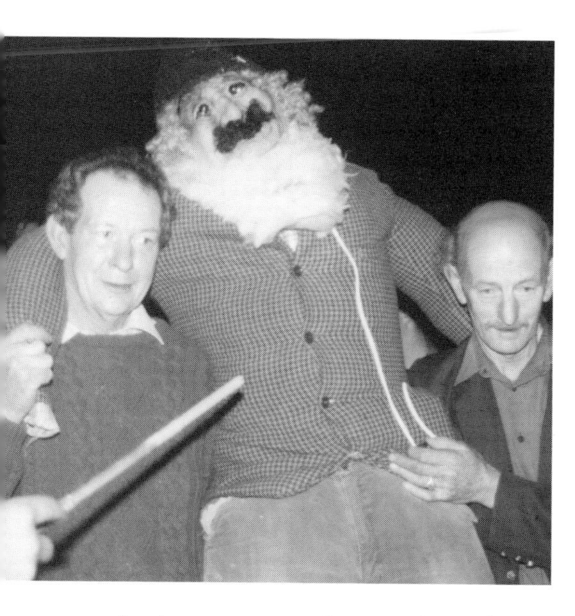

Old Bartle is carried to his fate.

400 years ago. Or it might simply be to remember the saint himself, although having been flayed alive in 44 AD what has he done to deserve a yearly roasting? Alternatively, in the absence of any historical evidence to support either of these theories, it might be just an excuse for an orgy of public singing guaranteed to wake the dead and an opportunity for a glorified knees-up.

Made of straw, old clothes and a mask, Old Bartle is ceremoniously taken round the village at 10 o'clock in the evening by two men, a large and usually well – inebriated crowd following his progress. At the last house, the effigy is held aloft as an ancient rhyme is recited in a high-pitched monotonous voice:

In Penhill Crags he tore his rags;
At Hunter's Thorn he blew his horn;
At Capplebank Stee he brake his knee;
At Grisgill Beck he brake his neck;
At Wadham's End he couldn't fend;
At Grisgill End he made his end.

At the end of the recitation, the man implores the crowd to 'shout, lads, shout!' (The word is pronounced 'shute'*). Then, Old Bartle gets the Guy Fawkes treatment, communal singing accompanying his last frizzled moments.

Directions: *West Witton is in the Yorkshire Dales National Park, four miles south-west of Leyburn on the A684. Map Landranger 99 – Grid Ref: 064884.*

---

* This is a call for a rustic huzzah and not an invitation for southerners in the audience to let fly at Old Bartle with their fowling pieces.

11. MIDDLEHAM: 'LOYAULTE ME LIE'

Richard III has been slighted more than any other English monarch in history. His chief caricaturist is Shakespeare, the play Richard III painting the image of a crooked-back ogre – a bad man and a worse king.

I that am curtail'd of this fair proportion,
Cheated of feature by dissembling Nature,
Deform'd, unfinish'd, sent before my time
Into this breathing world, scarce half made up,
And that so lamely and unfashionable,
That dogs bark at me, as I halt by them.

Richard spent much of his boyhood in Middleham Castle, having a real affection for the town and the surrounding area. This Duke of Gloucester became 'Lieutenant of the North' for twelve years, effectively governing the northern counties and earning a reputation for fairness, generosity and incorruptibility. He became king in 1483, history implicating him in the notorious murder of the Princes in the Tower. In two short years, however, he passed the most enlightened laws of the fifteenth century. He introduced a relay postal service, put an end to the intimidation of juries, initiated the bail system, outlawed benevolences, encouraged the importation of books and decreed that laws be written in English rather than Latin to foster greater understanding.

Despite his wider responsibilities, Richard always found time to champion Yorkshire affairs. Highly regarded in Middleham as a fond husband and an affectionate father, he secured a royal charter for the town to hold two annual fairs and he became a patron of the Yorkshire churches, having a particular regard for York's recently completed Minster. Keen to see justice served, on one occasion, he even intervened in a local dispute, declaring that obstructive fish-nets be removed from the Rivers Wharfe, Ouse and Aire.

Richard had a son, a strong and lusty child who, like his father thrived in the pure air of Wensleydale. But this prince died at the age of 11, his father – the only king from the north ever to rule England and the last English monarch to die in battle – meeting his own untimely end at the age of 32 at Bosworth Field in 1485.

Eclipsing every one of Shakespeare's weasel words, Richard's personal motto was: 'Loyaulte Me Lie.' Let that and the tribute of a contemporary be his lasting epitaph: 'No ordinary man was he, neither knight nor squire nor honest yeoman, but one possessed of such extraordinary strength and compassion that he should be forever loved and revered.'

Directions: *Overlooking the gateway into Wensleydale, Middleham is two miles south-east of Leyburn on the A6108. Now under the protection of English Heritage,*

Middleham Castle – the former home of Richard III – is set back south of the town centre. Dating from 1190, it has a keep second only in size to the Tower of London. In the higher of the village squares is an old cross, the Swine Cross. Although much weathered it is said to depict a wild boar – the emblem of Richard III. The king bestowed collegiate status on Middleham's St Mary and St Alkelda Church. The honour is celebrated in the red robes worn by members of its choir. Map Landranger 99 – Grid Refs: 128877 (Middleham Castle); 127878 (Swine Cross); 122879 (St Mary and St Alkelda Church).

12. RIBBLEHEAD: STIFFENING ENGLAND'S BACKBONE

Impressed into the wilderness with the force of hot branding iron, the monumental Ribblehead Viaduct smoulders on, steam trains still rattling its 440-yards span. One of the marvels of the railway age, it is the soaring climax of the Settle to Carlisle railway, the engineering challenge of the century opened after six years of prodigious work in 1876.

The centrepiece of a line that cost an amazing £47,500 per mile, the Ribblehead Viaduct took five years to build. It has 24 arches, the tallest reaching 165 feet above the moor. Some of its piers penetrate bedrock to a depth of 25 feet. The undisputed star of the whole line, Ribblehead is close to an only slightly less impressive black hole, the Blea Moor Tunnel to the north burrowing up to 500 feet underground in a 2,629 yards dash for the light. Costing a river of sweat and £45 per yard to construct, this tunnel was built by some 300 miners, labourers and bricklayers using drills, sledge hammers, picks, shovels and boxes of dynamite by the hundred. Accidents were surprisingly rare, although one miner named John Thompson, in attempting to dry off some wet explosive, blow himself up. His fellow workers found his mangled body next to an open fire!

Attracted by the promise of earning as much as 10 shillings per day, thousands of navvies, and many of their unsuspecting families, converged on Ribblesdale from all over England. They were billeted in the wild-west settlements of Batty Green, Jericho, Salt Lake City and other mushrooming shanty towns that provided primitive housing and makeshift stores, schools, hospitals, public houses and places of religion. Conditions, especially during the raging winters for which Ribblesdale is noted, were appalling; disputes, drunkenness, prostitution, injury, poor diet and diseases such as smallpox, leading to despair and a high death rate.

For a time, the entire line was threatened with closure. Happily, it survives as a monument to an army of men who stiffened the backbone of England.

Directions: *Ribblehead (just a railway station and a pub) is in the Yorkshire Dales National Park about 12 miles north of Settle (A65) at the B6479/B6255 junction. Ribblehead Viaduct is about 600 yards north-west of the pub. Batty Green (it alone* *accommodated 2,000 people) was on the flat ground to the north-east of the viaduct. The Dales Way footpath follows the line of the railway passing directly over Blea Moor Tunnel. Notice the air-shafts whose belching smoke and steam once gave Blea Moor the name 'Yorkshire's Smoky Mountain.' Down the B6255 from Ribblehead towards Ingleton in Chapel-le-Dale Church, is a memorial to the dead construction workers. Map Landranger 98 – Grid Ref: 760795 (Ribblehead Viaduct); 762819 (southerly entrance to Blea Moor Tunnel near the Dales Way); 738773 (Chapel-le-Dale Church).*

13. INGLEBOROUGH :THE BRIGANTES' LAST STAND

If the Germans had come, we too might have made our last stand on Yorkshire's fabled mountain. At a height of 2,373 feet with long distance views and precipitous sides, it made a stout citadel against the determined hordes of Rome. One of the final bastions of the Brigantes, it kept the legions at bay for years.

The third highest of our peaks, Ingleborough is capped with millstone grit, a hard and unyielding material used by our Iron Age ancestors to a construct a 15-acre camp and stronghold. A 1,000-feet-long rampart was built from millstone blocks to reinforce the summit crags, three entrances providing access to a collection of huts erected on the plateau.

It must have taken a fit and determined legion of soldiers to dislodge the Brigantes, overwhelming numbers perhaps breaching the walls and, with fire and sword, putting paid to a thousand years of history.

Much of the original rampart wall is damaged, large anonymous fragments of stone finding their way into the modern cairn. The original entrances, where the Romans poured through, can be seen on the north, south-west and east sides of the encampment. The stone foundations of the circular huts, predominantly with entrances facing south, are still visible.

Directions: *Ingleborough is in the Yorkshire Dales National Park about five miles on foot (public footpath) north of Clapham (A65). Map Landranger 98 – Grid Ref: 741746.* ☛ ***See also 79 (Almondbury)***

14. GAPING GILL: DOWN, DOWN, DEEPER AND DOWN

To the eternal regret of all Yorkshiremen, it took a Frenchie to conquer Britain's deepest hole. Regarded as a bottomless abyss for centuries, Gaping Gill plunges to a depth of 340 feet, its enormous main chamber remaining unfathomed until 1895.

Around 1842, Englishman John Birkbeck made the first unsuccessful attempt on the cave, his compatriot Alfred Ernest Clibborn having no better luck in 1882. The way was open for experienced French caver Edouard Alfred Martel to try his hand, and on the 1st August he stood on the brink, tested his rope and telephone link, and uttered the immortal words: 'Let go gently.'

Over aeons, the waters of the Fell Beck have carved out a space that would gobble up St Paul's Cathedral. On that particular day, the flow had been diverted but Martel soon found himself drenched and numb with cold. Down and down he went with the light growing ever dimmer. After twenty-three minutes he touched the bottom of the cave and looked up awestruck. Hearing news of an impending storm above, he quickly scribbled a sketch of the cave and made the following notes: '... there is the feeble light of day which, filtering through the spray, with millions of prisms formed by the drops, does not seem like anything upon which human eye has gazed. It affords one the impressive attraction of something never seen before. It is one of the most extraordinary spectacles it has been my pleasure to witness.'

Gaping Gill.

Directions: *Gaping Gill is in the Yorkshire Dales National Park about three miles on foot (public footpath) north of Clapham (A65). Annual descents of the cave by motorised cradle are organised by the local caving club. On the route to Gaping Gill, you will pass the floodlit Ingleborough Cave (open to the public) discovered in 1837. Map Landranger 98 – Grid Ref: 751727.*

15. SETTLE: HOMELIFE BC

Without question, the oldest, and most enduring abodes on the planet are caves. A vital element in the emergence of man, these rock dwellings attracted a variety of occupants over many centuries, human and animal remains and artefacts telling us much about life BC. In Yorkshire, most of the ideal homes of the period were located in the fractured limestone country of the dales, one celebrated cave investigated by a Settle tradesman, causing nationwide controversy and yielding one of the greatest finds of bones ever.

Victoria Cave – named in honour of Queen Victoria's Coronation – was first studied by Joseph Jackson in 1838 but, according to the history books, more scientific analysis was delayed until 1870. Surely though, generations of inquisitive children had been coming here for centuries? 'Take that horrible thing away Thomas. It's an old skull!'

Around 20 years of excavation revealed numerous bones, stratification suggesting that the cave had been first used as a hyena den. Occupation by hunters in the late glacial period left further layers of bones, intermittent use in later years by Stone Age tribes depositing the remains of animals such as mammoth, hippopotamus, bison, elephant and bear. From one such deposit appeared a singularly fascinating specimen that became known as 'The Yorkshire Bone of Contention'. Some eminent persons claimed that the relic in question was humanoid. Others begged to differ, the weight of scientific argument coming down on the side of a large bear.

But the cave produced not only bones. Attesting to habitation by Romano-British squatters of the third and fourth centuries AD, were fragments of pottery, beads, brooches, fish-hooks and a collection of Roman coins. But where was the nearest shop?

Directions: Settle is in the Yorkshire Dales National Park on the B 6480 (off the A65), around 15 miles north-west of Skipton. Victoria Cave is around two and a half miles on foot east of the town. Beyond Attermire Scar, a scrambling path leads up to the cave entrance where you will find an interpretation board. Map Landranger 98 – Grid Ref: 839651.

16. SKIPTON: HEART WOOD

Inert and soulless, ancient stones radiate the energy of past lives. So what forces emanate from the longest-lived breathing entities on the planet? Surviving trees in various parts of the world, span the recent history of man, one specimen in Skipton planted in the reign of Elizabeth I outlasting 10 generations.

A symbol of everlasting life, a yew tree was planted in the Conduit Court of Skipton Castle in 1659. Carefully treading-in its young roots, its planter would have pondered on her own mortality and wondered. 'What will the world be like when I'm long gone?' she might have said. 'And will this sapling become a tree? Thrive on young scion … and take some more water!'

Lady Ann Clifford planted the yew tree after her extensive restoration of her castle following the Civil War. Now with an eight feet girth surrounded by a circular seat, the spreading yew is as tall as the castle itself. Sit below its spreading branches and listen.

Directions: *Skipton is between Ilkley and Settle (A59/A65). The 900-year-old Skipton Castle (which is open to the public) is north of the market square. The yew tree is in the central court. Map Landranger 103 – Grid Ref: 993523.*

17. BOLTON ABBEY: 'THE WHITE HORSE OF WHARFEDALE'

There is no more menacing beauty spot in the whole of Yorkshire, the evil Strid – a riverine constriction synonymous with convulsing water and death – having claimed dozens of lives down the years.

For nearly all of its 69 miles length, from the bleak expanse of Cam Fell in Langstrothdale to its confluence with the Ouse in Cawood, the River Wharfe is picturesque and benign, only one awful compression defiling its character. This Strid, where the seething waters are funnelled through a deep and narrow gorge only four feet wide, has gone down in legend as the place where the 'Boy of Egremond' died.

This child was the son of Adeliza and William FitzDuncan 'one of the veriest old swashbucklers that ever cut a throat'. In the bravado of youth, the young gentleman attempted to leap the gap with his greyhound, the leashed dog hanging back and dragging him into the cauldron. So distraught was the mother at the death of her son, that legend suggests she founded Bolton Priory just downstream.

There have been numerous accidents and suicides at this spot down the years, the danger arising as much from the slippery rocks as the torrential flow. According to folklore, before every fatality, a vision appears, the spectral 'White Horse of Wharfedale' rising from the bed of the river below.

Before you get the urge to test your own virility, you need to be aware of the enormous flow of water that roars through the Strid canyon. Consider the sobering facts. The gap here is a strides width. Just a mile below, you may cross the Wharfe on 57 stepping stones.

Directions: *The Strid is just over a mile upstream from the Cavendish Pavilion, at Bolton Abbey (footpath on both sides of the river from the wooden bridge) The road access is via the B6160. Take the first right after the priory using the private signposted road (parking fee payable). Map Landranger 104 – Grid Ref: 065564.*

18. APPLETREEWICK: JUST WILLIAM

Apart from the cat, this poor farmer's lad was a regular Dick Whittington. In a romantic rags-to-riches life, he left the cowshed to become a wealthy man. But his ambitious spirit never allowed him to forget his native home, and, as we pass over the River Wharfe, we can thank him for his generous gift of Burnsall Bridge, tipping our caps to William Craven.

Born in 1548, young William spent his early days in the dale, his three weeks long journey to London in a carrier's cart at around thirteen years of age, beginning a stirring adventure that started with an apprenticeship to a city mercer and ended in a knighthood and the pomp of the Lord Mayor's Show.

Working his way up the ladder of fortune with hard work and entrepreneurial flair, William impressed himself on his employer to such an

The Mock Beggar Hall at Appletreewick.

extent that he was allowed to marry into the firm, further prosperity and distinguished municipal service leading to his appointment as Sheriff of London in 1600. In 1603, he received a knighthood becoming Lord Mayor of London in 1610.

When he left Appletreewick as a young man, William had bade farewell to its most prestigious building. Returning to the village with a bulging purse, he bought the place. High Hall was restored, much of William's remaining fortune paying for a new bridge over the Wharfe at Burnsall, and repairs to Burnsall Church. He also endowed Burnsall Grammar School.

A thoroughly unassuming, kind and gentle Yorkshireman who never forgot his roots, Sir William Craven is fondly regarded in Appletreewick, particularly in the Craven Arms that bears his name.

Directions: *Appletreewick is in the Yorkshire Dales National Park. The best access is from the A59 at Bolton Bridge, going north-west on the B6160 to Burnsall for about seven miles and turning east on a minor road for a further two and a half miles. The graceful Burnsall Bridge spans the Wharfe in the village of Burnsall. Burnsall Church and Burnsall Grammar School are a few hundred yards north of the bridge to the right of the B6160. High Hall in Appletreewick is opposite the small church of St John. This church was originally two cottages. One of these was Craven's birthplace. Map Landranger 98 – Grid Refs: 033612 (Burnsall Bridge); 033613 (Burnsall Church and Burnsall Grammar School); 055602 (High Hall and St John's Church).*

19. GRASSINGTON: ORE PERSPIRING

From as early as the twelfth century, Yorkshire lead kept the rain off some of the noblest heads in the country, thousands of miners toiling away for hundreds of years to extract the precious galena ores. It is somewhat ironic that the desecration from coal mining has been expunged from the urban landscape in a generation, while the spoil heaps, abandoned hushes, shafts, dressing floors and smelting houses associated with lead mining, continue to blight our National Park to this day. Nothing much grows on the earthy innards that were ripped and washed out, but the abandoned sites, where men sweated in appallingly difficult and dangerous conditions, are fascinating for all that. One of the busiest of the ore fields, and perhaps the best preserved, is the one on Grassington Moor. Limited mining had been carried on here for decades but exploitation began in earnest about 1730 when the output rose to 150 tons of smelted lead. By 1745, this had risen to 400 tons, the figure exceeding 600 tons in 1760. The formation of mining partnerships and the advent of new techniques and machines in later years, caused a further expansion in the industry, nearby Grassington growing to meet the demand for labour and raw materials.

The author (left) and a fellow Neanderthal on Grassington Moor.

Developed on the Duke of Devonshire's estate in the early nineteenth century, the more advanced Yarnbury mines were highly organised and well engineered, a complex system of shafts, known as the Masons', Barrett's, Tomkin's and Bowden Shafts, linking both working and drainage levels at various depths up to 50 fathoms. The operation was assisted by the use of whims or gins, whose winding gears were operated by two ponies, and by the construction of a site railway. Other power, to operate the stamps and dressing machinery, came from water wheels.

The first ingots of Yorkshire lead had Roman assay marks, the industry becoming ever more intensive over the succeeding centuries until the veins petered out and cheaper foreign imports brought the inevitable decline in the early twentieth century. Only piles of defiantly sterile spoil remain.

Directions: *Grassington is in the Yorkshire Dales National Park about 15 miles north of Skipton on the B6265. Grassington Moor is two and a half miles north-east of the village down Moor Lane to the start of Old Moor Lane (a track unsuitable for* *vehicles) at Yarnbury. The whole of the moor is littered with the remains of the lead mining industry. Ripped apart, gouged out and eaten alive like some piranha rattled corpse, its once heather-rich mantle is an industrial desert riddled with abandoned levels and shafts. Beware straying too far from the paths! Interpretation boards in front of the various ruined buildings, which include a chimney and its flues, give some idea of the layout of the site. In the centre of Grassington village, overlooking The Square in two converted former lead miner's cottages, is the Upper Wharfedale Museum. It is open from Easter until October and tells the often-harrowing story of the local lead mining industry. Map Landranger 98 – Grid Refs: 025665 (Grassington Moor lead mines); 003640 (Upper Wharfedale Museum).*

20. MIDDLESMOOR: ASTOUNDING IMPOUNDMENT

Only in recent years have we begun to appreciate the worth of piped water and the intricate voyage from dam to glass. With the explosion of urban development in the nineteenth century, came the great era of dam building, the construction of the twin dams of Angram and Scar House in Upper Nidderdale, producing two of the engineering marvels of the age.

Nearly 70 miles from Bradford, the highly ambitious scheme by the city's Corporation Waterworks called for the erection of two giant dams to contain the headwaters of the River Nidd, the construction demanding the importation of vast amounts of building materials and equipment to a remote site only accessible by an inferior track. The logistical answer to the access problem was the installation of a railway running for 13 miles between Pateley Bridge and the dam sites, the line opening in 1907. Work began in earnest soon afterwards, an army of men quarrying thousands of tons of rock, other workers building a mini city complete with dormitories, a canteen, a dispensary, a church and a cinema.

At nearly 160 feet high, Scar House Dam impounds 2,200 million gallons of water. It was completed in 1936.

Directions: *Scar House Dam is around 13 miles north-west of Pateley Bridge on a minor road (cross the river and go first right passing by Gouthwaite Reservoir and through Ramsgill and Lofthouse). Continue uphill to Middlesmoor and walk from here using the picturesque moorland track, or turn right at the foot of the hill on the waterworks road, passing the abandoned railway line and continuing in a broad arc left for about two miles to the parking area near the dam wall. The distinctive site of the workers' town is on the flat ground below the spillway. Looking west from the dam top walkway, you can see Angram Dam and Great Whernside (2,310 feet). To really get a feel for the pioneering achievements of the Bradford engineers, follow the hoots of the old tank engines* Craven, Gadie, Kitchener, Watson and Trotter, *walking on what is now a public footpath from Pateley Bridge. Map Landranger 99 – Grid Ref: 067767.*

21. ILTON: TEMPLE OF BOON

In the old days, there was no such thing as unemployment benefit, only begging or the meagre crusts of the poor house warding off starvation. In times of economic uncertainty and dwindling markets, most landowners and industrialists of the nineteenth century were reluctant to help their laid off workers in any way. But there were exceptions in the callousness and indifference, the intervention of William Danby of Swinton Hall pricking the conscience of employers everywhere.

In the general slump following the Napoleonic Wars, when thousands of men where thrown out of work, Danby came up with a unique solution to the scourge of unemployment. Inspired perhaps by the extensive earthworks at nearby Carlesmoore, he decided to erect his own tribute to ancient man, instructing his workers to build him a miniature Stonehenge.

The 10 feet-high monoliths for this perfect replica of the famous Druid temple, took months to cut and erect, Danby using this most eccentric of landscape ornaments for soirees and picnics. The henge is orbited by a number of cromlech like structures and outliers.

Directions: *Standing on its own in a publicly accessible wood, the temple is best reached from the A6108 going west through Masham and Fearby for two miles. Before reaching Healey, drop down, travelling on for a further mile or so, crossing the River Burn and following the road round a 90° bend and going next right to the temple. Map Landranger 99 – Grid Ref: 175787.*

The Druids' Temple at Ilton.

22. GREWELTHORPE: HACKFALL – A MAGICAL GARDEN

A wild and wonderful 100 acre landscape garden that exploits the most dramatic river gorge in Yorkshire, Hackfall was begun by William Aislabie around 1750, a profusion of trees and flowers, labyrinthine paths, waterfalls and a collection of outlandish follies attracting delighted crowds for over 200 years.

Centuries ahead of its time, Hackfall rejoiced in a sublime and unfettered Nature, visitors confronting stupendous views and a green and joyous rampancy unknown elsewhere. Designed to contrast with the formal and regimented plantings at nearby Studley Royal, Hackfall took its inspiration from the scenery of the Alps, Aislabie funding the project from yields on investments in the South Sea Bubble.

For a while, Hackfall was threatened by commercial logging, the Woodland and Landmark Trusts' coming to its rescue in the 1980s and protecting its long-term future.

Directions: *Hackfall is a short walk on sign-posted public footpaths north-east of Grewelthorpe (three miles south of Ripon and A6108 on a minor road). Will you find Mowbray Point (a tea-room during the 1920s and 30s), Mowbray Castle, the Rustic Temple, Fisher's Hall and a golden beach to compare with any in Europe? Map Landranger 99 – Grid Ref:230763 (footpath access in Grewelthorpe).*

23. WEST TANFIELD: 'SHITTE ON FROM A GREAT HIGHTE'

In the Middle Ages, relieving oneself in a castle served a dual purpose, the jettisoning of waste matter both voiding the system and helping repel boarders in one fell swoop. Built into high projections strategically placed above ditches or moats, these relieving stations or garderobes as they were known, were the height of medieval luxury, offering private closets with a view and the opportunity of indulging in an early form of chemical warfare. Some garderobes even had primitive flushing systems, diverted rainwater from roofs, helping to ensure an even spread of deterrent on scaleable walls. Not all the sluicings, however, clung to the verticals, gravity taking some material into the ditches below. Over time these receptacles became full, the stench, the offensive yards-high piles and the tendency of the material to crusting, whereby lightweight besiegers might make a somewhat precarious crossing, all calling for the services of the gong fermers.

These highly specialised and handsomely paid cleaners were charged with digging or scooping out the accumulated filth into carts. Unpleasant in the extreme, the job, which was usually done by torchlight at night, was not without its attendant dangers, the possibilities of catching disease, the build up of explosive gas in the confined spaces and the risks of falling into the crud, making it precarious work.

The fifteenth-century garderobe at West Tanfield.

Directions: *West Tanfield is about six miles north-west of Ripon on the A6108. There is a fine example of a garderobe set into the southern wall of the porter's lodge (together with the Marmion Gatehouse, this is all that survives of the once extensive castle). Both structures (part open to the public) are adjacent to the church on the north bank of the River Ure. Map Landranger 99 – Grid Ref: 268788.*

24. FOUNTAINS ABBEY: 'A PLACE REMOTE FROM ALL THE WORLD'

The Dissolution of the Monasteries was the worst regal act of larceny in British history, at the stoke of a quill, hundreds of millions of pounds worth of property at current values transferring into the coffers of Henry VIII. One of the biggest appropriations of them all was Fountains Abbey.

Within a few months of the infamous edicts of 1536 and 1539, England had lost her soul and much more besides, the monasteries providing much of the social infrastructure of the day. Gone were the centres of learning, medicine and poor relief. Gone too were the only hotels of the day. Suddenly, the monastic services that provided education, employment and succour to vast numbers of people across the country, had disappeared and there was hardship on a massive scale. The distress was particularly acute in the monastery rich county of Yorkshire, whose premier abbey at Fountains suffered more than most.

Founded as a mere group of huts in 1132 by a breakaway group of disgruntled Cistercian brothers in 'a place remote from all the world, uninhabited, set with thorns … fit more, it seemed, for the dens of wild beasts than for the use of mankind,' 'Sancta Maria de Fontanis' grew prosperous on wool, successive abbots acquiring up to 60,000 acres of land. It was said that the abbot could walk from Ripon to the heights of Penyghent without stepping off his own land. As well as 18,000 sheep, the monastery also owned vast stores of cattle and horses together with assorted lead mines, stone quarries, game preserves and fisheries. The income from these investments supported a lavish building programme.

Fountains was a thoroughly independent and highly organised community of monks and laymen. Built near and partly over the River Skell, it had a magnificent church as its focus, ancillary buildings including the abbot's lodge, chapter house, cloister, kitchen, refectory, a sacristy and library, dormitories, infirmary and the at the end of the piped water supply, a cleverly designed arrangement of monks' reredorters or lavatories.

At the dissolution, one Yorkshire eye-witness to a typical scene of desecration said: 'It would have made a heart of flint melt and weep to have seen the breaking-up of the house, the sorrowful departing and the sudden spoil that fell the same day of their departure from their house.'

The plunder from Fountains filled innumerable carts, scores of silver and gilt chalices, dozens of pairs of candlesticks, censers, incense boats, mitres, vestments of velvet and damask, multitudes of silver basins and ewers, salt cellars, spoons, rings, buckles, cruets and silver icons together with countless more utilitarian items such as pots and pans, crockery, chairs, tables and benches all being trundled away. And the monks were dispersed along with their possessions. But that was not the final ignominy. In around 1611, Sir Stephen Proctor, the official Collector of Fines on Penal Statutes, 'an unscrupulous and unsqueamish man', ravaged the south-eastern parts of the abbey, quarrying its stone for his Fountains Hall. Despite this vandalism, though, Fountains Abbey remains as the best-preserved and most romantic monastic ruin in the country.

Directions: *Fountains Abbey is about four miles south-west of Ripon (B6265 and then on a minor road south). The abbey and its grounds – a World Heritage Site – are in the care of the National Trust and are open to the public. Map Landranger 99 Grid Ref: 274683.*

25. NEWBY PARK: FOXHUNT KILLS SIX

> *Death is more fearful when it is in direct contrast with pleasure, and the little ferry on the Ure will be remembered so long as that river rolls its dark waters from the moors to the Ouse as the scene of the most fearful tragedy in hunting history. Yorkshire could hardly believe the sad tidings.*

This lament in *Saddle and Sirloin* refers to the appalling accident that occurred on the River Ure on 4th February 1869, when the pursuit of a fox went tragically wrong.

The renowned York and Ainsty Hunt assembled over a stirrup cup on that fateful winter's morning, a specially charted train bringing hunters and

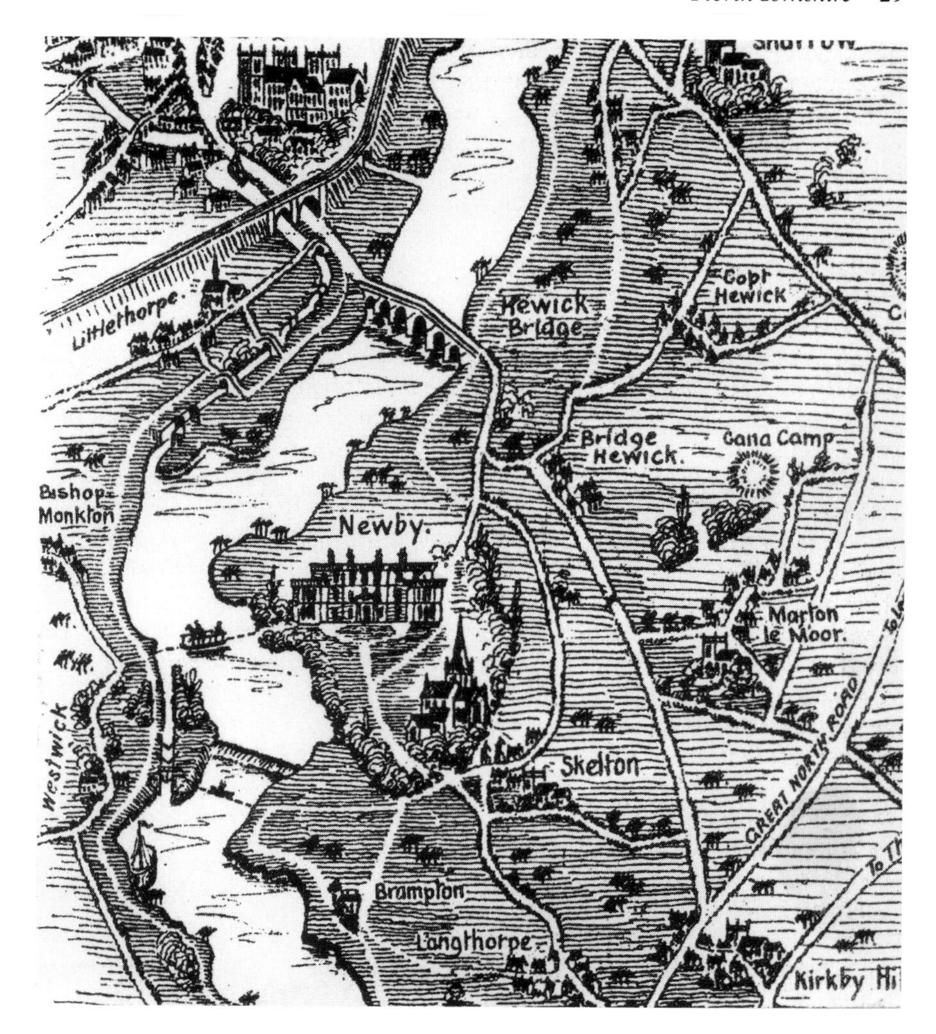

The Newby Hall Ferry is clearly shown on this map from 1891.

spectators from all over Yorkshire to the starting point at Stainley. At the head of the pack, mounted on his famous horse Saltfish, was the redoubtable Sir Charles Slingsby of Scriven Park.

Soon after the hunting horn sounded, a fox was flushed from cover. It was thought to be the same animal that had twice that season evaded capture by crossing the river, and it repeated the ruse, jumping into the swollen waters opposite Newby Hall. This time, however, Sir Charles and his fellow huntsmen were determined to outwit the fox, the anxious party electing to cross the river on a ferry.

A Heath Robinson contrivance consisting of a boat and a heavy chain operated by a cog-wheel, the ferry was immediately overloaded, spate conditions in the river and instability caused by the current and the cargo of frightened horses, spelling immediate disaster. The terrified Saltfish reared up and jumped into the water. Frantically thrashing out with its legs, the hunter became entangled in the chain and upset the ferry, throwing the rest of the horses and their riders into the torrent.

Sir Charles Slingsby struck out for the far bank but never made it. His friend Mr E. Lloyd, a former Eton swimming champion, made a valiant attempt at reaching safety but his heavy riding boots and the weight of his saturated riding apparel pulled him down and he became exhausted. Captain Robert Vyner and Mr William Ingilby, who had managed to pull themselves out of the river, jumped to his assistance:

> *For some time they sustained him, but he was a heavy man and soon overpowered them. In the last extremity he never lost his presence of mind. There was a total abnegation of self. He did as they directed him, putting his hands on their shoulders, and when he found they were exhausted he calmly removed them like the noble fellow that he was rather than imperil their lives as well as his own. No three men could have behaved more gallantly.*

Four more men were drowned that day; Mr Edmund Robinson, Mr William Orveys (First Whip), Mr C. Warriner (gardener at Newby Hall) and his son Mr J. Warriner. All the horses apart from one were also drowned. Ironically, the aptly named Saltfish struggled to the side and was saved.

Directions: *Newby Hall is near the village of Skelton, about three miles south-east of Ripon (B6265 and a minor road). The site of the ferry is opposite Newby Hall and its riverside gardens. The hall is open to the public. A commemorative stained glass west window to Sir Charles Slingsby, who tragically was the last male of his line, is in Knaresborough Church. Map Landranger 99 – Grid Ref: 350672.*

26. RIPLEY: 'ONE MOVE SIR ... AND YOU'RE DEAD'

The most powerful man in England fingered his warts nervously for hours on end, staring at the pair of pistols protruding from the lady's apron strings. History does not record much of the conversation that ensued on that long July night between Oliver Cromwell and the mistress of Ripley Castle, only the lady's parting words, on a document preserved in the castle records, showing us how the whole history of England might have been dramatically changed.

In pursuit of Royalist stragglers after his resounding victory at Marston Moor, Oliver Cromwell came to Ripley Castle on the morning of 3rd July 1644 demanding admittance and refreshment. In the absence of Sir William Ingilby, however, the lady of the house refused to let Cromwell in, only the sternest intimidation on the part of his soldiers, causing her to relent. Perched on the edges of their respective sofas in the castle's great hall, these unlikely opponents are said to have spent a restless night together, Lady Ingilby sending her uninvited guest packing at day break with these words: 'It is well that you have behaved in so peaceable a manner, for had it been otherwise, you would not have left this house with your life.'

Directions: *The village of Ripley is just north of Harrogate off the A61. Ripley Castle, which is open to visitors, is a few strides north-west of the church. The marks on the east wall of the castle, were made by Roundhead firing-squad bullets following the execution of Royalist prisoners. Map Landranger 99 – Grid Ref: 283605.* ☛ ***See also 39 (Newburgh Priory)***

27. HARROGATE 'GET IT DOWN LAD, IT'LL DO THEE GOOD.'

Until 1576, Harrogate was a collection of cottages and muddy fields. In that year, William Slingsby cautiously tasted a sample of the local spring water, setting in motion a multi-million pounds health industry that survives to this day.

At the height of its popularity, Harrogate had 87 saline, sulphur and iron springs, a hotel, boarding house and bathhouse building boom creating a

The Royal Pump Room Museum at Harrogate.

vibrant and fashionable spa town, royalty, landed gentry and rich and fashionable people from all over Europe coming to 'take the waters.'

For wealthy patients, the three weeks long 'cure' was properly supervised by those who could advise on the most efficacious treatments for leprosy, baker's itch, fish-skin disease, apoplexy, chlorosis, diabetes, dropsy, gout, scrofula, the vapours and other vile complaints. Other less well-endowed sufferers had to run the gauntlet of scruffy street vendors and so called water-women who, on occasions, adopted the most bullish of tactics. Bursting into the bedrooms of sleeping visitors at dawn with their pitchers, they cried out:

> *I am pretty Betty let me serve you,' or 'Kate and Coz Dol, do let we tend you.' One irate gentleman who suffered such an intrusion observed: '… their faces did shine like bacon rind. And for beauty many vie with an old Bath guide's ass, the sulphur waters having so fouled their complexions.*

Miraculously, the waters were sometimes effective, although the constant draining and purging of the system made some people quite ill. With the advent of mechanised torture in the early twentieth century, when 75,000 deluded souls were visiting the town every year, came the introduction of new machines and treatments, the Harrogate System of Intestinal Lavage matching any procedures of the Inquisition in its treatment of nervous disorders, fibrositis, appendicitis and the dreaded runs.

Directions: *Harrogate is north of Leeds on the A61. The spring discovered by Slingsby – the Tewit Well – is preserved under a cupola on The Stray (at the south side of the town – turn right at the Leeds Road/Hookstone Road crossroads down Tewit Well Road). Going east from Tewit Well, walk along the edge of The Stray down Slingsby Walk to Wetherby Road and St John's Well. In the town centre, the Royal Pump Museum, on Crown Place, houses the original sulphur wells and tells the history of the spa industry. There are the sites of other wells opposite in the Valley Gardens. Map Landranger 104 – Grid Refs: 305545 (Tewit Well); 315555 (St John's Well); 298555 (Royal Pump Room).*

28. KNARESBOROUGH: SINNERS AND A SAINT

For fourteen tormented years, schoolmaster Eugene Aram kept the darkest secret. A fugitive from Yorkshire, he fled to Norfolk in 1744 becoming a popular school usher in the village of Lynn. But his demeanour was not that of a contended man, one former pupil describing his constant fear. 'He always wore his hat *bangled,* which is bent down, or slouched,' she said. 'And in looking behind him, he never turned his head or his person partly round, but always turned round at once bodily.' He needed to look behind

St Robert's Cave at Knaresborough.

him quick, for in 1758, the constable came and led him away in handcuffs. His crime? The murder of Daniel Clark.

Daniel Clark was the third member of a trio involved in the theft of property from their Knaresborough neighbours. In the process of dividing the spoil, Clark was killed and his body hidden in St Robert's Cave. Aram fled the town but his accomplice, Richard Houseman stayed, denying all knowledge of his partners in crime. The disappearance of the two men was a complete mystery, until a chance discovery sparked a murder hunt.

A labourer found a skeleton in a local quarry. Suspicious that this might belong to Clark, a coroner interviewed the long deserted Mrs Aram, her testimony raising doubts about Houseman. Under interrogation, he thoughtlessly grabbed a piece of the skeleton and declared: 'This is no more Daniel Clark's than it is mine!' Under further questioning he confessed to his guilt and the constable set off hot-foot for Norfolk.

Eugene Aram was taken to York Castle, where he was tried for murder. At his trial, 'he delivered a written defence, so admirable for its ingenuity, and so replete with erudition and antiquarian knowledge, that it astonished the whole court.' Despite this attempt to escape justice, he was condemned to death, a botched attempt at suicide causing him to be brought to the scaffold 'almost in a state of insensibility.' Finally before he was executed, Aram confessed to murder.

On the morning of his execution – August 16th 1759 – a letter was found in his cell, concluding thus: 'I slept soundly and wrote these lines:

Come, pleasant rest; eternal slumber fall;
Seal mine, that once must seal the eyes of all.
Calm and composed, my soul her journey takes,
No guilt that troubles, and no heart that aches,

Adieu! thou sun; all bright like her arise;
Adieu! fair friends, and all that's good and wise.

Directions: *Knaresborough is four miles north-east of Harrogate on the A59. The scene of Daniel Clark's brutal murder could, ironically, have hardly been in a more hallowed spot. St Robert's Cave – carved into the rock on the hillside above Abbey Road, just below Low Bridge – was the abode of the hermit St Robert, who spent 40 years in his cell until his death in 1218.*

A little, lowly hermitage it was,
Down in a dale, hard by a forest side,
Far from resort of people that did pass,
In traveill to and fro a little wyde,
There was an holy chapelle edifyde,
Wherein the holy hermite dewly went to say,
His holy things each morn and eventyde.

Tread in the footsteps of thousands of medieval pilgrims and visit St Robert's Cave. It is open to the public. To the right of the cave, carved into the rock face is a niche reached by steps. Map Landranger 104 – Grid Ref: 351563.

29. KNARESBOROUGH: HORRIBLE ORACLE

With a face like that, who needs a petrifying well? I refer of course to that Yorkshire legend Old Mother Shipton whose 'boat race' was not her only distinguishing mark.

A soothsayer who achieved international acclaim for her predictions, Old Mother Shipton was born in the eponymous Knaresborough cave around 1488. Christened Ursula Southell, she married Tobias Shipton, a farmer from York. That poor gentleman must surely have been under some magical spell at the altar. For who but a blind man would have said 'I do' to this?

She was very morose and big boned, her head very long, with great, goggling, sharp and fiery eyes, her nose of an incredible and unproportional length, having many strange pimples of diverse colours ... which, like vapours of brimstone gas gave such lustre in the dead of night. She had in addition a chin of the nutcracker order, yellow skin shrivelled and wrinkled, one solitary big tooth standing out of her mouth like a tusk, neck so distorted that her right shoulder supported her head, legs crooked with feet and toes turned towards her left side, so that when she walked to the right it seemed as if she were travelling to the left.

Although there is little historical evidence of her colourful life, tradition has been very busy with her name, various pamphleteers and owners of the Dropping Well earning a handsome living fostering the myths.

The hooked nosed sybil is supposed to have foretold the coming of the railways in the saying:

When carriages without horses run,
Old England will be quite undone.

Selling her nostrums in York, it was claimed she predicted the death of Cardinal Wolsey, the advent of ironclad ships and the destruction of the Crystal Palace. Nearer home, there were prophecies about events at Pickhill, a town in the North Riding and problems in the riverside village of Ulleskelf near Tadcaster. Shipton claimed that Pickhill would never thrive until a local family of note became extinct, the prediction coming true in 1850. She also boasted that the tithe barn in Ulleskelf would be demolished and that its public spring would dry up. Again both warnings came to pass although the old girl exaggerated somewhat in predicting the end of the world in 1881.

Directions: *Knaresborough is four miles north-east of Harrogate on the A59. Mother Shipton's Cave ('where she first drew breath') and Dropping Well is on the right bank of the River Nidd between High and Low Bridges (access from High Bridge). For centuries, visitors have left personal articles in the Dropping Well where they are 'turned to stone.' Adjacent to Low Bridge is the Mother Shipton Inn. Map Landranger 104 – Grid Ref: 345564.*

30. SELBY: MONK LIFTS FINGER

Books galore will tell you about the sober history of the marvellous Selby Abbey but you will find little in the literature about its founding monk. Perhaps this is a deliberate omission? After all, what pious abbot would want to admit fellowship with a rogue like Benedict?

An inmate of the monastery of Auxerre in France in the middle half of the eleventh century, Benedict was something of a sampler, 'with an innocent faculty for discovering things that belonged to his brother monks and appropriating the same.' With a cheery 'Amen Brother', he would sample his fellow brothers' beer, only the fixidity of the bald spots on their heads preventing wholesale looting. In short, to use the Yorkshire parlance, he was a hook of the first order … the Benedictine order.

Monastic tolerance has only certain limits and the good monks of Auxerre convened to discuss the tea-leaf in their midst. Miraculously, Benedict had a vision, St Germanus, the patron saint of the monastery, coming to him in a dream with instructions to leave for a certain place in England. The unpopular monk duly obeyed the call and quit his cell, taking with him Auxerre's most treasured relic – a finger from the patron saint's hand. The faded texts are unclear as to the motives for this crime but there is some suggestion that the over – riding temptation might have been the alcoholic fluid in which the holy digit was preserved.

And so, it came to pass that our monk sailed west. But Benedict was no Christopher Columbus. He got lost, or perhaps St Germanus' message was garbled? Anyhow, Benedict first went to Salesbyria (Salisbury) by mistake. 'No, your reverend; you want's Selebia. Turn left at the Humber.'

Eventually, the hapless and by this time penniless monk, came on a ferryboat up the Ouse. Pot-less, he had not the wherewithal to pay his fare and he ended up swimming, with all his might, to the place referred to in his dream. He had found Selebia!

Setting up home on the banks of the river, Benedict was noticed by the High Sheriff who brought William the Conqueror along to see the holy man for himself. Impressed by his fellow countryman's tale, the king gave the monk a rich gift of land for the endowment of an abbey.

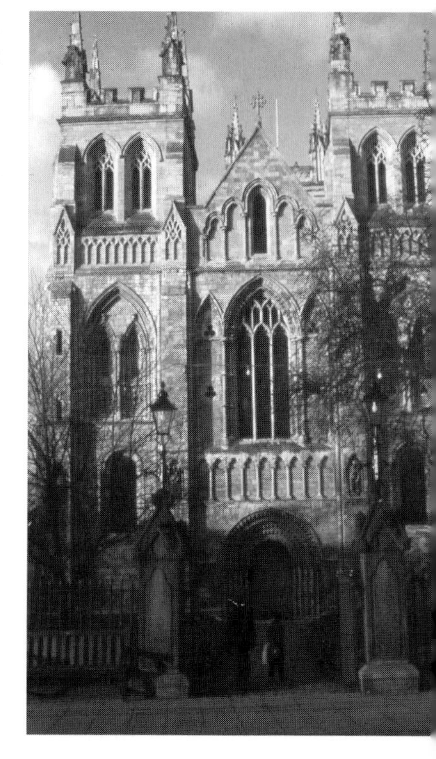

Selby Abbey.

The rest is boring old history ... but what about that finger?

Directions: *Selby is on the A19 about 10 miles east of the A1 (via the A63). The prominent Selby Abbey is in the centre of the town. Map Landranger 105 – Grid Ref: 616325.*

31. CAWOOD: THE MOTHER OF ALL BLOW-OUTS

Before its demolition on the orders of Parliament at the end of the Civil War, Cawood Castle was a medieval Hilton, kings and queens, bishops and archbishops and sundry blue-bloods by the score all enjoying its hospitality. Henry III, Edward II and Henry VIII all had many a gargantuan feast in its walls, but for sheer Billy Bunterian extravagance nothing could compete with the inaugural bash for the Archbishop of York ... although it was only three courses.

George Neville, brother of the Earl of Warwick, wanted to make a splash. And splash out he did, ordering so much food for his installation feast in 1466, that half of Yorkshire was denuded, 62 cooks, 515 kitchen hands and 1,000 waiters sweating over hot platters in one of the biggest mass catering marathons in history. And here is the menu:

A Grand Feast – On the Occasion of the Installation of His Eminence the Archbishop of York

MENU

Please note that restrictions on dish sizes preclude diners partaking of all choices.

FIRST COURSE

Pykes and Breams	608	Purpoises and Seals	12
Oxen	104	Wild Bulls	6
Muttons	1000	Veals	304
Porks	304	Kids	204

SECOND COURSE

Swans	400	Geese	2000
Capons	1000	Coneys	4000
Biterns	204	Heronshaws	400
Pheasants	200	Partridges	500
Woodcocks	400	Curlews	100
Egrittes	1000	Plovers	400
Quales	100 doz.	Peacocks	104
Fowls	200 doz.	Mallards and Teals	4000
Cranes	204	Chickens	2000
Pigeons	4000	Pygges	2000
Stags, Bucks and Does, 500 and more			
Pasties of Venison (hot)	1500	Pasties of Venison(cold)	4000

THIRD COURSE

Parted Dishes of Jellies	300	Cold Tarts (baked)	4000
Cold Custards (baked)	3000	Hot Custards	2000

Spices, Sugared Delicacies and Wafers – plenty!
Ale – 300 tuns Wine 100 tuns
Ypocrass 1 pipe

Directions: *Cawood is on the river Ouse between Tadcaster and Selby at the junction of the B1223 and the B1222. Only a gatehouse survives (south-east of the* *crossroads) an exquisite oriel window and a stair turret giving just an inkling of the castle's former opulence. Map Landranger 105 – Grid Ref: 575377.* ☛ ***See also 139 (Bishop Wilton)***

32. ULLESKELF: THE LAST BASKET MAKER

Moses floated to his destiny beholden to the basket-makers' trade, myriads of people ever since singing the praises of osiers. Wands of highly durable and elastic coppiced willow, osiers have been grown in England for thousands of years, many villages having their own basket-makers who produced a wide variety of receptacles and furniture for every conceivable purpose. An indigenous tree of river-banks and water margins, fast growing willow yields an annual harvest, providing a versatile raw material that in the earliest days of manufacture could be fashioned into utilitarian objects without tools.

Osier growing in Yorkshire was once concentrated along its tidal rivers, the tiny Viking settlement of Ulleskelf on the Wharfe having seven basket-makers along with its eel catchers, water fowlers and farmers. The last in a long line of makers, only John Taylor survives.

John Taylor can trace his basket-making ancestry back to the sixteenth century, and he still uses the river banks of his forebears to grow his crops. He plants four types of osiers – Champion Rod and Black Mole for basket work, Blue Bud for woven fencing and Longskin for hampers and mill skeps. Some plants are left to grow on for three years, although most are cut annually. Tools are minimal consisting of a knife and shears for cutting and trimming, a flat board to hold and turn the work, a flat weave – compacting hammer, a pricking knife which delicately scores the rods to make them pliable, and a bodkin. The rest is down to skill and the old techniques of 'randing', 'slewing' and 'whaling', which produce baskets and other wicker products in the traditional time-honoured way.

Directions: *Ulleskelf is two and a half miles south-east and downstream of Tadcaster on the River Wharfe (A162 and the B1223). John Taylor's basket making workshop and showroom is on Ings Road next to the river, about one mile east of the railway station, opposite the Ship Inn. Map Landranger 105 – Grid Ref: 537396.*

33. TOWTON MOOR: PALM SUNDAY FIELD

Towton Moor has the dubious distinction of being the most blood drenched stretch of land in all England, upwards of 28,000 corpses staining its soil after a tumultuous battle that marked the end of the War of the Roses on Sunday 29th March 1461.

Henry VI, the symbolic leader of the Lancastrian army, refused to fight on the Sabbath and fled to York with his wife, leaving the Duke of Somerset at the head of a 40,000 strong army. In opposition was the Earl of March,

Bloody Meadow at Towton Moor.

Edward Plantagenet and 36,000 men. A previous skirmish had left Edward's father dead and decapitated and the eighteen year old Yorkist general, recently declared King Edward IV, was vowed to vengeance, driving his troops forward with the chilling shout: 'No quarter! No prisoners!.'

Better tactics and the cruellest of spring weather conspired a victory for the white rose. Aided by a blizzard raging from the south, Edward's archers flung a single volley of arrows into the enemy ranks, instantly retreating out of range. The Lancastrians responded with their own fusillade but it fell short in the wind, the Yorkist bowmen collecting the arrows and repeating the ruse. Then, the armies fell upon each other like wolves, the orgy of stabbing and hacking with sword, bill and mace continuing for several hours. For a while, the contest hung in the balance until the arrival of 5,000 reinforcements led to a breach in the Lancastrians' left flank. Terrified, they retreated northwards, the wounded and injured troops funnelling into a defile near a crossing of the Cock Beck, the frenzied flash of steel creating a mound of bodies and a tidal wave of blood, whose taint discoloured the water for miles downstream. True to his word, Edward left not a single Lancastrian alive, the butchery continuing for three days in a merciless pursuit of stragglers.

An abiding legend persists in the melancholy hedgerows of Towton. The copious seepage of blood on that mad March day is supposed to have so conditioned the soil that the petals of the white Towton Rose were thereafter tinged with crimson:

There still wild roses growing,
Frail tokens of the fray,
And the hedgerow green bears witness
Of Towton field that day.

Directions: *Towton Moor is south-west of Towton on the B1217 – access from the A1/M1 Interchange at Hook Moor – three and a half miles. Roadside is a memorial known as Lord Dacre's Cross (he fought for the Lancastrian cause) the short path west leading to the valley of the Cock Beck where the rout of the Lancastrians took place. Overlooking this spot, an interpretation board gives details of the battle. The aptly named Bloody Meadow lies a few hundred yards to the south. In the nearby village of Saxton, in the graveyard of All Saints' Church, is Lord Dacre's tomb chest – he was buried with his horse having died after improvidently removing his gorget to drink a cup of wine, a cross-bow bolt hitting him in the neck. On the B 1217 west of Saxton is the Crooked Billet inn. This was the Yorkist headquarters. Opposite and accessible by a field path is the tiny thirteenth-century Lead Chapel. This was used as a makeshift mortuary and hospital during the conflict. Map Landranger 105 – Grid Ref: 478387 (Lord Dacre's Cross).* ☛ ***See also 123/145 (York/Londesborough)***

34. MARSTON MOOR: 'I COMMAND AND CONJURE YOU ... TO THE RELIEF OF YORK'

With the English Civil War ravaging on into its second bloody year, the fortunes of war hung in the balance. York was imperilled. If the great city fell, the whole Royalist cause might be lost. King Charles was impelled to act, writing prophetically to his victorious general Prince Rupert with these words:

I command and conjure you, by the duty and affection which I know you bear me, that, all new enterprise laid aside, you immediately march, according to your first intention, with all your force to the relief of York; but if that be either lost, or have freed themselves from the besiegers, or that, for want of powder, you cannot undertake that work, that you immediately march with your whole strength to Worcester, to assist me and my army; without which, or your having relieved York by beating the Scots, all the successes you may afterwards have, most infallibly will be useless unto me.

On the evening of 30th June 1644, Rupert, who was flushed with success from recent skirmishes at Newark, Stockport, Bolton and Liverpool, occupied

Knaresborough and Boroughbridge. Marching into York on the 1st July, he raised the siege, the Parliamentarians withdrawing to Marston Moor. With around 26,000 troops on either side, the scene was set for the battle that would decide the King's future. But the troops were reluctant to fight.

Between the opposing forces was an open moor, a hedge and ditch in its centre, protected by Royalist field guns and a detachment of musketeers, causing apprehension on both sides. Waiting for each other to make the first move on that pleasant summer day of 2nd July, the generals contented themselves with occasional salvoes, one cannon shot, that killed Cromwell's nephew, supposedly bringing on a Roundhead attack. At around seven o'clock in the evening, just as Rupert began to eat his supper, the Earl of Manchester attacked the ditch – with fatal consequences.

The monument at Marston Moor.

Deadly showers of bullets and cannon balls were fired into the Roundhead lines, Cromwell coming temporarily to the rescue. With his trademark impetuosity, Rupert entered the fray, leading his cavalry against the Parliamentarians' left wing. Flinging the opposition aside, he pursued the fleeing troops for some miles, Royalists in the rear causing havoc to such an extent that three generals – Manchester, Lord Fairfax and Leslie, believing all was lost, fled in the direction of Tadcaster and Cawood Castle. The old Ironside himself, however, fought on with utmost tenacity and great valour, Cromwell completely routing the Royalists. In a desperate melee, the Marquis of Newcastle's 'White Coats' fought a rearguard action, flinging their spent pistols at the enemy and fighting hand-to-hand with dagger and sword. 'Disdaining all offers of quarter, they perished almost to a man. They fell in their proper battle order, and presented a ghastly spectacle as they lay upon the field in rank and file, their white coats cruelly slashed with many a crimson stain.' Returning from his rash charge, Rupert, who was expecting a glorious victory, was roused to anger. Leading the last of his troops, he waded into the Parliamentary throng.

Cromwell was wounded in the neck but the attack was repulsed and Rupert fled in disarray.

Cromwell remained all night on the field in anticipation of a Royalist counter attack that never came, summoning his fugitive generals to re-join him at Marston Moor. When the order reached Leslie, who was already in bed in Leeds, he exclaimed: 'Would to God I had died on that place!'

Some 4,150 bodies were buried where they fell on the moor, the defeat severely affecting the Royalists' ability to wage war. Rupert's aura of invincibility was shattered, Newcastle fled to the Continent together with about eighty gentlemen who thought that the cause was hopeless, and the King lost a host of able men including Lord Kerry, Sir Francis Dacres, Sir William Lampton, Sir Charles Slingsby, Sir William Wentworth, Sir Marmaduke Luddon and Colonel John Fenwick. He also lost much of his logistical capacity to continue with the struggle, the parliamentary inventory of captured items listing 25 artillery pieces, hundreds of carbines and pistols, 130 barrels of gunpowder and 10,000 assorted hand weapons.

This bloodiest battle of the entire campaign totally destroyed the King's power in the north, the Parliamentarians marching into York on the 16th July and giving thanks for their victory at the Minster.

Directions: *Marston Moor is about seven miles east of York just north (on the minor lane to Tockwith) of the B1224 near the village of Long Marston. An obelisk, at the junction of the minor lane and Moor Road (overgrown), marks the site of the battle. An interpretation board shows the deployment of the opposing troops. Map Landranger – Grid Ref: 490521 (obelisk).* ☛ ***See also 26/39 (Ripley/Newburgh Priory)***

35. BENINGBROUGH: BOMBS AND JUST A LITTLE BOOZE

Feted one minute and shot at the next, many RAF airmen during the war led the life of gladiators, having to cope with two starkly contrasting worlds. Billeted in the beautiful early eighteenth-century Beningbrough Hall, the flyers from Linton-on-Ouse, some two and a half miles distant, felt the contrast more than most.

The hall, completed by John Bourchier, High Sheriff of Yorkshire, in 1716, was home to a number of squadrons. The most famous of these was 76 Squadron under the command of the legendary Leonard Cheshire VC. The hall was stripped of its valuable furniture and artwork when the new occupiers moved in, the owner of the property, Lady Chesterfield, relocating to Home Farm nearby. The airmen had their dormitories on the top two floors of the hall, using the ground floor as a mess.

With tranquil views of the river Ouse over water meadows to the confluence with the Nidd in the impossibly picturesque village of Nun

Monkton, Beningbrough Hall was the epitome of peace and tranquillity. But many crews left this halcyon place on their nightly bombing raids over Germany, never to return. Sergeant Clifford Hill, who was a gunner in a seven-man Halifax bomber flying from Linton in 1943, wrote an account of the his bitter sweet memories of the old hall:

> *After debriefing and breakfast, the seven of us would cycle along in the early morning to a dawn chorus along country lanes to Beningbrough.*

Later in 1943, Linton became the base for two squadrons from the Royal Canadian Airforce – the 426 'Thunderbird' Squadron and the 408 'Flying Goose' Squadron.

The infrequent interludes of rest and relaxation between missions were incongruent in the extreme. Evocative of the English idyll that the flyers were sworn to preserve, Nun Monkton with its ancient church, maypole and wide village green overlooked by the most inviting inn in Chistendom, was tantalisingly close. There was no road to the Alice Hawthorn from the Beningbrough side, so the aircrews took the ferry, spending their few precious hours in the bar of the Alice Hawthorn. Despite the full beer loads and the absence of navigation lights on the return crossing, there were only a few reported casualties.

Directions: *Beningbrough Hall (it is now a National Trust property open to the public) is about nine miles north-west of York (A19 to Shipton and left on a minor road). The Alice Hawthorn Inn is in the village of Nun Monkton (turn right down Pool Lane, about seven miles north-west of York off the A59 York to Knaresborough road. During the war the 'Alice' became a 'home from home' for many aircrews, some of who spent their last nights in its bar. Others customers, who were subsequently shot down and interred, wrote to the wartime landlord saying how much they missed the inn's hospitality and friendship. In November 1943, the landlord and a number of villagers, together with representatives of the Canadian bomber crews, made a wireless recording. It was transmitted from the inn to North America and Canada. There are photographic reminders of the bombers and their crews on the walls of the bar, nostalgic ex-servicemen still returning to the inn from time to time. Map Landranger 105 – Grid Refs: 516586 (Beningbrough Hall); 508578 (Alice Hawthorn Inn, Nun Monkton).*

36. ALDBOROUGH: BRIGANTES AND THE EARLY BATH

With a constant wind up their kilts, the Brigantes were not given to bathing or lounging about. So what did they think of the sweet-smelling invaders from across the seas?

'They might be a bit lively with the gladius and shield but have you smelt the buggers?' commented one old man. 'Do you know what they've done?

They've only gone and built a town on our old stomping grounds. And do you know what they've had cheek to call it? *Isurium Brigantum.* As if that would keep us quiet. I'll tell thee. Watter's bad for a body. Tha'll not get me near them baths not even with a trident up my arse!'

Our Yorkshire ancestors always had a way with words, the above verbatim report from the *Tile and Stilus* of 23rd Mars 87, recording a tribal chief's reaction to a guided tour of the newly opened Roman town.

Begun in the first century AD, the Roman town was of typical design, rectangular walls with four gates protecting an area of some 55 acres, a linear pattern of streets radiating out from a central forum. The town had a rich treasury of mosaic pavements. Discovered in 1848, one of these, showing a central eight-pointed star surrounded by four decorative borders, is in near perfect condition. Around this conversation piece, the Roman couches would have stood, Smithosus and Jonesopus reclining and discussing the affairs of empire before they retired to the town baths. A number of excavated toiletry articles, demonstrate considerable attention to personal hygiene, the commentary of our tribal leader shedding much light on the Yorkshireman's ancestral antipathy to soap.

'And do tha knows what else they showed me?' added the old man. 'It baffles me son. They had a bronze pick for cleaning tha lugs out and another tool for scraping muck from under t'finger nails. But there was summat even worse than that. The tribune said it were a strigil. I'd seen nothing like it afore neither. It were a fancy looking blade. Not so fancy that you could kill any bugger with it, no. Well it were obscene it were. Do you know what they did with it? They scraped their skins wit thing. Yus. Took off the lot it did. Muck and all that lovely hair that keeps the likes o' you and me warm. And this is the daftest bit. After they stood there shivering like new-born pups, they lights a fire under t'villa to keep their teeth from chattering. And they've conquered the world. Woden help us!'

Directions: *Aldborough is adjacent to Boroughbridge just east of the A1 on the B6265. Parts of the remains of the Roman town of Isurium Brigantum, which is in the centre of the village, may be explored on foot. Isurium is managed by English Heritage who charge an entry fee. Many artefacts discovered on the site are on display in a small museum. Built alongside a Roman road, St Andrew's church occupies a central position in what was the old town. Stone for part of its walls was plundered from the Roman ruins and the church is said to occupy the former site of the Roman temple of Mercury. Inside the church (to the right of the tower steps) is a statute of the god. This was unearthed when foundations for the church were dug in the fourteenth century. Map Landranger 99 – Grid Ref: 404663.* ☛ ***See also 140 (Kirkby Underdale)***

37. MYTON-ON-SWALE: RIVER RUNS RED

The barbarism perpetrated by the Scots at this still largely anonymous Yorkshire village, could have set alight an ethnic conflict to rival any in the world. But atrocities were the stock-in-trade of professional soldiers and mercenaries in the fourteenth century, history saying little about the appalling slaughter of a largely peasant and priest army at Myton-on-Swale on 20th September 1319.

With Edward II's army preoccupied in an assault on Berwick-on-Tweed, the Scots decided to invade England, Earl Murray and Lord James Douglas making a bold attack on York with a force of 10,000 men. The fortified city resisted, the Scots rampaging through the countryside with little opposition. Without the support of regular troops, the clergy felt impelled to act and they quickly recruited a rag bag assembly to match the Scottish force, farm labourers, serfs and around 400 of their own number taking the field. With the Archbishop of York, the Bishop of Ely and the Abbot of Selby in the van, the English rabble prepared to meet the hardened veterans of the 1314 victory at Bannockburn. Untrained and tactically guileless, overweight and unfit and possessing only the most rudimentary rustic weapons, this motley crew assembled on Myton Meadows, the Scots immediately luring them into an ambush.

Praising God, the white robed priests led the attack, pursuing the enemy over Myton Bridge. The Scots led them on, retreating under a smoke-screen provided by burning haystacks. Then the claymores set to work, taking the bridge and cutting off the retreat, the terrified English scattering in disarray. Many of the conscripts were hacked to pieces. Many drowned in the river that flowed red with blood. By nightfall, Myton Meadows was littered with some 4,000 corpses. Amongst their pitiful ranks, were the bodies of 300 clergymen, their gored and crimsoned bodies lying sodden in the grass.

According to one old account of the battle, the priests were 'arrayed in full canonicals … the Scots, who lost few men themselves, treating the slaughter of the churchmen as a pleasant joke …'

After their success, the Scottish army drove south and crossed the Aire in Castleford, marching on, with terrible devastation and plunder, through Airedale, Wharfedale and the lands of Craven.

Directions: *Myton-on-Swale is somewhat isolated by the rivers Swale and Ure and is best approached from the east via Tollerton (go eight miles north of York on the A19 and left on a minor road through Tollerton for a further five miles). The battle, variably known as the Chapter of Myton (by the Scots), the White Battle of Myton (in allusion to the white surplices of the priests) and the Battle of Myton Meadows, was fought out on the banks of the Swale near to the existing bridge. Many bodies were buried in the nearby churchyard of the thirteenth-century church of St Mary's. Map Landranger 99 – Grid Ref: 438668.*

38. CASTLE HOWARD: A SOARING SEPULCHRE

The Earls of Carlisle must have had egos and bank balances the size of airships. Why else would they have built a mausoleum that could accommodate an entire necropolis? Designed by Nicholas Hawksmoor in 1728, this enormous bone repository was 11 years in the building, its ridiculous size, cost and opulence being compared to a Wren church in the city of London. Seeing this undeniably beautiful building in 1772, a gobsmacked Horace Walpole said the mausoleum 'would tempt one to be buried alive.'

Located three quarters of a mile from the mansion, the mausoleum was reckoned to be the first building of its kind, unconnected with a church, in England. Essentially it is a Doric temple with a dome and a peristyle of twenty Tuscan columns. No expense was spared in its construction or decoration, embellishments including a triglyph frieze, banded rustication, carvings and brass inlay.

Directions: *Castle Howard (which is open to the public) is around 15 miles north-east of York via the A64 (take the signposted minor road north at Barton Hill). The mausoleum is not open to the public but it can be viewed from a public footpath starting in the village of Welburn just east of the access road to the south of Castle Howard (Follow the signpost north, near the War Memorial building, going down Water Lane and through the wood for about three quarters of a mile). Map Landranger 100 – Grid Ref: 727697.*

39. NEWBURGH PRIORY: OLIVER CROMWELL R.I.P.

Time has a habit of repaying evil acts in spades, the juxtaposition of two severed heads reminding us all just how perverse life can be. Charles I had his head chopped off in 1649 at the command of Parliament, one of the signatories to his death warrant giving scant thought to the vulnerability of his own neck. If Oliver Cromwell had known what destiny had in store, he might have thrown down his quill in terror.

The great dictator died in 1658. He did not rest in peace. On the 30th January 1661, along with the corpses of other regicides, his body was exhumed and beheaded on the twelfth anniversary of the execution of the king, the trophy being impaled on a pole raised above St Stephen's Hall. The ignominy might have ended there but for the clandestine efforts of a Yorkshire lady.

Lord Fauconberg married Cromwell's third daughter Mary who brought her father's remains back to Newburgh Priory. There, they were placed in a vault that has remained unopened in 340 years. According to one description, the vault was affixed with an inscribed metal plate concluding with the letters 'R.I.P', someone, over the years, having attempted to scratch them out. There have been numerous inquisitive requests for the vault to be opened, King Edward VII and Winston Churchill ranking among the disappointed visitors. Former priory owner Sir George Wombwell, spoke for generations of Cromwell's descendants when he fumed: 'No! No! We do not make a show of our great relative's tomb, and it shall not be opened. In this part of Yorkshire we no more dig up our remote great uncles than we sell our grandmothers. The Protector's bones shall rest in peace.'

Directions: *Newburgh Priory is half a mile south-east of Coxwold (access off the A19 north of Easingwold). The tomb of Oliver Cromwell is on display in Newburgh Priory, which is open to the public. Map Landranger 100 – Grid Ref: 543765.* ☛ ***See also 26/34 (Ripley/Marston Moor)***

40. COXWOLD: 'I AM AS HAPPY AS A PRINCE'

Laurence Sterne, the famous author of *Tristram Shandy* and *A Sentimental Journey*, was contentment personified. Coxwold's parson for the eight happiest years of his life, he lived in the delightful Shandy Hall, opposite St Michael's Church, between 1760 and 1768. Sterne had a reputation as a somewhat doleful sermoniser, but he was a demon with a pen, his novels and eulogies about his Yorkshire home creating queues of would be clerics!

'I am as happy as a prince at Coxwold, and I wish you could see in how princely a manner I live,' he wrote to a friend. ''Tis a land of plenty. I sit down alone to venison, fish, and wild fowl, and a couple of fowls or ducks, with curds, strawberries and cream, and all the simple plenty which a rich valley (under the Hambleton Hills) can produce, with a clean cloth on my table, and a bottle of wine on my right hand to drink your health. I have a hundred hens and chickens about my yard, and not a parishioner catches a hare or a rabbit or a trout but he brings it in as an offering to me.'

Directions: *Coxwold is around three and a half miles north-east of the A19 (turn off three miles from the Easingwold Bypass and go through Husthwaite. Shandy Hall is a museum to Sterne's memory and is open to the public. Map Landranger 100 – Grid Ref: 533773.*

41. KILBURN: THE FAMOUS WHITE HORSE

But for a phalanx of spades and the determination of a London businessman, Kilburn would be largely unknown. A tiny village at the foot of an escarpment of the Hambleton Hills, it slept on in anonymity until 1857 when local schoolmaster John Hodgson returned from a visit to the capital with the drawing of a horse. Inspired by the thousand year old Uffington White Horse in Berkshire, Kilburn's steed was commissioned by Thomas Taylor, a proud native of Kilburn who, with his brother, ran a prosperous grocery store in

London. Determined to put his home village firmly on the map, Taylor planned to carve a distinctive horse into the slope of his beloved Roulston Scar. He recruited the enthusiastic Hodgson, whose pupils marked out the outline of the horse, the task of scrub and turf removal falling to thirty-one Kilburn stalwarts.

At 314 feet long and 228 high, the horse was liberally covered in lime, its distinctive flanks shining out ever since. But the nag has suffered from recurring mange. Most classical subjects of leucippotomy – for that is what the hillside carving of equine figures is called – are to be found on a chalk ground. Kilburn's horse though, stands on rock of a dun colour, only regular grooming with lime keeping its coat gleaming.

By 1920, however, the underlying rock had been eroded to such an extent that the horse was destined for oblivion, a trust fund administered by the local vicar, a farmer and the celebrated 'Mouseman' Thompson of furniture fame, coming to its rescue. One donation of £100 was invested in a 5% War Loan, but the dwindling returns on interest purchased ever reducing quantities of lime and by the 1960s, the horse was threatened again. A renewed plea for funds led to major restoration work that included the removal of loose scree and the construction of a cement-overlay incorporating chalk chippings. Since then, chemical and engineering science has further spruced the distinctive mare, ensuring that the famous horizons horse can be seen from as far away as Brafferton, Boroughbridge, Wetherby, Harrogate, York and parts of the Yorkshire Dales.

Directions: *The White Horse overlooks Kilburn and the Vale of Mowbray. Kilburn is three miles south of Sutton Bank summit. Take the minor road south near the Hambleton Hotel. Affording an excellent view of the horse, a footpath runs north from the village bisecting Roulston Scar and Hood Hill. The horse can also be seen from a designated Viewpoint (parking available) off the minor road. Map Landranger 199 – Grid Ref: 514813.*

42. KILBURN: MICE MEN

There's not a church in Yorkshire worth its cruets without an oaken mouse. This 'wee, cowering timorous beastie' is the trade-mark emblem of Kilburn's furniture makers, their crafted wares gracing hundreds of churches, stately mansions and private homes alike.

The founder of the business was Robert Thompson. Born in 1876, he was apprenticed to his father, the Kilburn joiner, carpenter and wheelwright. Not content with the more rudimentary aspects of the business, Robert began to produce quality furniture, some using fourteenth-century medieval patterns from his extensive library. And he took up the carver's chisels and the age-old adze, using this ancient tool to produce a characteristic dimpled and undulating finish that marks out the firm's speciality oak furniture to this day. He also left his unique signature on each and every piece, thousands of life-sized mice, running up clocks, crawling down table legs, scampering along church pews and generally creeping about, sometimes in the least obvious places. The mouse was adopted around 1925, Robert Thompson revealing the origins of the beast to his grandsons.

> *I was carving a beam on a church roof when Charlie Barker, another carver, murmured something about us being as poor as church mice, and on the spur of the moment I carved one. I thought how a mouse manages to scrape and chew away the hardest wood – and it works quietly. I thought that was maybe like this workshop; it's what you might call industry in quiet places, so I put my mark on all my work.*

A quiet, dedicated and contented craftsman whose work adorns Westminster Abbey, York Minster, Workington Priory, St Peter's School in York, Ampleforth College and innumerable chapels and churches both in Yorkshire and elsewhere, Robert continued working until his death at the age of 79 in 1955. He was keen to ensure that his legacy continued, reputedly saying to his grandsons just before he died: 'Make sure you keep your timber yard full.'

Today, that timber yard is replete with slowly seasoning English oak, his ancestors still producing quality furniture in the same old way. And the mouse tiptoes on.

Directions: *Kilburn is three miles south of Sutton Bank summit (A171). Take the minor road south near the Hambleton Hotel. The Mouseman Visitor Centre is in the centre of the village. Visitors can watch working craftsmen and inspect native hardwoods prior to manufacture. Map Landranger 100 – Grid Ref: 514795.*

43. THIRSK: HYMNS AND HERDS

Scotsman James Alfred Wight saw more blood, sweat and pigs ears than 10 Yorkshireman and deserves his proud place in the Tyke's hall of fame. A Dales vet who joined J Donald Sinclair's practice in Thirsk in 1940, he remained in the area, apart from three years absence in the RAF, until his death in 1995, chalking up thousands of veterinary visits and five internationally famous books based on his exploits in surgery, yard and field. Published in 1972 under the pen name James Herriot, the first of these, *All Creatures Great and Small*, inspired the immensely popular BBC Television series of the same name, his equally successful *All Things Bright and Beautiful, All Things Wise and Wonderful, The Lord God Made Them All* and *Every Living Thing* following on in subsequent years. Remarkably though, Wight only began writing in 1966, over 25 years of wrestling with '... hard-bitten old characters with their black magic cures ...' enabling him to conjure up stories that have the provenance of a Yorkshire pud.

Directions: *Thirsk is about 23 miles from York on the A19/A170. Alf Wight lived and worked in Thirsk at No 23 Kirkgate, off the Market Square (on the B1448 to Northallerton). The period-restored house and surgery, which is now known as 'The World of James Herriot', has 1940s and 1950s rooms, and exhibits of veterinary artefacts. There are numerous Dales locations with Herriot connections. He was married in Thirsk's local church and in later life he owned a house in the nearby village of Thirlby. The long running TV series introduced the Yorkshire Dales to the world, places such as Langthwaite in Arkengarthdale (opening sequence) and Askrigg in Wensleydale (house used as Skeldale surgery) drawing thousands of visitors every year. Map Landranger 99 – Grid Ref: 428822 (The World of James Herriot).*

44. BUSBY STOOP: AN ELECTRIC CHAIR

Heroic, exotic, bucolic and bizarre, inn names are inspired by famous battles, heraldic arms, streaming flags, crossed keys, multiple kings' heads, red lions, black swans, golden fleeces, dusty millers and two-headed swans. But what of the unusually titled *Busby Stoop*? It has the dark shadow of Uriah Heep about it. And well it might, for it commemorates a public gibbeting that surely gave rise to the most chilling pub name in England.

In 1702, local reprobate and drunkard Thomas Busby murdered his father-in-law Daniel Auty. The pair may have quarrelled about Busby's ill treatment of his wife. The more likely explanation for the argument, however, is a dispute over money, both men having a reputation for involvement in the coining trade. Auty was reported missing, a subsequent search by the constables leading to the discovery of his corpse. Busby, who was an obvious suspect, was arrested at home, the officers finding him in a befuddled state, slumped in his favourite chair. He was promptly arrested, summarily tried and condemned to death, legend suggesting that before he went to the gallows, he cursed his chair and its

The infamous Busby Stoop chair.

future occupants. The sentence was carried out and Busby's limp body was hoisted in display on a post or 'stoop', at the prominent Ripon to Thirsk crossroads. The inn had its name.

Rotting corpses were the warning notices, the cautionary billboards of the day. The most graphic and hideous of deterrents, they were meant to be constant and long-standing reminders of the need for good behaviour. It was an offence to interfere with them in any way, only the processes of putrefaction and decay and the depredations of insects, crows and wild animals being allowed to intervene. In May 1703, the ragged cadaver was still on its stoop, the Leeds antiquary Ralph Thoresby passing the body and describing the 'doleful object of Thomas Busby, hanging in chains for the murder of his father-in-law Daniel Auty.' Eventually, every hair and scrap of skin had gone and the chains were removed. But the story did not end there.

Busby's accursed chair was taken into the newly named inn as a novelty, but it soon acquired a sinister reputation. For a century or more, it worked its dark magic, pilots, who used the inn during World War Two, associating it with bad luck. In the 1970s, several fatal accidents were linked with the chair, the inn's landlord successfully arranging for its banishment in 1978.

Today, it resides in the Victorian kitchen in Thirsk Museum, where it is somewhat of an attraction. With bravado and not a little trepidation, local schoolboys commit their rear-ends to its seat in a sort of right-of-passage: 'I double-dare you!'

Quick, the curator's not looking. Dare *you* take the plunge?

Directions: *The Busby Stoop inn is three miles west of Thirsk (through the village of Carlton Miniott) at the A61/A167 crossroads. Thirsk Museum is in Kirkgate, Thirsk (just north of the centre). Map Landranger 99 – Grid Refs: 383809 (Busby Stoop inn); 428823 (Thirsk Museum).*

45. OSMOTHERLEY: SOME WALK!

For most of its recorded history, Osmotherley was a fairly ordinary and largely anonymous little village that hardy warranted a mention in the guidebooks. Then in 1955, up popped a lunatic with brains in his boots. Cleveland smallholder Bill Cowley issued a challenge in the August issue of the *Dalesman* magazine, inviting walkers to join him in a traverse of the North York Moors at their highest and widest point in 24 hours. His starting point was Scarth Wood Moor, near Osmotherly. His destination was Ravenscar, some 42 miles to the east!

Incredibly, several addled pedestrians joined the advance party, paving the way for thousands of other sloggers in the years ahead. Osmotherley was put firmly on the map and, a torrent of blister fluid and nearly 50 years later, the appeal of the so called Lyke Wake Walk shows no sign of abating, its trio of

Osmotherley – the author made it!

last-rites pubs continuing to pull some of the most sadly unclasped pints in the world.

The walk crosses a moorland wilderness, springy with heather and soggy with bog. Frequent bad weather and rugged terrain, which involves climbing some 5,000 feet, demands thorough preparation and fitness, and speaking from personal experience, a dogged determination to get to the finishing line in the bar of the Raven Hall Hotel. 'The last one in buys the ale!.' The walk passes a number of intriguing marker stones – the Face Stone, Blue Man I't Moss, the Head Stone and Fat Betty.

The name of the walk is inspired by the ancient funereal history of the moor, the word *'lyke'* referring to a corpse, the word *'wake'* meaning a watching of the deceased. Until comparatively recent times, the isolated communities in these parts believed that the 'soules of the dead went over Whinny Moore', the coffin recital of an ancient dialect dirge running to 40 lines. It begins:

This yah neet, this yah neet,
Ivvery neet an' all,
Fire an' fleet an' cannel leet,
An Christ tak up thy saul.
When thoo frae hence away art passed

Ivvery neet an' all,
Ti Whinny Moor thoo cums at last,
An' Christ tak up thy saul.

Walkers who complete the walk automatically become Dirgers and members of the Lyke Wake Club. So what are you waiting for?

Directions: *Osmotherley is at the western edge of the North York Moors, one mile east of the A19/A684 junction at Lane End. The Lyke Wake Walk effectively starts in the village. Map Landranger 99 – Grid Ref: 456974 (Start of Lyke Wake Walk).*

46. KIRKDALE TIME STANDS STILL

A real Tom Thumb of a church, St Gregory's Minster lies in the valley of the reclusive Hodge Beck. Of great antiquity, it incorporates Saxon, Norman and Early English styles of architecture, two of its former priests leaving us a message written in time. Their 900-year old sundial, set on a massive beam of stone above the doorway, can be dated to the reign of Edward the Confessor, a translation of its unique inscription reading:

Orm, the son of Gamal, bought StGregory's Minster when it was all broken and fallen, and he caused it to be made anew from the ground, for Christ and St Gregory, in the days of King Edward and in the days of Earl Tosti, and Hawarth wrought me and Brand the prior.

For centuries, the sundial was buried under a covering layer of plaster, only a chance discovery in 1771, leading to its cleaning and renovation.

In a sylvan spot, the church looks out over a dry river-bed incrusted with ancient fossils, the prominent cave above yielding Stone Age tools and the bones of elephant, rhinoceros, hippopotamus, lion, tiger, hyena, wolf, ox and bear when it was first explored in 1921.

Directions: *St Gregory's Minster is two miles south-west of Kirkbymoorside on a minor road off the A170. The famous Kirkdale Cave is on the left bank of the beck, just 100 yards or so north of the road crossing. Map Landranger 100 –Grid Ref: 677858.*

47. LASTINGHAM: SPIRITUAL CURRENTS

The subliminal power of this subterranean shrine to Saint Cedd is quite astonishing. For Christians and atheists alike, its aura knocks the spiritual Geiger counter off the scale.

Raised by monks on the site of the saint's grave around 1080, it remembers the holy pioneer who came to Yorkshire in 660 and founded the monastery

St Mary's Church.

at 'Laestingaeu.' The crypt is dominated by an eye-drawing apse and altar lit by a sensual shaft of light, visitors hypnotically descending a flight of steps from the nave of St Mary's Church above.

A retreat for meditation and reflection, this church in miniature has a chancel, nave and aisles, four stout columns supporting groin vaults. For nearly 50 years between 1831 and 1879 it was transformed into a Greek temple. Today, it serves its original purpose, a collection of ancient cross heads and other artefacts adding to the interest of this very special place.

Directions: *Lastingham is about six miles north-west of Pickering. Take the A170 and turn right in Wrelton going via Cropton. St Cedd's crypt is underneath the nave of St Mary's Church. Near the church are the inscribed sites of two holy wells. Map Landranger 100 – Grid Ref: 728905.*

48. ROSEDALE: IRON IN ARCADIA

Not many of the ironstone workers in the dramatically beautiful Rosedale worked beyond the age of 21. Furnace and machinery accidents, rock falls, overcrowding in one up and two down hovels and disease saw to that. The perilous large-scale extraction of iron ore began in the area around 1800. By 1850, a dramatic 100-feet high chimney spewed out its smoke and ash over the shivering one in three gradient that is Rosedale Chimney Bank, a mineral railway soon cutting a swathe through the purpled moors en route to the smelting works at Battersby on the Tees. In the 1870s, the population of Rosedale parish rose tenfold, a church, five chapels, a hospital, five public houses and a police house complete with cells serving a Klondyke community of nearly 4,000 souls. In 1926 following a terminal decline in the industry, the kiln fires finally went out leaving the village virtually empty and the scarred moor-top abandoned to the sheep. Following a strike by lightning that rendered its foundations unsafe, the towering legend that was Rosedale Chimney was demolished in July 1972.

Some workers endured a daily trudge up and down the steepest road in England. At an elevation of 1,000 feet, the remains of their recently conserved kilns can still be seen and visitors can walk along the greened track of the former mineral railway. Back in the valley bottom is the village of Rosedale Abbey and the church of St Mary and St Laurence whose Burials Register for the years between 1871 and 1902, confirms the average life expectancy of just 21 years. In the churchyard are a number of poignant reminders of the fragility of miners' lives.

Directions: *Rosedale is about 13 miles north-west of Pickering (leave the A170 at Wrelton, travelling via Cropton) Rosedale Chimney Bank is unmistakable! Map Landranger 100 – Grid Refs: 724955 (top of Rosedale Chimney Bank);725960 Rosedale village.* ☛ ***See also 52 (Port Mulgrave)***

49. GOATHLAND: HEARTS BEAT FAST AS ROPE SNAPS.

Even the sheep are members of Equity in Goathland, its traditional ways having been swamped in TV fame. Goathland is, of course, the backdrop to the Yorkshire Television series 'Heartbeat', fans from all over England clamouring to be photographed alongside Ewe and Shawn on its village green. But there is more to Goathland than the Aidensfield Arms.

Goathland has a remarkable mention in railway history. The village was on part of the route of the Whitby to Pickering line. Opened as a horse railway in May 1836 and converted to steam in 1847, this picturesque line had George Stephenson as its consulting engineer, the 24-miles-long route costing £4,000 per mile. The severe one in 15 gradient to nearby Beck Hole, however, demanded an ingenious form of traction. The engine tarried in the sidings as its coaches were hauled up the hill on a cable wound onto a revolving drum, a four ton tank filled with water acting as a descending counterbalance. Charles Dickens rode 'this quaint old railway along part of which passengers are hauled by rope' but in 1864, a serious accident saw coaches careering back down the slope towards Beck Hole. This persuaded the engineers to divert the track onto its present route.

Directions: *Goathland is in the North York Moors National Park between Pickering and Whitby. Road access is from the A169 (go north from Pickering for about 13 miles, and turn first left after Eller Beck Bridge). But why not maintain the railway theme and travel by steam-hauled engine from Pickering to the station in Goathland? A path, at the start of a Historical Rail Trail, follows the line of the old railway down to Incline Cottage. Map Landranger 94 – Grid Ref: 833014 (start of rail trail).*

50. GLAISDALE: A SONNET IN STONE

Yorkshiremen are not the most romantic lovers in the world. They occasionally pick hedgerow flowers for their sweethearts, but as a token of love, they prefer something a little more perennial and longstanding. Tom Ferris was a typical Tyke. He built his girl a bridge.

This young farmer's son from Lastingham was apprenticed to a Hull ship owner. Returning home on leave, he fell madly in love with beautiful Agnes Richardson, a local squire's daughter. Much to the displeasure of her rich father, Tom proposed marriage, a rebuttal only stoking his ardour and ambitions to tie the knot. He suggested a bold scheme. 'If I return from sea with a fortune to match your own, will you relent?' he asked boldly. The squire agreed, and in May 1588 Tom packed his kitbag. Bring on the Armada and Spanish treasure! But Tom just had to say goodbye.

His usual route to the squire's house in Glaisdale was over the brawling Esk. But heavy rains had made the ford impassable, the raging torrent thwarting all Tom's attempts at crossing. The lovers signalled to each other with candles and Tom reluctantly turned away, sailing off to confront the enemy.

Having helped capture a galleon, hero Tom returned to Glaisdale as a rich man. The couple were married, soon settling in Hull, where Tom became a successful businessman. In 1618 Agnes died. A year later, Tom remembered his love in the most enduring of ways. He raised a bridge over the Glaisdale ford, impressing his initials in the parapet. The bridge has stood these 400 years.

The bridge at Glaisdale.

Directions: *Glaisdale is in the North York Moors National Park. The best access is from the A169 Pickering to Whitby road, going west for about seven miles through Grosmont and Egton. Thankfully relieved of its traffic burden by a more modern structure, the Beggar's Bridge is east of the village near the railway line. Map Landranger 94 – Grid Ref: 783055.*

51. EGTON BRIDGE: THE PRIEST OF THE MOORS

The Catholic priest Nicholas Postgate needs no monument. No plaque or roadside shrine need mark his passing. But search and you will find him. Come to Egton Bridge where he was born, and come to the wild uplands where he wandered in all seasons for twenty selfless years, bringing comfort to the poor and needy. Here, in the muffled cottages where he celebrated Mass, and here beside the ancient moorland crosses where he preached, you will find the man, incense on the wind conjuring a picture of a gentle priest bounding across the heather, his brown tunic and white cape billowing and his old bone cross bouncing on his chest.

Nicholas Postgate – quietly passionate, undemonstrative, totally dedicated, and as stubborn as a mule. Nicholas Postgate – a simple servant of God who just wanted to be left alone to perform his holy life's work. Nicholas Postgate – a gentle and increasingly frail priest of 82 who was arrested as he baptised a child in 1678 and taken away for trial and ultimate execution.

Nichloas Postgate shown on an inn sign at Egton Bridge.

Postgate was born into a recusant Catholic family in Egton Bridge around 1600. At the age of 21, against a background of continuing religious persecution under the reign of James I, he entered the English College at Douai in Flanders to study for the priesthood, returning to England in 1630. For some years, he acted as chaplain to various prominent Catholic Yorkshire families, clandestinely visiting places such as Barnbow Hall and Saxton Hall near Leeds, Hazelwood Castle near Tadcaster and Everingham Hall near Pocklington in the East Riding. In the early 1660s, as an old man of over 60, he decided to quit the homes of the Yorkshire gentry and return to his roots on the North York Moors.

Settling into a humble cottage at Ugthorpe, near Whitby, Postgate began to serve a vast parish, stretching from the coast to Guisborough and south to Egton, Eskdale and over the Goathland moors to Pickering. Moving stealthily to avoid suspicion, with his simple chalice and cruets, he toured the district, taking the Holy Communion into cottagers' homes, attending the dying and offering spiritual nourishment to all. For two decades the work went on unabated until 7th December 1678. On that day, as he visited a house to baptise a Catholic child, Postgate was arrested, two men, in the process of searching for arms and ammunition, finding 'popish book, relicks and wafers, and severall other things,' including a 'supposed priest.' When interrogated about the discoveries, Postgate admitted to ownership, explaining that they were required for 'severall persons who desired them for help with their infirmities.' When asked if he was a priest, the dour Postgate, with typical Yorkshire bluffness, exclaimed: 'Let them prove it!'

The authorities did prove it, and hideously, Nicholas Postgate was hung, drawn and quartered on 7th August 1679. Before he died, the martyr composed a hymn. It is sung in the church at Egton Bridge to this day:

O Gracious God, O Saviour Sweet,
O Jesus, think of me.
And suffer me to kiss Thy feet,
Though late I come to Thee.

Behold, dear Lord, I come to Thee
With sorrow and with shame,
For when Thy bitter wounds I see
I know I cause the same.

O Sweetest Lord, lend me the wings
Of faith and perfect love,
That I may fly from earthly things
And mount to thee above.

For there is joy both true and fast
And no cause to lament.
But here is toil both first and last,
And cause oft to repent.

But now my soul doth hate the things
In which she took delight,
And unto Thee, O King of Kings,
Would fly with all her might.

But oh, the weight of flesh and blood,
Doth sore my soul detain:
Unless Thy grace doth work, O God,
I rise but fall again.

And thus, O Lord, I fly about,
In weak and weary case.
And, like the dove Noe sent out,
I find no resting place.

My weary wing, Sweet Jesus, mark,
And when thou thinkest best,
Stretch forth Thy Hand out of ark
And take me to Thy rest.

Directions: *Egton Bridge is in the Esk Valley in the North York Moors National Park, two miles west of Grosmont. Nicholas Postgate is thought to have been born in Kirkdale House in Egton Bridge. The site of the house is just beyond the bridge, to the left of the road, on the right bank of the river.*

On the left bank of the river is St Hedda's Catholic Church, which accommodates the Postgate Centre. The focal point of pilgrimages, the church has a number of Postgate relics displayed in an illuminated niche to the right of the altar. These include his chair, two altar candles, two pyx bags (used for taking the Blessed Sacrament to the sick), a rosary, a scrap of brown fabric possibly from his tunic and a small book on theology bearing Postgate's signature. Several of these items were discovered in the nearby Old Mass House. A model of the Mass House is also in the church – to the left of the entrance.

North of the church, on Brown Hill just above the school on the left as you descend into Egton Bridge, is the Old Mass House. It was the scene of a remarkable discovery in 1830, when a girl accidentally broke through a plaster wall to find an altar, complete with a crucifix, candlesticks, a missal and vestments, already prepared for the celebration of mass. Map Landranger 94 – Grid Refs: 804052 (site of Kirkdale House); 804054 (St Hedda's Church); 809059 (Old Mass House).

52. PORT MULGRAVE: ORE INSPIRING

On my 1895 map of the Yorkshire coast, Port Mulgrave is a nameless cove. Now, it's anonymous once more, only twin wave-crashed piers and blocked up tunnels suggesting its brief importance as an iron ore terminal.

Developed to feed the furnaces of the rapidly expanding smelting industry in Jarrow, Port Mulgrave is a prime example of fevered exploitation and summary abandonment, its investment requiring the excavation of a two-mile long tunnel to the ironstone mine in Grinkle, near Dalehouse and the construction of a narrow gauge railway to the sea. By 1920, the industrial fortunes turned and the business was rendered uneconomic. Today, the trundle of the ore wagons and the noise and dust of offloading are gone, only the creak of a few crab boats breaking the silence.

Directions: *Port Mulgrave is between Runswick Bay and Staithes. Take the A174 and turn right on a minor road at the northern end of Hinderwell. A steep, old miners' track leads to the bottom of the cove. The steps, which were once packed with 'slapes' of hard clay, are now part of 'Wilf's Way' and are in a good state of repair. The piers were blown up with explosives during World War II to prevent use by the enemy. There are several former miners' cottages at the top of the cliff. Map Landranger 94 – Grid Ref: 799177.* ☛ ***See also 48 (Rosedale)***

53. KETTLENESS: KEEP THE STONE PYRES BURNING

Shiploads of urine, mountains of seaweed and millions of tons of shale once desecrated Yorkshire's finest landscape, smoke and steam from the belching and bubbling pyres and cauldrons, nauseous smells and the eternal sounds of digging marking out the alum fields.

Alum was used in medicine, for tanning and as a fixing agent for dyes, Yorkshire producing most of the nation's mineral from cliff top sites between the early seventeenth to the late nineteenth century. The bluish alum rock was mixed with urine and seaweed and slowly roasted over vast bonfires of brushwood and coal, the vast heaps reaching 200 feet in length and over 100-feet high. Coal came from Sunderland and urine from London and elsewhere, ships contemptuously named 'Vasa Urinae' transporting tens of thousands of 25-gallon casks. After burning and calcification, the brick–red alum was repeatedly washed and boiled in lead-lined troughs, at the end of the months long process, the liquors eventually becoming crystalline and ready for use.

Thousands of men worked on alum extraction on dozens of sites between Scarborough and the river Tees, only advances in chemical science halting the industry.

Directions: *Kettleness was one of the main producers of alum, the detritus of its extraction bequeathing a moonscape quality to the local cliffs, which are halfway between Whitby and Staithes on the coastal path. Travelling from Whitby on the A174, turn first right after leaving Lythe, going through the hamlet of Goldsborough to Kettleness. The steep path down to the old workings is off right (left of the Cleveland*

Way track). Remnants remain of the track made from beach boulders. In places, the footprints of buildings and parts of old surface conduits can be seen. Map Landranger 94 – Grid Ref: 835160.

54. WHITBY: THE ABLEST SEAMAN

Captain James Cook worked his exploratory magic across the globe from the coast of Newfoundland in Canada to the Cook Strait in New Zealand. In three remarkable voyages aboard the *Endeavour* and *Resolution* between 1768 and 1779, he extended the boundaries of the known world, discovering and naming islands and charting coastlines in feats of seamanship and navigation unparalleled in naval history.

Cook was born of humble parents in Marton in 1728. His early career was ordinary in the extreme, his boredom as a farm labourer and a haberdasher's assistant in Staithes sparking the passions that were to take him around the world. But at the age of eighteen, he came to Whitby as an apprentice to local ship-owners John and Henry Walker who were in the colliery trade.

The monument to Captain James Cook at Whitby.

Learning the ropes, Cook spent most of his formative years plying the coal routes between Newcastle and London, later voyages taking him to England's west coast, to Ireland and to Norway. His vessels were the immensely practical but aesthetically unappealing colliers – 'a cross between a Dutch clog and a coffin' – whose remarkable broad-beamed, flat-bottomed design was to be adopted in building the *Endeavour* and *Resolution*. In these formative Whitby years, the tenacious Cook devoted himself entirely to the sea, spending his infrequent off-watch hours and shore leave in the study of navigation, astronomy and mathematics. Declining the captaincy of a commercial vessel in 1755, he took the amazing decision to join the Royal Navy as an able seaman. Thirteen years later, he was the captain of his own ship about to embark on one of the most adventurous voyages of all time.

Directions: *Whitby is on the Yorkshire coast between Scarborough and Redcar (A171). Cook spent three years as a lodger with John Walker who lived in Grape Lane (east side of River Esk off Church Street) overlooking the harbour. The house with a date plaque of 1688 is now a museum, Cook's attic bedroom forming the centrepiece of displays that include period furnished rooms, models and memorabilia. The Whitby Museum in Pannett Park (west side of River Esk off Church Hill Road) also has a wealth of Cook treasures.*
Looking out to sea, on a pedestal on the West Cliff (East Terrace), is a statue of Cook. On one side of the monument is a representation of the Resolution *and an inscription: 'For the lasting memory of a great Yorkshire Seaman this Bronze has been cast, and left in the keeping of Whitby; the Birthplace of those good Ships that bore him on his Enterprises, brought him to Glory, and left him at Rest.' Map Landranger 94 – Grid Refs: 901111 (Cook Museum – Grape Lane); 894109 (Whitby Museum); 898115 (Cook's statue).* ☛ ***See also 87/104 (Foulby/Birstall)***

55. WHITBY: STAKE AND NIPS

In Whitby, garlic is as popular for necklaces as its famous jet, scores of stakes also gracing the kits of its would-be vampire hunters. The literary devil Dracula first came to the Yorkshire port in 1897, part of Bram Stoker's novel of the same name using Whitby as a backdrop for the dark tale of animal transformations and neck puncturing.

In the guise of a black dog, Dracula scrambled ashore from a ship and bounded up the abbey steps. Later in the story, he appears as a bird, the scene being set, according to a local boarding house owner, in a tourist roost on the East Crescent: 'She was fast asleep, and by her, seated on the window- sill was something like a full sized bird … as I came into the room she was moving back to her bed, fast asleep and breathing heavily; she was holding her hand to her throat as though to protect it from cold.'

Today, the count is most often seen at twilight, flitting over the harbour in the form of a flying fox. He can also be examined at close quarters in a permanent exhibition on the harbour side.

A Dracula Trail visits all the Count's well-known haunts.

Directions: *Whitby is on the Yorkshire coast between Scarborough and Redcar (A171). Map Landranger 94 – Grid Ref: 901113 (start of Dracula Trail).*

56. ROBIN HOOD'S BAY: LIFEBOAT TOBOGGANS TWELVE MILES

Communal enterprise and determination can move mountains, Everests coming no bigger than that faced by the lifeboatmen of Robin Hood's Bay on

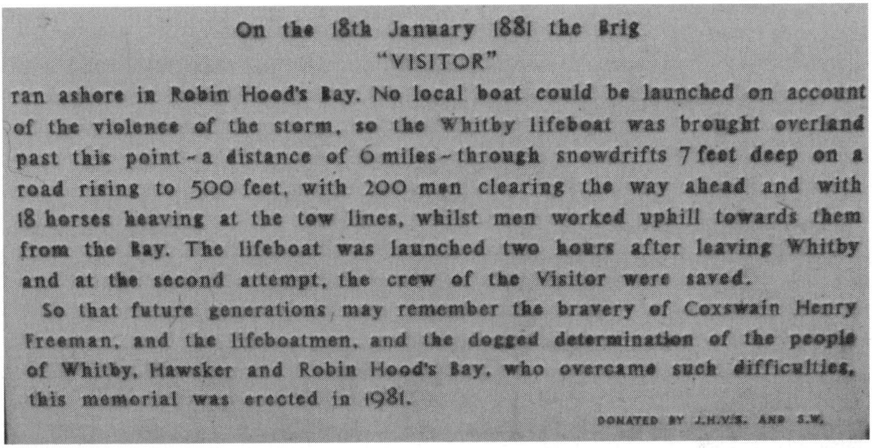

On the 18th January 1881 the Brig
"VISITOR"
ran ashore in Robin Hood's Bay. No local boat could be launched on account of the violence of the storm, so the Whitby lifeboat was brought overland past this point – a distance of 6 miles – through snowdrifts 7 feet deep on a road rising to 500 feet, with 200 men clearing the way ahead and with 18 horses heaving at the tow lines, whilst men worked uphill towards them from the Bay. The lifeboat was launched two hours after leaving Whitby and at the second attempt, the crew of the Visitor were saved.

So that future generations may remember the bravery of Coxswain Henry Freeman, and the lifeboatmen, and the dogged determination of the people of Whitby, Hawsker and Robin Hood's Bay, who overcame such difficulties, this memorial was erected in 1981.

DONATED BY J.H.V.S. AND S.W.

Plaque in Robin Hood's Bay marking the rescue of the Visitor.

the dire day of 18th January 1881. With the brig *Visitor* foundering in the bay and in danger of sinking in heavy seas, the lifeboatmen were faced with an awful dilemma. Should they risk attempting a rescue and see their craft smashed to smithereens even before they had left the slipway? Or should they seek help from their fellow lifeboatmen in Whitby? Standing by their braziers in a torment of indecision, they chose the latter option. But the seas off Whitby were equally treacherous and deemed too dangerous to launch a boat. Ordinary men in this predicament would have wrung their hands in despair and prayed. Not so our Yorkshire band of Titans who elected to drag their lifeboat overland … through the snow.

Using over 200 men and 18 horses, this bigger, more seaworthy boat was dragged up hill and down dale through snowdrifts seven feet deep, more volunteers lending their muscle with every mile. After nearly three exhausting hours, the boat was on the precipice of the grain shoot that passes for Baytown's main road, hundreds of blistered, rope-burned hands guiding it down the final incline to the sea. At last, the lifeboatmen had the means of salvation and they committed their oars to the waves, affecting a famous rescue of the six-strong crew of the sinking ship.

Directions: *A plaque at the top of The Bank records the details of the rescue. Forget the ice – rink underfoot and the four tons weight pulling on your arm sockets; just try walking down The Bank in summer attached to nothing more than a child's pushchair. It's strenuous man! The lifeboat was launched opposite the Bay Hotel on the slipway known as Way Foot. A Leo Walmsley novel inspired the pre-war movie the*

'Turn of the Tide.' Scenes of a lifeboat rescue were filmed here. Map Landranger 94 – Grid Ref: 952052 (Bank Top).

57. RAVENSCAR: THE TOWN THAT NEVER WAS

The Romans coveted every eminence and, inevitably, they built a fort on the isolated cliff of rock that is Ravenscar. In 1774, when the foundations were being dug for the mansion that was to become the *Raven Hall Hotel*, an inscription stone was discovered, dedicating the defensive work to 'Justinian, governor of the province and Vindician, general of the forces of Upper Britain.' The Vikings too knew a strategic location when their banners swelled, and, in 876, they planted their famous raven standard here, giving the place its name. Apart from the raising of Raven Hall – it was acquired by the royal surgeon Dr R.C Hall, who used its recuperative isolation as a treatment for King George III's madness – nothing much happened in Ravenscar in the succeeding millennium. Apart that is, from speculation.

Ravenscar: a road to nowhere.

A compulsive gambler who was almost as crazy as his royal patron, Doctor Hall bet his property on the outcome of a race between two bugs. He lost the wager, Raven Hall and the entire headland coming into the possession of a group of businessmen whose investment interests had been aroused by the completion of the Scarborough to Whitby railway line. In 1895, they embarked on an ambitious scheme to develop a holiday resort on the cliffs to rival Scarborough.

A blueprint was drawn up and, attracted by the grandiose ideas and special cheap rails fares from places like Bradford and Leeds, investors flocked to an auction of the seventy-nine plots. With plans and extravagantly worded sales literature flapping in the wind promising '... some splendid shop plots in Station Road and sites for marine villas of every size ... on a dry, rocky subsoil open to sunlight and bracing breezes', the company agents escorted the bidders round the site and the sale began. Thousands of pounds were raised for the new resort and preliminary work began using a workforce of 300 recruited from a wide area. Wide boulevards were constructed, sewers were laid and two or three isolated blocks of houses, complete with fenced gardens, were erected in advance of a building bonanza that never came. Ravenscar has stupendous views but no sandy beach, and the public never took the wind-scoured site to their hearts. Through lack of interest, the development company went bankrupt and the roads to nowhere were abandoned.

On reflection, the two bugs might have been a better bet.

Directions: *Ravenscar is about 12 miles north-west of Scarborough (A171 to Cloughton and then a minor road). The site of the proposed holiday resort is south-east of the Raven Hall Hotel. The tumbleweed infrastructure – the roads and the thistled-plots – is still there. Most noticeable are the kerb stones and the cast iron grates that reveal a sophisticated and expensive network of road drains. Map Landranger 94 – Grid Ref: 984015.*

58. HAYBURN WYKE: THE GHOSTS OF 'HALF THE GERMAN NAVY!'

Penetrated by a dark, serpentine path amidst the thickest trees, Hayburn Wyke cries out for exploration, visitors following an equally tangled stream whose merry waters make a final leap for the beach. A popular attraction in the Victorian era when a railway line delivered day-trippers to a nearby hotel, this delectable cove once held a dark secret. Had you been here on the fogbound morning of 16th December 1914, you might have strained your ears and peered into the mist. And dumbfounded, you might have seen the ghosts of 'half the German navy!.'

In 1914, Britain was at war with Kaiser Wilhelm. Reluctant to confront our fleet in an all out naval battle, he opted for a more cautious deployment of his forces, setting out to ambush our ports in a series of dawn raids. The German capital ships *Seydlitz, Moltke, Von der Tann, Derfflinger* and *Blücher,* together with a number of auxiliary vessels, moved off that morning to their rendezvous points. Their targets? Hartlepool and Scarborough.

At precisely 8.05 am, two cruisers began firing into the Yorkshire town, the unopposed barrage of 500 high explosive shells lasting 20 minutes. Nineteen people were killed in the attack and another 80 lay injured but with typical phlegm one lady remarked: 'Hey! Is it only guns? I was frightened it was thunder.' With Scarborough in flames, the ships turned north to loose the remainder of their ammunition on Whitby.

The people of Britain were outraged at the atrocity, the slogan on a famous war poster 'REMEMBER SCARBOROUGH' helping to stiffen the national resolve.

Directions: *Hayburn Wyke is about six miles north-west of Scarborough. Take the A165 and the A171 to Cloughton (four miles) and at the sharp left hand bend, keep forward on a minor road for a further one and a half miles to the right hand turn for the Hayburn Wyke Hotel. Footpaths lead down to the beach and the waterfalls. Map Landranger 101 – Grid Ref: 011971.*

59. SCARBOROUGH: SNAP, CRACKLE AND DROP

Erosion is an eternal curse, the sea consuming billions of tons of our Yorkshire coast since Roman times. In the worst affected area between Filey and Spurn Point, a vast area of land, up to three miles in depth, has been lost in the last millennium, villages such as Monkwike, Auburn and Ravenser Odd having been ground away. The low mudstone cliffs near Mappleton and Holmpton are the most vulnerable to attrition by the sea, but even the higher and seemingly more geologically robust cliffs further north are not immune.

On the morning of the 4th June 1993, the breakfast cereals in the luxury four-star Holbeck Hall Hotel in Scarborough, were not the only things making strange noises. A million tons of earth was on the move and guests had to get out quick.

News teams from all over the world reported the scene of devastation as the hotel began to tumble over the edge. Built in 1883, the 29-bedroom Holbeck Hall had once been owned by the family of the famous Hollywood actor Charles Laughton, extensive renovations making it one of the most luxurious in the resort. 'The hotel was our dream,' sobbed joint owner Joan Turner. 'I was in the main lounge this morning and I could see the walls cracking in front of me. The windows were breaking and I was told to get out for my own safety.'

'CLIFF – HANGER!' screamed the headlines of the local paper. 'The atmosphere is something like a cross between carnival and public execution,' reported another. Thousands of sightseers watched the Holbeck's Hall's last moments, some straining in pleasure boats offshore for the best views. A few days later only a pile of rubble remained.

The landslip was blamed on a series of dry summers leading to cracking, water penetration and lubrication of underlying sand and gravel beds. In 1994, hundreds of tons of rock from Norway were used to bolster erosion protection at the foot of the cliffs nearby. The Holbeck Hall site was cleared and landscaped.

Directions: *Scarborough is between Whitby and Bridlington. The main routes from the west are the A170 and the A64. The site of the Holbeck Hall Hotel is off Esplanade Crescent (take the Filey Road for one mile south from the town centre and turn left on Holbeck Road). Map Landranger 101 – Grid Ref: 047872.*

60. SCARBOROUGH: GRIMMY THE MOONLIGHT

A policeman's son, born in Leeds in 1836, John Atkinson Grimshaw had a natural talent for painting that his strict Baptist mother attempted to snuff out. She destroyed his paint box and persuaded him to pursue less frivolous interests, the thwarted artist eventually becoming a clerk at the Great Northern Railway in 1852. For nine years, the pen dominated his professional life but, inspired by the work of Holman Hunt and others, he persevered at his easel, taking up his brushes full time in 1861. Still lifes and a few landscapes were the predominant subjects of his early works, steady sales enabling him to move out of the city into Knostrop Old Hall.

The large and imposing seventeenth-century manor house two miles south-east of the city inspired the blossoming artist. Its raised garden and pleasance adorned with stone figures, and its splendid interior decorated with antique furniture, old armour and bric-a-brac, laid the foundation of 'that dreamy representation of the shadowy realm of the past which lives in his work, of which he was famed as a master of unquestionable ability.' From his new home, Grimshaw travelled by carriage all over Yorkshire, painting well-known scenes at Adel, Barden, Bolton Abbey (the Strid) and Semerwater. He also executed studies of Liverpool and the Thames.

By 1880, he was producing the tranquil night scenes for which he is best remembered. Few artists before or since have captured the genre so perfectly – the crepuscular communion of light and dark, the moon-dusted skies shot with blue and vermilion, the reflections of lamplight and the spars of ancient ships shimmering on the sea, and, in the shadows, lovers entwined in a last farewell. But some critics denounced Grimshaw, suggesting that his pointillist technique, by which tiny dots of colour were applied onto the canvas by stippling, debased art. Steady sales and exhibitions proved otherwise, one of his rivals, the noted artist James McNeill Whistler remarking: 'I thought I had invented the Nocturne until I saw Grimmy's moonlights.'

Nocturnal seascapes were one of Grimshaw's favourite subjects and he made many excursions to his favourite resorts of Bridlington, Whitby and Scarborough, painting a number of famous canvases such as 'Moonlight on the Esk – Whitby', 'The Harbour Flare' (real title 'In Peril'), and a 'View of Scarborough at Night.' Without relinquishing his Knostrop home, in 1876, he built a beautiful house to his own design in Scarborough. This castellated home and belvedere, perched on the cliffs near the castle with views of both bays, was called 'Castle-by-the-Sea.' It is still there.

Directions: *Scarborough is on the Yorkshire Coast (A64). Knostrop Old Hall was demolished and obliterated by sprawling sewage works before World War Two, but Grimshaw's evocative Scarborough house on the cliffs survives. The symmetrical mansion, Castle-by-the-Sea, is on Rutland Terrace off Castle Road. Grimshaw's paintings are in private collections and galleries all over the world. Locally, they may be enjoyed in the public galleries in Scarborough, Whitby and Leeds. Map Landranger 101 – Grid Ref: 046891 (Castle-by-the-Sea).*

61. BROMPTON: THE 'FATHER OF AERIAL NAVIGATION'

Born into an aristocratic family in1773, inventive genius Sir George Cayley changed the skyscapes of the world. One of his minor achievements was to engineer a flood relief channel to take surplus water to the sea from the River Derwent, his other credits including a design for caterpillar traction and a self –righting lifeboat. But it was his pioneering work on aerodynamics and manned flight that put this visionary scientist in the hall of fame, one prestigious society suggesting that his name should be 'inscribed in letters of gold on the first page of the aeroplane's history.'

As a child, Cayley read and experimented widely. He was fascinated by the achievements of the early balloonists but he was also a keen observer of birds and fish, concluding that 'a globe is by no means the best shape for obviating resistance to the air.' His thoughts on aerodynamic streamlining were inspired by the actions of the dolphin and the trout!

Pursuing his theories in his Brompton workshop, he built kites, balloons, airships and a model glider, elucidating the fundamentals of mechanical flight: 'To make a given surface support a given weight by the application of power to the resistance to air.' Sketching and theorising all the while, he defined the primary elements of aeroplane construction, examining the potential of an internal combustion engine and a 'whirling arm' as a method of propulsion. He also propounded the concept of integrated weight control, air resistance and longitudinal stability. By 1853, he had built

Plaque on Sir George Cayley's workshop at Brompton Hall.

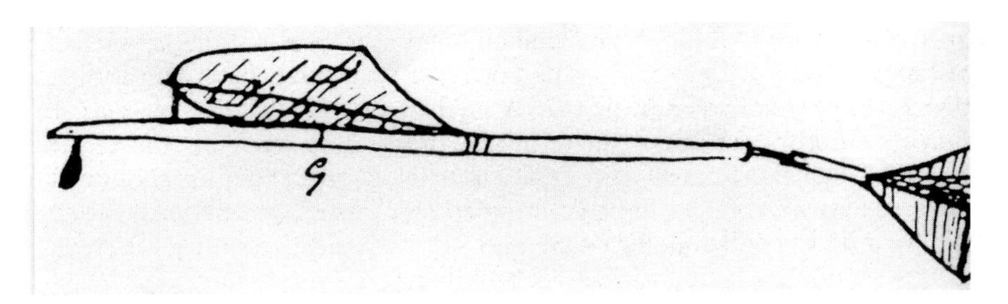

A sketch from Sir George Cayley's notebook.

a prototype to put his theories to the test, the world's first manned test flight of a heavier-than-air craft taking place in Brompton Dale.

Sir George died at Brompton Hall on 15th December 1857. One hundred and twenty years later, on the occasion of the opening of Washington's Air and Space Museum in 1977, it was declared: 'Sir George Cayley has earned the title 'Father of Aerial Navigation.'

Directions: *Brompton is on the A170, seven miles south –west of Scarborough. Marked by a plaque, Sir George Cayley's workshop is on the roadside, about 300 yards west of the Cayley Arms. Adjacent to the worshop is Brompton Hall which is now a school. Brompton Dale is north of the village. Map Landranger 101 – Grid Ref: 945823 (workshop).*

62. FILEY BAY: TRIREMES AND THE PRIDE OF THE U.S. FLEET

From the cliffs of Carr Naze, Roman sailors looked down on their galleys at anchor in Filey Bay. Protecting this great arc of water on the northern side is a famous reef – the Brigg – galleys chaffing on their moorings and leaving indelible marks to this day.

It is said that Filey Bay was shown on a Greek map drawn a century before the legions came, Roman occupation leaving us the remains of a signal station, fragments of a pier and several carved stones believed to have been part of a lighthouse.

A myriad tides have flooded and ebbed since the Romans left these shores in the fourth century, the gentle waters of Filey Bay hardly seeing an offending ripple in all those years. Then along came a pirate named John Paul Jones, his attack on an English convoy marking the birth of the United States Navy.

During the American War of Independence, US ships harried the English coast, John Paul Jones using a converted French merchantman renamed the *Bonhomme Richard* as his flagship. On Thursday 21st September 1779, he intercepted a flotilla of English ships and hoisted his colours, the resultant day long Battle of Flamborough Head ending in the defeat of the English and the capture of the *Serapis*. Locked together, the two vessels had pounded each other in bloody broadsides, hundreds of men dying of fearful wounds. By midnight, both craft were dead in the water and shot to pieces, the commander of the English ship crying quarter. Transferring his men to the *Serapis*, Jones abandoned his own crippled ship, which sank two days later. John Paul Jones recorded the moment: 'I saw with inexpressible grief the last glimpse … the stars and stripes were still flying.'

Directions: *Filey is between Scarborough and Bridlington on the Yorkshire Coast. The sea battle took place in fine weather, hundreds of spectators lining the cliffs of Flamborough Head to witness the contest by moonlight. The two ships closed at 7.20 pm in the southern quadrant of Filey Bay where the Bonhomme Richard sank. A few dedicated divers have attempted to locate the famous ship in recent years, one wreck, in less than 100 feet of water, exciting a number of archaeologists. Radiocarbon analysis of recovered timbers has dated the fire-damaged vessel to between 1776 and 1880. John Paul Jones is regarded as the 'Father of the American Navy' and even a plank from his flagship would be hugely prized. Map Landranger 101 – Grid Ref: 225795 (approximate coordinates of the wreck of the* Bonhomme Richard*).*

63. FILEY: THE WALKING PARSON

He should be the patron saint of perambulists the world over. At the start of the automobile age, he trumpeted a clarion call to legs that still has the pull of a spring tide. Inspirational and unconventional with a passion for physical exercise and the great outdoors, he toured most of Europe on foot, recording his adventures in a series of books that paved the way for all walking men. Impish, with a great joy for living, he was the incumbent in Filey's St Oswald's Church for over 55 years. He was the 'Walking Parson.'

Arthur Neville Cooper, to give him his Sunday name, was born in 1850. A robust child of eight, he attended a London boarding school, its strict regimes and poor diet only serving to strengthen his indomitable spirit. 'Our only clothing was a shirt and a coat, with the addition of a yellow petticoat in winter' he confided. 'When it rained, we played just as usual, our hair getting as wet as our clothes. No one ever thought of drying them. Sir Walter Scott relates that when a Highlander in the days before Flodden made himself a pillow of snow on which to rest his head at night, another Highlander kicked it away as a new fangled luxury.'

After leaving school, Cooper joined the Civil Service, spending the next 10 years studying for the ministry, which he entered in 1865. He came to Filey in 1868 and became an instant celebrity with his trade – mark frock coat, breeches, black hat and knapsack. Shunning the enfeebling luxury of hot water, he bathed regularly in Filey Bay in all seasons and he toured the county on foot, often tramping in excess of forty miles per day. Baggage, he counselled, should be reduced to the barest minimum, only a single change of shirt and stockings, a razor, comb and brushes and a pair of slippers being permitted. He carried with him no compass, map, waterproof clothing or rations, preferring the certitude of the open road. He was a generous man but was an eager convert to the Yorkshire creed of 'eating all, supping all and paying nowt', warming to the idea of enjoying hospitality at what he termed 'open houses', various landowners welcoming him with open arms. A raconteur with a love of good company that knew no social bounds, he was equally at home with fishermen, farmers and country landowners like the famous Sykes family of Sledmere. Cooper travelled all over Yorkshire and in a remarkable series of odysseys on foot, he visited London, Dublin, Limerick, Italy, Venice, Hamburg, Denmark, Belgium, Portugal and Iceland recording his adventures in his books, *Quaint Talks about Long Walks, The Tramps of the Walking Parson, A Tramp's Schooling* and *Round the Home of the Yorkshire Parson.*

A thoroughly stout fellow, a rustic Socrates with a profound appreciation of life, Cooper wrote this compelling commentary on the final page of a manuscript written in 1908: 'Everywhere there is a desire to return to a natural life, for it is evident from the health of the nation that something has gone wrong. The ancient philosophers who sought the Elixir of Life failed in their search, because they looked in every direction but the right one … it lies in the deep draughts of oxygen one drinks in from the air around us.'

I think it's time for lacing up.

Directions: *Filey is between Scarborough and Bridlington on the Yorkshire Coast (A64/A1039). St Oswald's Church is on the northern edge of Filey, overlooking Church Ravine. Cooper lived at the now demolished parsonage just over the ravine (use the footbridge) on Church Street. He died in 1943. His grave is about 100 yards east of the church porch (walk towards the sea) on the left of the path. Inside the church, in the sanctuary, is a plaque to his memory. The 'Walking Parson' is also recalled in Filey Museum on Queen Street (walk south, down Church Street and go first left). Map Landranger 101 – Grid Refs: 118812 (St Oswald's Church); 117810 (site of parsonage); 117809 (Filey Museum).*

64. NORTH GRIMSTON: '... HEAR HIM SWING HIS HEAVY SLEDGE.'

With his biceps gleaming in sweat and his hands wielding a great hammer, the blacksmith of old cut a noble figure. Looking for all-the-world like some leather-aproned apprentice to Hercules, he was an elemental and sensual exponent of fire and water, the sounds of his asthmatic bellows, hot-quenched iron and the clanging of his anvil, giving the smithy an almost magical appeal. Is it any wonder that blacksmiths were credited with special powers?

And children coming home from school
Look in at the open door:
They love to see the flaming forge,
And hear the bellows roar,
And catch the burning sparks that fly
Like chaff from the threshing floor.
– H.W. Longfellow

For hundreds of years, blacksmiths were as essential to the rural economy as seed corn, offering a vital service in shoeing horses and in making and repairing a whole variety of farming tools. They were consulted on more esoteric matters, having it was said, the ability to cure ailments of horses and to miraculously draw out stones or nails that had become lodged in the hooves. With a reputation as rural doctors, some were invested with the ability to cure humans, many anxious patients subjecting themselves to strange incantations and bizarre rituals with hammers and tongs. Famously, they were also thought to have the right to sanctify marriages.

There was a village smithy in North Grimston for decades. Similar to other smithies that once abounded in every settlement with a horse, it was greatly in demand with local racehorse owners from nearby Malton and Norton. Evidence of its popularity were the piles of old horse-shoes at its entrance, one of the stacks rising to a height of 14 feet and containing hundreds of rusted shoes.

A North Riding blacksmith's account ledger for 1833, gives a fascinating insight into the other types of work undertaken in the forge, as the following extracts show:

2 oxen shoeing 2/s
1 fork grathing and sock sharpening 5 and a half d
1 gavelock and swingletree grathing 6d
1 beast chain grathing 9d
2 cloggs ironen for servant boy 1 and a half d.

Directions: *North Grimston is about four miles south-east of Malton (A64) on the B1248. The smithy was in the centre of the village opposite the pub. Map Landranger 100 – Grid Ref: 843678.*

65. WHARRAM PERCY: GHOST VILLAGE

What happened to the villagers of the long abandoned Wharram Percy? Were they slaughtered in their beds? Did some terrible invader torch their houses? Or did some natural catastrophe or plague drive them out? The answer is prosaic indeed.

Wharram Percy.

Their agrarian economy, dating from the twelfth century, probably turned sour, unproductive fields forcing the entire population to seek pastures new. After hundreds of years, they abandoned a village whose archaeology continues to tell us much about early life in rural England.

Utterly peaceful and unsullied by any modern developments of any kind, the deserted medieval village covers some 10 acres of a 550 feet plateau, archaeological excavations between 1950 and 1990 uncovering a multitude of bones and revealing the sites of two manor houses, peasant cottages, a vicarage and a brace of mills. Of Saxon origins, the ruined church of St Martin's sits quietly nearby in a depression overlooking a former fish-pond. Until 1949, the church was used by parishioners from nearby Thixendale. In the absence of a road, they had to walk three miles to mass.

The bones from over 1,000 graves have revealed much about the physique and health of the local population. According to detailed scientific analysis, they were brachycephalic (they had short, squat heads!) and they suffered from gall and bladder stones and rheumatic disease, although, compared with modern man, they had fewer dental caries. The identification of animal bones shows a heavy dietary dependence on cattle, ox, sheep and pigs. Interestingly, the skeletons of some of the beasts show evidence of poor nutrition.

Directions: *Wharram Percy is eight miles south-east of Malton off the B1248. Go 700 yards south of the crossroads in Wharram-le-Street village and turn right on the lane for just over half a mile, passing Bella Farm to the parking area. There is no road access to the site, visitors having to walk the three quarters of a mile from the English Heritage car park (follow the signposts). A number of interpretation boards explain the history of the site. Map Landranger 100 – Grid Ref: 858644.*

West Yorkshire

66 to 105

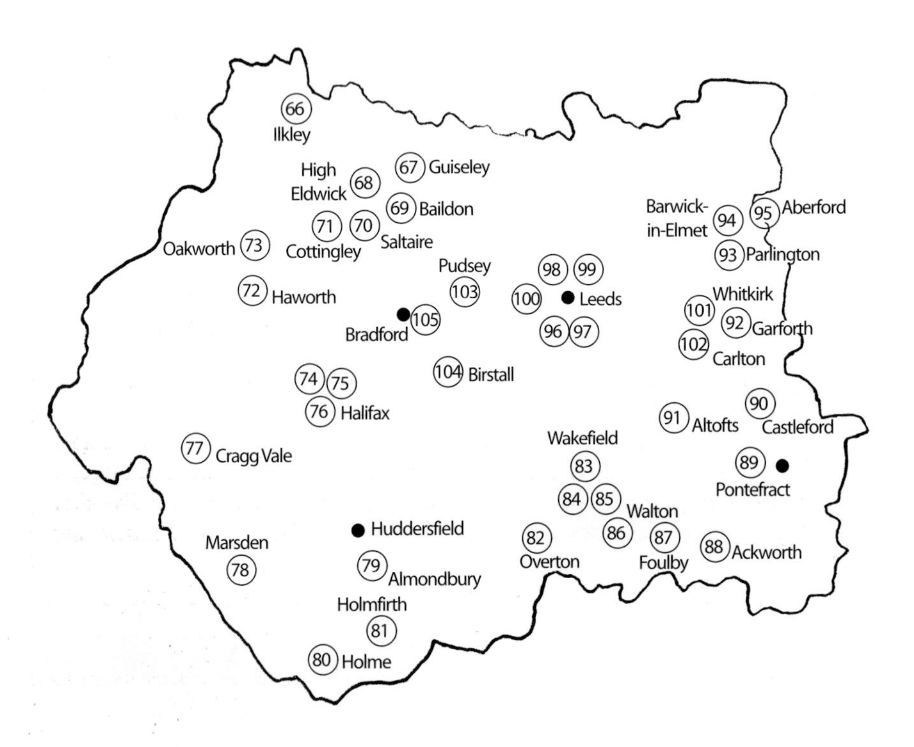

Rural and industrial in equal measure, gritty and uncompromising West Yorkshire was the birthplace of the Industrial Revolution, prodigious supplies of wool, water power and coal coupled with pioneering invention and ingenuity, helping to change the world. This Yorkshire Texas boasts the biggest and best of anything you would care to mention, its hall of fame including a man who created the world's first commercial railway, an eccentric who rode on a cayman and founded the modern science of anaesthetics and a larger than life parson who, with whisky in his shoes, walked the 741 miles distance to Italy in just six weeks on 10 shillings a day expenses. Read on and you will also come face to face with a young Russian chap who had the ultimate experience with a tree …?

HALIFAX BUGLE – APRIL 30th 1650

GIBBET CLAIMS TWO MORE VICTIMS

A large crowd gathered today at the execution ground to witness the beheading of John Wilkinson and Anthony Mitchell, both of this township. The unusual twin spectacle was attended by a great clamour of the populace, many side-shows, jugglers and acrobats adding to the entertainment.

GARFORTH GAZETTE – 1st APRIL 1903

RUSSIAN PRINCE DISAPPEARS WITHOUT A TRACE

Dozens of police officers scoured Parlington Woods late last night following reports of the disappearance of Crown Prince Zmronge, a prominent and popular Romanoff who is sixth in line to the Russian throne. The alarm was raised by Lady Gascoigne who claims she last saw the young man cavorting through the trees.

66. ILKLEY: THE SWASTIKA STONE

There is no more strange, enigmatic and thought provoking image in the whole of Yorkshire. Intricately and expertly carved on a monumental lump of rock on a bluff overlooking the town of Ilkley, it has cast its spell for thousands of years, its meaning lost in the mists of time. What manner of fur clad man scratched out this fylfot? And why?

Protected by a rusting iron fence, the stone could have been a sacred altar, just one of scores of incised boulders that are scattered liberally across Rombald's Moor. The Swastika Stone. See it. Study it. It shouts out for

On Ilkley Moor: The Swastika Stone.

examination and conjecture. Shaped like a writhing, four-legged octopus with a tail, it is attended by 10 spheres, one of the raised discs being slightly asymmetrical. Are these the planets? Is this a compelling image of the night sky? Not reckoning the earth, our ancient ancestors are said to have only known the existence of four planets. So what other message is written here? Stare on.

Directions: *Ilkley is between Leeds and Skipton on the A65. At the fringe of the moor east of the town, the Swastika Stone can be reached by public footpath, going through the very picturesque Heber's Ghyll. Follow the winding footpath up over a series of bridges and turn right at the summit for about 400 yards. Rombald's Moor has many other magico-religious carvings and prehistoric remains. Wander at will to find rock-engravings (especially those with a 'cup and ring' motif) stone-circles, cairns, field systems, hut-circles, round barrows, entrenchments and enclosures. Map Landranger 104 – Grid Ref: 096096.*

67. GUISELEY: T'BIGGEST CHIP SHOP IN'T WORLD!

A prolific spud basher by the age of five, Harry Ramsden worked in his father's chip 'ole in Bradford, diversionary stints as a lather-boy in a barber's shop, a taxi proprietor and a licensee only serving to heighten his ambitions in the frying trade. He opened his first fish and chip emporium at the Wibsey Fair, repeating his success in premises at the corner of Manchester Road and Bower Street in Bradford, its coal-fired ranges burning 365 days a year.

Buying a wooden lock –up shop in the more commercially favourable district of White Cross in Guiseley, Harry embarked on his most ambitious project yet. Opened in 1931 at a time of chronic unemployment, his new business was initially based on bulk out-sales to working class customers but a growing reputation for excellence soon led to investment on the grandest scale, Harry creating a 200 seater restaurant complete with fitted carpets and chandeliers. The opulence of the surroundings was best summed up by the reactions of one wide-eyed young customer who asked: 'Is this where God comes for his fish and chips dad?.'

A stickler for quality and detail and a tyrant where money was concerned, Harry was constantly attuned to staff pilfering. On one occasion, he spied a plaice fillet hanging from an employee's jacket left in the cloakroom. Without haranguing the man, he removed the fish, filling every pocket with the entrails from the slop bucket.

An innovative showman and entrepreneur who was way ahead of his time, Harry organised entertainments and attractions to draw the crowds, providing facilities for snooker and live music. He arranged fairs and brass band concerts at the rear of his restaurant in the summer months, and he even provided a delivery service for local mill workers. On the 21st anniversary of the opening of White Cross in 1952, he offered fish and chips at 1912 prices as an acknowledgement to his humble beginnings, thousands of people eagerly queuing to spend their one and a half pennies in the sun.

Harry Ramsden died in 1963 but his fish and chip shop is still as busy as ever, the brand name having inspired a number of similar restaurants across the world.

Directions: *Harry Ramsden's is on the A65 at White Cross, Guiseley (junction of A65 and A6038). Telephone 01943 874641. Map Landranger 104 – Grid Ref: 182425.*

68. HIGH ELDWICK: HAM SHANKS

Dick Hudson's forays onto Ilkley Moor are as familiar as ham and eggs. This champion of Yorkshire pubs rose to prominence in 1850 on the edge of a vast upland bristling with burial mounds and carved stones. Dick Hudson, a man 'who knew a thing or two about grub', lured his customers with a smell irresistible to man. Curled to perfection in a 30-inch frying pan from morn until dusk, his famous rashers: 'Scented the air with the aroma of home fed ham so that the wanderers over the moor twitched their noses like camels coming to water and lengthened their stride for the last quarter of a mile.' Sweet, fresh, unadulterated air by the lungful; appetites honed by unbridled miles of glorious tramping … and platters drooped with ham and eggs. What a combination! Ham, oh my! 'It's not only delicious' reported one disciple of the boot, 'but it bestows upon its devotees a calm and profound view of life.'

In his 1934 publication *English Journey*, J.B. Priestley wrote powerfully of the lure of Ilkley Moor, generations more ramblers answering his siren call: 'However small and dark your office or warehouse was, somewhere inside your head the high moors were glowing, the curlews were crying, and there blew a salt wind as if it came straight from the Atlantic.'

Dick Hudson's continues its victualling of walkers (ham and eggs are still on the menu), the path from its door leading across the heather to a thought provoking circle of stones – the Twelve Apostles.

Directions: *Roadside, at the southern edge of Ilkley Moor (Rombald's Moor on the map), Dick Hudson's is on a minor route between Menston and East Morton, about two and a half miles north of Bingley. Map Landranger 104 – Grid Ref: 125421.* ☛ ***See also 69 (Baildon)***

69. BAILDON: TICKET TO GLIDE

On one summer day alone in 1911, 17,000 passengers travelled on Yorkshire's most unusual tramway, the journey taking excited parties from the smog-choked mills of industrial Bradford, through bluebell woods to Baildon Moor. A magical one in 12 ascent through Shipley Glen – whistle the airs from 'Funiculee, Funicular' and you could well imagine yourself en route to some Alpine peak – the ride, which first opened in 1895, came to epitomise the wholesome Victorian temperance day out, lashings of fresh air washed down with copious pots of tea, drawing people in droves.

Local businessmen Samuel Wilson and H. Wilkinson installed the cable-operated tramway, using an eight horse-power gas engine to haul the four open, 12-seater carriages up the 386 yards long narrow-gauge line. The 'toast-rack' carriages were so called because their seats were arranged in single rows with the backrests pivoted so that passengers could face downhill on the return journey. The fares were 1d up and 1/2 d down, the whole joyous experience lasting about a minute. Children loved it, the only disappointment coming when the carriages came into the station. But what's that?

At the top of the glen, inside the grounds of Vulcan House, was an amusement park for children and a miniature Japanese garden said to be the most unusual in the country. Its owner described it thus:

In the grounds were eight or nine big arches, through which people could easily walk. I built four large greenhouses, full of plants and flowers. Inside were the same big arches. All the walls were built up with clinker and cement pockets for all kinds of ferns and plants. There was a castle built on a little island (I remember it well!) *surrounded by a moat. The castle was large enough for six or seven persons to go into it. It could only be reached across the water, which was wide enough for a little boat to sail round with twelve to fifteen children in it. I fitted up a chime of bells inside the castle, worked with a penny-in-the-slot mechanism. In the centre of the garden was a large fountain and surrounding it were a lily pond, a watercress pond, rose beds and numerous other flower beds. There was a beautiful studio and a rose garden filled with three of four hundred rose trees and an orchard filled with fruit trees.*

Other attractions in this wonderland, included a room bursting with slot machines, cases of old curiosities and displays of butterflies, a grotto housing a polyphon and a phonograph operated by a water wheel, and a well-patronised tea-room. Further along the lane in summer, you would find visiting fairs, boxing booths, shooting galleries and side-shows and on the Green, on the moor proper, was a hair-raising aerial glide. The return tram-car journey to the bottom took a full minute; this wire – whizzed descent just a few seconds!

On the Green was a famous rendezvous point – a large rock marked with a number nine. A local comedian, Reg Bolton, sang a ditty about the boulder as follows:

Meet me Gwen on Shipla' Glen, on Sunday afternoon.
Near No.9, we'll have a good time,
It's just the place for a spoon.
When you're up there you get salt –air,
You fancy yourself by the sea.
And if you are willing, and I have a shilling,
We'll call at Dick Hudson's for tea.

Most of the attractions had disappeared by the mid-1960s when vandalism nearly destroyed the tramway. Happily, it was repaired in 1969 and refurbished in time for its anniversary in 1995.

Directions: *Baildon is north-west of Shipley, immediately across the River Aire. The Shipley Glen Tramway (top station) is on Prod Lane, Baildon. From Baildon centre, go left at the roundabout on West Lane. To get to the bottom station, take the A6038 northbound from Shipley and go first left after crossing the river, continuing for just under a mile to the large turning circle to the right of the school. The tramway is at the* *foot of the hill at the woodland edge. It is open from Easter to October. Vulcan House is on Prod Lane. The revitalised Shipley Glen Pleasure Grounds and Fun Fair operate at weekends from March to December. Map Landranger 104 – Grid Refs: 138385 (Shipley Glen Tramway); 136388 (Vulcan House).* ☛ ***See also 68 (High Eldwick)***

70. SALTAIRE: A GOOD YARN

Some of the catalysts of the Industrial Revolution ground their workers into the dust and toasted their endeavours in champagne. In an age when exploitation was the norm, however, one pioneering Yorkshireman, created a model that was to become an international benchmark for industrial enterprise and harmony.

Sir Titus Salt was a businessman whose shrewd purchase of a seemingly worthless consignment of alpaca set him on the road to an amazing fortune. Introducing new methods of weaving, he transformed the inferior fibres into a whole new range of cloths, his success leading to an ambitious expansion programme involving relocation from the grime and squalor of Bradford.

Driven by his deep religious convictions, the visionary and philanthropic Salt proposed a radical and futuristic scheme consolidating the production of five scattered mills on a greenfield site strategically placed near the Leeds and Bradford turnpikes, the River Aire, canal and the newly opened railway. The project involved the creation of an entire industrial village built around a modern mill. One of the architectural wonders of the age, this was completed in 1853.

A colossus built in the Italianate style it rose to six storeys, having a frontage to the railway of 550 feet and a top floor room reckoned at the time to be the longest in the world. Built to accommodate 1,200 looms powered by four beam engines generating 1,000 horse power, the mill's massive weaving shed occupied some 8,400 square yards, 3,000 workers producing some 30,000 yards of cloth a day. The new mill was the central feature of the newly christened Saltaire, modern workers' housing with properly paved and drained streets, an infirmary, communal baths and a wash-house, a school, a Wesleyan chapel and Congregational church, forty shops, a library, and a 14-acre riverside park following on in subsequent years.

People from all over the world came to marvel at Saltaire. And they are still coming to see what is today an industrial heritage site, Salt's famous mill becoming a display centre for arts, crafts, housewares, designer clothes and furnishings.

Saltaire is between Shipley and Bingley off the A650. A heritage trail (information available locally and on the internet – search word saltaire*) takes in the entire model village. Workers' housing such as that in Titus Street is particularly fascinating. The* *converted and modernised Saltaire Mill houses the 1853 Gallery, displaying over 300 works by the Bradford-born artist David Hockney. Map Landranger 104 – Grid Ref: 140380 (Saltaire Mill).*

71. COTTINGLEY: AWAY WITH THE FAIRIES

In 1920, an illustrated article in *Strand* magazine shocked the world. An article by Edward L. Gardener and Sir Arthur Conan Doyle, no less, confidently reported that fairies had been observed in a Yorkshire village. But they had not only been observed, but photographed as well. And there, on the very page, were the illustrations to prove it!

The photographs that purported to show 'a group of fairy like figures dancing on the bank of a stream in front of a little girl' and 'a winged gnome like creature' prancing in the grass before her friend, took the readership by storm. The magazine sold out in three days, the story reverberating around every continent as the news hounds beat a path to Cottingley.

The young lady who took the remarkable photographs was Elsie Wright, who, along with her playmate Frances Griffiths, regularly cavorted with fairies in Cottingley Glen. She spoke with great animation to her father about her little friends but he, sceptic that he was, refused to believe her. Tired of her constant boasts, one day he thrust a camera in her hands and exclaimed: 'Prove it!.'

Elsie obliged, to the great astonishment of her father, whose interrogations revealed no trickery. Onward fluttered the photographs to Gardner and Doyle, examinations by an expert on fake photography and a Kodak film specialist, proving indecisive. The photographs were deemed genuine and the girls were despatched with more film for a further romp with the

The author spied this twenty-first century fairy at Cottingley.

goblins. The little fellows duly obliged and three more photographs were sent to Gardner, one showing a 'fairy poised on a bush as she offered a posy to Elsie', a 'leaping fairy in front of Frances', and 'a dense mix up of grasses and harebells with intertwined figures and faces.' This last image was solemnly scrutinised by people familiar with the Lilliputians' ways, their expert eyes pointing out a 'magnetic bath', a 'special restorative vessel used by the fairies after lengthy spells of dull weather.'

In reporting the astounding discovery, the global news media spawned a rash of similar outlandish stories in every continent. Hundreds of people had enjoyed similar enchanting experiences, the further testimony of a clairvoyant who accompanied the girls on one outing to Cottingley Glen, proving the existence of fairies beyond doubt. With her own eyes she witnessed gnomes with puckered faces and knocking knees, dancing fairies and a real live naked water nymph. Subscribers to *Strand Magazine* and other, more adult publications, came flocking to the glen in droves.

The two girls steadfastly stuck to their story, millions of people falling for the ruse. Vast amounts of time, money and adult prestige had been invested in the plot and the girls, no doubt, were frightened to reveal their secret? So they kept their faces straight for decades, hiding their little cut-out figures from prying eyes. Eventually, however, they could suppress their laughter no longer and they confessed the truth, some disbelieving and disappointed leprechauns rushing to the glen with their own cameras.

The theory was, that the girls had been brainwashed by the fairies, to put the inquisitive off the scent ...?

Directions: *Cottingley is three miles north-west of Bradford on the A650. Cottingley Glen is in Cottingley Park on the western side of the village off Beckfield Drive (use public footpath to March Cote Farm). Map Landranger 104 – Grid Ref: 108374 (Cottingley Glen).*

72. HAWORTH 'OUT OF THE WORLD'

As bleak as *Wuthering Heights,* nineteenth-century Haworth was described by Charlotte Bronte as 'a strange, uncivilised little place', its cramped yards and open sewers impressing themselves vividly on the minds of six frightened children who first ascended its lonely hill in 1820.

The Bronte's came only reluctantly to Haworth Parsonage. Within a few short years, three of the family were dead, one had drifted into melancholia only relieved by opium and three quite amazing sisters had achieved literary fame.

Charlotte, Emily and Anne Bronte initially scratched away to relieve the tedium of that dour place, even writing anonymously under the male pseudonyms Currer, Ellis and Acton Bell. Later though, motivated by angst and inspired by the surrounding moors they wrote some of the finest books ever written, *Wuthering Heights, Jane Eyre, Shirley, Villette, Agnes Grey* and the *Tenant of Wildfell Hall* going on to sell hundreds of thousands of copies worldwide.

A shrine to the memory of the famous sisters, Bronte parsonage has been preserved as a museum, its atmospheric rooms containing many of the family's personal items, manuscripts, books, letters, furniture and paintings.

Directions: *Haworth is eight miles west of Bradford (B6144) and three miles south of Keighley (A6033). The Bronte Parsonage Museum is at the top of the cobbled Main Street. Visitors can follow the Bronte Trail on foot from the parsonage, footpaths leading to Top Withens and other places described in the novels. Map Landranger 104 – Grid Ref: 039372.*

73. OAKWORTH: WHAT THE JUICE!

Some men invest their fortunes in palaces. Others indulge in foreign travels, South Sea Bubbles and illicit snuggles. So what did textile magnate Sir Isaac Holden blow his breadfruit on? Why, in the pre-Del Monte age, he developed a taste for the sweetest peach of all, spending a vast fortune on glasshouses.

A highly successful inventor and textile manufacturer who owned factories in Bradford and France, Holden developed a compulsive taste for exotic fruit. His passion for peaches would, though, have been unrequited but for a huge investment in hot-house technology. To keep the supply of fruit going during the winter months – the production of a pineapple for the Christmas table was seen as a status symbol – Sir Issac installed forty hot-houses in the grounds of his Oakworth House home, fourteen boilers, 37,000 feet of piping, three purpose built reservoirs, hundreds of tons of coal and dozens of gardeners, stokers and cinder-shovellers keeping the peaches and oranges from blushing with cold. Such was the outlay on this vast enterprise that each fruit was worth its weight in gold.

Also in the lavishly laid out grounds was a Winter Garden with a Turkish Bath at the rear. Fed from a moorland pool and roofed with coloured glass, this sumptuous winter wallow is estimated to have cost up to £120,000.

Between 1864 and 1874, Italian and French craftsmen fashioned further eccentricities to delight Sir Issac, cascades, temples, statues, caves and grottoes adding further intrigue to a garden already bursting with surprises.

Directions: *Oakworth is in the Worth Valley, two and a half miles south-west of Keighley on the B6143. Oakworth House was largely demolished after Sir Isaac Holden's death in 1897. Only one tower of the Italianate, mid-nineteenth-century Oakworth House remains. The Winter Garden has also disappeared, its site now forming part of a municipal park. Elements of the grand indulgence survive, however,* *the Summer House, grottoes, a cascade, masonry walls and simulated fossilised trees reminding us of the huge profits that were made in the woollen trade. Map Landranger 104 – Grid Ref: 034389.*

74. HALIFAX: PIECE DE RESISTANCE

Not for us the navel-gazing piazzas of Paris and Rome. We pragmatic Yorkshire folk demanded more for our brass than fresh air and perambulation. And we got it, the Piece Hall in Halifax, providing just the right mix of practicality and panache.

In the eighteenth and nineteenth centuries, the West Riding was the biggest producer of woollen and worsted goods in the world, the cottagers of Halifax producing myriad lengths of cloth every year. Before the Piece Hall was built, individual weavers would bring their 'pieces' into town for sale either on the streets or in the local taverns, unscrupulous dealers and landlords ensuring a lively trade. After the hall was opened for business in 1779, the town made considerable commercial strides, the availability of over 300 merchants' offices and a vast concourse measuring 100 yards long by 91 yards wide, bringing added business and prestige to the town.

This large rectangular structure, which rises to three storeys on the eastern side, has elegant colonnades all round, the whole edifice making only limited use of wood in the interests of fire prevention. A colourful trading bazaar, it was a hotbed of head shaking, hand slapping and deal-making, the old Yorkshire adage of: 'see all, hear all, say nowt; eat all, sup all, pay nowt; an' if thoo does owt fer nowt, do it for thisen,' having been honed to perfection here.

The Piece Hall has been utilised for a variety of events down the years, massed hymn singing, preaching, a balloon ascent and an exhibition by the dare-devil Charles Blondin all drawing large crowds. In 1861, Blondin performed above the concourse on a 300 feet long rope suspended 60 feet above the ground. With their hearts in their mouths the gasping spectators watched him walk, run, somersault and stand on his head. For a grand finale he placed a sack over his head, completing his performance by carrying a man on his back.

The Piece Hall now houses an art gallery and specialist shops.

Directions: *Halifax is in the Calder Valley about eight miles south-west of Bradford. The easiest access is from junction 24 of the M62. The Piece Hall is in Thomas Street, 250 yards north-west of the railway station. Map Landranger 104 – Grid Ref: 096252.*

75. HALIFAX: HEADS YOU LOSE

The very name of this West Riding woollen town had criminals cringing, its novel way with miscreants who stole 'cloth or any other commodity of the value of thirteenpence half-penny' preceding the methods of Madame Guillotine by centuries.

The draconian Halifax Gibbet Laws were introduced to combat the theft of cloth and livestock, upon conviction, the law decreeing decapitation, 'after three market days or meeting days.' The instrument of execution was a machine that came to be known as the 'Sharp Maiden of Halifax.' It consisted of a wooden framework, two 15 feet high uprights held apart at the top by a four feet wide transverse beam. The uprights were grooved on the inner faces to take a wooden block fitted with a seven and a three-quarter pound axe head 18 inches long and 12 inches wide. This was hauled to the top of the twin posts by means of a rope and pulley, a removable peg holding the block in place until the victim was taken kicking and screaming to his doom.

In the Records of the Crown Office is a list of the names of fifty-three people executed on the gibbet between 20th March 1541 and 30th April 1650. One man and his daughter were beheaded within minutes of each other. On another occasion in 1542, one victim went to his death without revealing his name, the register of executions referring to him as 'a certain stranger.'

Directions: *Halifax is in the Calder Valley about eight miles south-west of Bradford. The easiest access is from junction 24 of the M62. When it was built, the Halifax Gibbet was some distance west of the town. Urban expansion assimilated the execution site and it was lost until its remains were re-discovered in 1840. Today, it survives as a sinister grass mound at the junction of Gibbet Street and Bedford Street North near Burdock Way.*

For many years, the actual gibbet blade was kept in Wakefield but it was returned to Halifax in 1970, now forming part of an exhibition of the town's gruesome past (including a model of the gibbet) in the Bankfield Museum on Boothtown Road (just north of the town centre). Map Landranger 104 – Grid Refs: 088253 (site of gibbet); 091263 (Bankfield Museum).

76. HALIFAX: 'SMOKIN'!'

Pisa has its leaning tower; we have our thunderingly more exciting Wainhouse's Chimney. Of a fantastical design, it soars to 253 feet above the Halifax skyline, culminating in a spectacular corona.

The chimney started out prosaically enough. Commissioned in 1871 by John Edward Wainhouse, it was designed to vent smoke from his local dyeworks. Using around 9,000 tons of ashlar stone from nearby quarries, it took four years to build, at an astronomical cost of £15,000. But, as the last stone was put in place, it was made redundant, Wainhouse having sold his business. After the new owner declined all interest in his chimney, Wainhouse converted it to an observation tower, the architect Richard Swarbrick Dugdale adding 400 stone steps, a look-out gallery and his incredible corona.

In the 1920s, such was the tower's state of disrepair that plans were proposed for its demolition. Its proximity to nearby houses ruled out the use of explosives and the tedious business of demolition stone by stone would have cost more than the value of the recovered materials. So perversely, the tower was saved, a public fund providing enough money for its repair.

The tower is open to the public on selected Sundays and Bank Holidays. The splendid views from its summit take in all of Halifax, parts of the Calder Valley towards Heptonstall and the windswept Widdop Moor.

Directions: *Halifax is in the Calder Valley, about eight miles south-west of Bradford. The easiest access is from junction 24 of the M62. Wainhouse's Chimney is on Washer Lane about one and a half miles south-west of the town centre down Burdock Way and King Cross Road. Map Landranger 104 – Grid Ref: 076240.*

77. CRAGG VALE: COINING IT IN

Easy money and crime go together like a noose and its knot, the lure of riches spawning criminal invention, ingenuity and opportunity in every age. And what could be more opportunistic than this:

> *I have a purse simply bursting with gold and silver coins. Alas, we are so quickly parted! But you'll buy me a new pocket-watch, a pair of breeches and that embroidered waistcoat I've always coveted. And you'll help settle my bill with the man who brings me the smuggled tea and brandy. But before I bid you adieu my shiny friends, you can perform for me one extra service. Brace yourself for the knife and I will pare you!*

When precious metals formed the basis of the nation's currency before effective milled edges and quality minting became the norm, the temptation to remove slivers of gold or silver from coins was enormous. Here was a crime you could commit from the anonymity of your own armchair. And there were no apparent victims. Short of using a weighing scale, the purblind pot-man in the Shoulder of Mutton would never know the difference and, after all, if he became wise to the ruse, he, in turn, could repeat the subterfuge.

Many normally law-abiding citizens nibbled away at the nation's specie, mounds of gold and silver parings depressing the economy snip by snip. But the problem was to come to a violent head in 1769 when the assault on the currency become a highly organised and an efficiently operated business, the intensive coining activities of a gang of crooks located in one of the remotest parts of Yorkshire, attracting national attention.

The leader of the notorious gang was David Hartley from Bell House Farm in Cragg Vale, near Hebden Bridge. Working from his isolated farmhouse high above the sinuous and tortuous valley of the Cragg Brook,

'King David', as he was known to his 70 strong band of followers, ran an intensive operation, taking advantage of the poor state of the national coinage. Battered and clipped and brought under suspicion to such an extent that tradesmen, particularly in the Halifax area, began to fear to trade, the currency had been supplemented by the gradual introduction of foreign coins, silver-rich Portuguese moidores attracting the coiners like no other. Not only did the gang clip them. Using their own primitively crafted dies, they smelted their own!

Such was the alarming escalation of the problem, that local manufacturers petitioned the government to act, excise-man William Dighton infiltrating the gang and engaging the services of an informer, James Broadbent. On his testimony, Hartley was arrested and taken, along with one of his associates, to York Castle to await trial. Seething from the arrest of their leader, the gang, meanwhile, resolved to murder Dighton, assassins Robert Thomas and Matthew Norman killing the excise-man with a single blunderbuss shot to the head on the night of 10th November 1769. Outraged, the government was at last stung into action, offering a reward of £100 – matched by a similar sum put up by the gentlemen and merchants of Halifax – for the arrest of the killers. By Christmas, action to root out the coiners, spurred on by a mass meeting of concerned parties, resulted in the arrest of 30 suspects. 'King David' was hanged for his crimes in York on 28th April 1770 and the bloodshed should have ended there. However, there was one sanguinary toss of the coin left, the barbarity of one final act ensuring that the remaining coiners would be pursued to extinction.

The coiners ruthlessly murdered a labourer who had bragged about knowing the identity of Dighton's killers. Cornered in a blacksmith's forge, he was despatched with gruesome brutality, a contemporary account recording his last moments: '... they immediately threw him against the fire and thrust his head into or under it ... one of them heated the tongs red hot, clasping them fast around the poor creature's neck, and kept them there ... but their inhumanity not being yet satiated, they actually filled his breeches with burning coals by which the poor fellow died in the greatest of agonies.'

Incited by such vile crimes, the pursuit of the remaining coiners intensified, and by 1774, their reign of deceit and terror was at an end.

Directions: *Cragg Vale is two miles south of Mytholmroyd (A646) on the B6138. The passage of time has inevitably softened the image of a thoroughly unscrupulous and often violent gang, the locality in which they operated now romantically being referred to as 'Coiners' Country'*

On the edge of Bell Hole, the isolated Bell House Farm (a restored private property) is on Heseltine Lane, Cragg Vale. A public footpath passes the house. To get a real feel for the area, follow in the footsteps of the coiners and walk from Cragg Vale. Turn right at the church to cross the Cragg Brook and pass the Hinchliffe Arms continuing on the lane – Calderdale Way – to Withens Reservoir. Turn right here for half a mile to a fork and go right to Bell House Farm, continuing onto Bell House Moor and Erringden Moor and on to Hebden Bridge. Other similarly located houses in the area were also used for coining.

The district's ale-houses were frequently the venue for clandestine meetings between Hartley and his men, two local hostelries – the Hinchliffe Arms in Cragg Vale and the Shoulder of Mutton in Mytholmroyd – having small collections of coining tools, dies and memorabilia. David Hartley is buried in the churchyard at Heptonstall. Maps Landranger 103/104 – Grid Refs: 103/996246 (Bell House Farm); 103/986280 (churchyard at Heptonstall); 103/999233 (Hinchliffe Arms, Cragg Vale); 104/013259 (Shoulder of Mutton, Mytholmroyd).

78. MARSDEN: TUNNEL VISION

The Gods guffawed at the news, Zeus himself laughing the loudest. 'The puny, arrogant fools!' he bellowed. 'They might as well contrive an emptying of Windermere with a spoon.'

Back on earth, legions of navvies ignored the thunder, picking up their picks and shovels and preparing to hack away at a mountain. Their task? To dig out the deepest, the highest and the longest canal tunnel in the world.

Part of the 20-miles long Huddersfield Narrow Canal, the Standedge Tunnel was begun in 1794. It took a back-breaking 17 years to complete using only the most primitive tools and dynamite. The cost in human suffering was huge, although the resolve of the excavators never waivered. By the time the canal was opened in 1811, the health of hundreds of workers had been shattered by arthritis, bone fractures, crush injuries, emphysema and blindness. The three and three-quarter mile slog resulted in 50 deaths – one every 100 yards – the whole operation averaging just 337 yards per year. In 1944, only 133 years after the navvies broke through, the tunnel was abandoned, competition from the railways making the canal uneconomic.

Progressive silting up, filling in and development along and over the line of the waterway, resulted in near extinction for the canal, only a band of amateur enthusiasts halting its decline in the 1970s. Their persistence and dogged determination resulted in the launch of a massive Millennium Commission funded scheme in 1997, nineteen different engineering projects restoring the entire canal for a grand reopening in May 2001. A depth of four feet of silt was removed from the length of the Standedge Tunnel alone.

Directions: *Marsden is about seven miles south-west of Huddersfield on the A62. Poor ventilation does not permit boats to navigate the Standedge Tunnel under their own power, but craft can be towed in convoys using electrically powered tugs (notice the original pick marks and blast holes). In the old days, bargees would lay on their backs* *with their legs against the tunnel ceiling, 'legging it' for three hours, their women crossing the moor above with their horses. The Standedge Experience at Tunnel End, Marsden, organises short tunnel trips for visitors, exhibits charting the history of its excavation. The Standedge Trail – a 12-mile circular walk linking both ends of the tunnel – has a unique concentration of artefacts from the canal, turnpike and rail eras. Some of the 50 tunnellers who died in Standedge are buried in Mardsen Church. Map Landranger 110 – Grid Refs: 040120 (the Standedge Experience); 046117 (Marsden Church).*

79. ALMONDBURY: QUEEN B

Pronounce her name wrongly and you could well have lost your legs. Cartimandua,* Queen of the Brigantes, the conniving ruler of the largest and most powerful tribe in Roman Britain. But for her, we might have sent the legions packing.

From 41AD to 60AD, Cartimandua held sway over a kingdom that included much of modern Yorkshire, legend suggesting that she chose Almondbury's Castle Hill as her base. In 43AD, she signed a non- aggression pact with the occupying army, placing herself under the protection of Rome. At a stroke, the northern flank of the province was protected, allowing the hard-pressed legions to be deployed elsewhere. Dissident forces revolted, however, their opposition to the traitorous liaison with Rome forcing the queen to seek imperial assistance in quelling a rebellion. And the scheming continued.

The Welsh leader Caratacus, who had waged a constant war of attrition against the invaders, sought sanctuary on Castle Hill. In 51AD, Cartimandua promptly turned him over to the Romans as a sign of loyalty. Sent to Rome as a public spectacle, Caractacus asked the famous question: 'Why do you, with all these great possessions, still covet our poor huts?.'

Denounced again, this time by her consort Venutius who attempted a coup, the queen again asked the Romans for help. They obliged, her highness eventually divorcing Venutius after another failed overthrow attempt. She then hitched her chariot to Vellocatus, a royal armour-bearer, sending her new husband off to fight the old! Dynastic strife and a breakdown in the stability of the Brigantian territories finally convinced the Romans to act. Newly arrived in Britain in 71AD, Petillius Cerialis mobilised the IX Legion based at the newly constructed fort in York, using them as the spearhead to smash the native tribes, Cartimandua drifting from the scene.

Directions: *Almondbury is on the southerly outskirts of Huddersfield. Go south from the ring road on the A616 for about two and three-quarter miles and go left just after the B6108 at Armitage Bridge, on minor roads for a further mile or so north-east to Castle Hill, which is off Lumb Lane.*

---

* pronounced 'kar-timan-juwu'

Queen Cartimandua's Iron Age citadel stands on a 900-feet high bluff covering eight acres. It was probably begun around 300 BC *and protected by huge ramparts. Abandoned for a thousand years after the conquest, the site of the fort was later occupied by a medieval castle. Numerous Roman coins were discovered on the hill in 1829. In 1588, bonfires were lit on the summit, as part of the chain of beacons warning of the impending invasion by the Spanish Armada. In 1899, the impressive Victoria Tower was built on the hill to commemorate the Diamond Jubilee of Queen Victoria. The tower is open to the public. Map Landranger 110 – Grid Ref: 153141.* ☛ ***See also 13 (Ingleborough)***

80. HOLME: WATER TORTURES

When not roused to ire, water is a spiritual and elemental life force. When, however, it is foamed to temper, it poses a serious threat to man, violent floods accounting for many Yorkshire fatalities down the years. One of the severest inundations to afflict the county, occurred on 5th February 1852, a wall of water estimated at some 86 million gallons descending on the sleeping population of Holmfirth and surrounding villages.

Heavy winter rains had saturated Wessenden Head Moor, water surging down Marsden Clough into the straining Bilberry Reservoir, weakening its dam. Just before midnight, the dam burst, a tidal wave racing down the valley and carrying away everything in its path. Some 78 unsuspecting victims still in their night attire were drowned, the list of destruction including four mills, ten dye-houses, seventeen shops, twenty seven houses, three churches and two iron foundries. In total 700 people were thrown out of work, the estimated cost of the damage amounting to £250,000.

Holmfirth looked like a war zone, artists of the *Illustrated London News* capturing the awful scenes in their edition of 6th March 1852. The accompanying article read: 'A more complete wreck, a more melancholy scene than Holmfirth presented to the thousands who visited it on Thursday, has never been beheld. The streets were filled with broken furniture, carding machines, huge iron boilers, bags of wool and other things; and the graveyards had their dead dislodged, and their contents borne again to the doors of the living.'

A national appeal was launched aided by the publication of a specially written song whose first verse was:

It rushed down the hill when people lay still
Roaring and rolling like thunder.
It cam in its might like a demon at night,
And left survivors in wonder.
It bore in its course a battlefield force,
Defying what stood in its way.

It recognised none but travelled along.
Like a giant in fearful array.

Directions: *Holme is just under three miles south-west of Holmfirth on the A6024. Bilberry Reservoir is north of Holme down Fieldhead Lane (one mile). Visitors can view Bilberry reservoir from a public footpath that goes west (half a mile) from the picnic area by Digley Reservoir or they can walk from Holme on a public footpath (one mile). The Old Genn monument in Towngate, Holmfirth (opposite the White Hart pub near the bus station), commemorates the flood, a brass plate marking its height. Map Landranger 110 – Grid Ref: 103070 (Bilberry Reservoir dam wall); 144083 (Old Genn monument).*

81. HOLMFIRTH: BILL'S BATTY BRUSH-OFF

There has been many a brandishment on these famous steps, the wrinkled-stockinged Boudicca with a broom, making regular assaults on Compo's rear-end a national obsession for nearly thirty years. Nora Batty and her admirer lived in adjoining cottages overlooking the River Worth, much of the TV hit series 'Last of the Summer Wine' being filmed in the hitherto quiet town of Holmfirth.

Nora's home, Sid's Café and the White Horse Inn where the dynamic trio dipped their wicks, have all become tourist attractions, a permanent exhibition to the antics of Compo, Clegg and Foggy and the rest, flourishing in what was Compo's TV house.

The whole cast of the series became naturalised Tykes, actor Bill Owen (and his wellies) going to his rest in the local churchyard at Upperthong.

Directions: *Holmfirth is six miles south of Huddersfield (A616/A6024). Nora Batty's and Compo's cottages are in Scarfold, off Hollowgate near the centre of the town. Sid's Café is opposite*

Holmfirth: Nora Batty's House.

the church on South Lane. The White Horse Inn is not in Holmfirth but in Jackson Bridge about three miles south-west of the town (A635/A616). Bill is buried in the churchyard at Upperthong. Go left at the A635/A6024 junction after crossing the river for about 250 yards and fork right uphill on Upperthong Lane for about 500 yards to St John's Church. Take the path to the left of the entrance uphill for 75 yards. The grave is to the right of the path. Map Landranger 110 – Grid Refs: 133082 (Scarfold); 143083 (Sid's Café); 165075 (White Horse Inn, Jackson Bridge); 137082 (churchyard at Upperthong).

82. OVERTON: OLD KING COAL

Underground Yorkshire has more black holes than the final frontier, mining operations over thousands of years creating a vast subterranean labrinthe of abandoned adits, shafts and passageways. Mining has claimed thousands of lives since our ancestors grubbed out their first primitive bell pits, the relentless pursuit of lead, iron, potash and particularly coal, fuelling an expansion that made Britain the industrial powerhouse of the world.

From the time of the Roman occupation until the eighteenth century, wood and charcoal were the principal fuels, domesticity and burgeoning industry changing the arboreal landscape forever. Mechanisation brought demands for a more efficient fuel with higher burning temperatures, readily available coal from surface deposits and shafts up to 200 feet deep, providing energy for industries such as metal-working, brick-making, sugar-refining, brewing and soap boiling. In the eighteenth century, insatiable energy demands particularly from all branches of the iron industry, led to the sinking of hundreds of new pits, the national output of coal rising from some 2,500,000 tons in 1700 to about 10,000,000 tons in 1800. The voracious appetite for coal, coupled with advances in mine technology and the introduction of ventilation and water pumping systems, saw a meteoric rise in production, the national network of newly-constructed canals helping distribute an estimated 287,000,000 tons of coal in 1913.

West Yorkshire sat on a veritable coal mine, vast measures conveniently extending from the Aire Valley southwards through Sheffield into Derbyshire. For generations, black gold was the mainstay of local economies, the shape and appearance of whole towns and villages and the lives of their inhabitants being dictated by coal.

Pitstacks, spoil heaps, mineral railways and dreary back-to-back colliery houses dominated the landscapes of these communities, the siren klaxons of the pits, the daily spin of winding wheels, the eternal assault on blackened collars with soap and scrubing brushes, and the images of graze – kneed children playing marbles in the coal dust, marking out the lives of mining families.

Falling rocks and subsidence, foul air and methane, accidents and explosions and the hideous long-term effects of dust inhalation led to an appalling catalogue of death and ill health. Despite this and despite the subsistence wages, poor housing and occasional debilitating strikes, mining communities in places like Thornhill, Allerton Bywater, Fryston, Wheldale, Ryhill, Silkstone, Aston, Darfield, Denaby, Dodworth and Tankersley, were some of the most cohesive and fiercely independent in the country. As tribal as the best Scottish clans, miners made their own entertainment, whippet racing, pigeon fancying, ferret keeping and the raising of prize flowers and vegetables – with the added attractions of welfare clubs, brass bands, galas and annual outings – creating a vibrant social scene that is sorely missed. Ask any miner about the demise of the industry and he will pass over the hardships to recount some humorous tale. 'I've seen more work in an Asprin', recalls one former manager remembering 'some blokes who were asked to do a bit of shovelling.' Another miner proudly announces: 'Whether I needed it or not, I'd wash missen in t'tin bath in front o' fire once a week. But I'd never wash me back. It makes you weak.' And then there's the story of a face worker who, forty years on, swears me to secrecy. 'Before they opened the pithead baths, I used to call at a fancy woman's on my way home from shift. We got to know each other quite well. Anyhow, after a while the wife gets a bit suspicious. "How come", she says, "that every part of your body is black except that thing?" Oh! I said. Yes, well. I stopped for a pee on the way home. I don't know whether she swallowed it or not, so I took to blackening t'thing wi me cap before I got home.'

In little more than a generation, hundreds of coalmines have been closed in Yorkshire alone, a massive programme of site restoration and regeneration removing the last vestiges of a once totally dominant industry. It is amazing to think that in 1855, the total West Riding coal output from 333 collieries was 7,747,470 tons. Now, there are but a handful of mines. In the rush to renewal, the national mining heritage and the social fabric of the industry have largely been obliterated, but one former Yorkshire pit preserves something of the history of old king coal.

The National Mining Museum for England is based on the site of the Caphouse Colliery where mining has been carried out for centuries. Caphouse was linked by underground roadway to Denby Dale Colliery in 1981, its final shift in 1987, marking the beginning of its conversion to a museum. Packed with exhibits, the museum charts the development of the mining industry, attractions including exhibition galleries, machinery displays and an underground tour.

Directions: *Overton is about six miles south-west of Wakefield (through Horbury and Middlestown) on the A642. The National Mining Museum for England is open every day. Map Landranger 110 – Grid Ref: 252164.* ☛ ***See also 114 (Silkstone)***

83. WAKEFIELD: YORKSHIRE'S PARLIAMENT

Built as the local government flagship for the whole of the West Riding, the monumental County Hall captures the spirit of the age. Erected at the end of the Victorian period between 1894 and 1898, it competes for the Wakefield skyline, presenting a confident and classical façade, the integrity and stature of its purpose reflected in a crowned dome, dormer-gabling, a series of oriels capped by a long balcony and the generous use of stained glass. An oratorical castle fitted with a grand staircase, a debating chamber that would grace Whitehall itself and a series of imposing committee rooms, the hall is embellished internally with tropical hardwoods, marble and a collection of exquisite sculptures and friezes depicting all the tenets of the democratic process – debate, wisdom, law, power, meditation, honesty, industry and the rest. As befits the home of this Yorkshire parliament, the banner of county history is triumphantly flown in the ante room to the council chamber, a frieze, in modelled and coloured plaster, showing four episodes from the Wars of the Roses – the Battle of Wakefield, the crowning of Henry VII on

Detail of the frieze in the ante-room at Wakefield Town Hall.

Bosworth Field, the procession of Henry VII and Queen Elizabeth of York through Wakefield, and Margaret of Anjou consigning her son into the care of robbers. But County Hall might not have been built in Wakefield.

In choosing a site for the new building, one of the prime considerations was its accessibility for elected officers. Of the 90 electoral divisions within the county, 34 were more accessible from Leeds and 38 from Wakefield, with the rest being equally accessible from either city. The fact that Wakefield was already home to the council's administration department swung the vote and an open architectural competition, with a first prize of £200, was launched with a comment that the 'Queen Anne or Renaissance School of Architecture appears suited to an old town like Wafefield.' The competition was won by James Gibson and Samuel Russell of Grays Inn Square, London, the firm also designing the Middlesex County Offices in London.

Directions: *Wakefield is easily accessible off either junction 40 (A638) or junction 42 (A650) of the M1. County Hall, which is now in the ownership of the Wakefield Metropolitan District Council, is on Bond Street and Wood Street overlooking Castrop-Rauxel Square. Guided tours are arranged of the building, visiting the council chamber and the committee rooms. Map Landranger 104 – Grid Ref: 335208.*

84. WAKEFIELD: A TROUBLED PEN

In lancing the boils of squalor and social injustice, George Gissing is said to have dug his pen even deeper than Dickens. The author of some twenty one novels and hundreds of other minor works, he was born into a middle class Wakefield family on 22nd November 1857, the son of a local chemist who died prematurely leaving five young children.

A brilliant history and literature student who won a scholarship to Owens College Manchester at the age of 15, Gissing seemed destined for a bright future, but, motivated by his infatuation for a young prostitute, Nell Harrison, he was caught in the act of stealing money from the students' cloakroom. He was sentenced to one month in prison, his 'guilty secret', casting a shadow over his entire life. After a year in America, he married Nell in 1887, her drunken and sluttish ways resulting in the unhappiest of unions and her early death from syphilis in 1888. Gissing's second marriage to Edith Underwood, a vicious virago of a woman, ended in equal torment and, by 1897, the author was left alone to brood.

Gissing's tortured imagination was fuelled by frequent penury, misery and feelings of inadequacy, his personal experiences of life amongst London's down and outs gushing from the pages of a series of dark so called 'slum novels' beginning with the *Workers* and ending with the reasonably successful *The Nether World.* His undoubted masterpiece, and the best known of his works, is *New Grub Street*, this and other novels such as *The Odd Women*, *Born in Exile*, *In the Year of the Jubilee* and the *The Whirlpool*, dealing with the searing social problems of the day.

For a passionate and dedicated author, one of the greatest tragedies of Gissing's life was the lack of financial reward for his efforts. In desperate financial straits, he sold the copyright of his works outright to publishers, never receiving more than a few pounds for his efforts. A disillusioned man of 46, he died of emphysema at St Jean Pied de Port on the Bay of Biscay on 28th December 1903.

Directions: *Wakefield is easily accessible off either junction 40 (A638) or junction 42 (A650) of the M1. George Gissing's boyhood home – now the Gissing Centre – is open to the public on Saturdays from April to October. It is located in an alley at 2-4 Thompson's Yard, off Westgate (north of) – about 275 yards east and uphill of the railway station. Gissing refers to his childhood home in his books. In 'Reminiscences of My Father' published in 1896, he writes: 'I was oil painting in the little spare bedroom which I used as a studio one day in 1870, when Father came in to tell me that the Franco-Prussian war had begun.' One of the Gissing family rooms was above the chemist's shop, the author describing the outlook in A Life's Morning: 'The uppermost windows commanded a view of the extensive cattle market, of a long railway viaduct, and hilly fields beyond.' Map Landranger 104 – Grid Ref: 330207.*

85. WAKEFIELD: HOLY TOLL

The best of only four such shrines that remain in England, St Mary's Chapel on Wakefield's fourteenth-century bridge over the River Calder, was erected around 1350. In a pragmatic church that always had one hand on the cross and another on its purse, it served the dual purpose of offering spiritual comfort to pilgrims and the levying of tolls.

Finely wrought in the elaborate Decorated style with a profusion of arches, tracery and a fine collection of reliefs depicting the Annunciation, Nativity, Resurrection, Ascension, and Pentecost, it has suffered much down the years, but successive restorations have restored it to former glories.

In its chequered history, the chapel has served a number of secular uses. At various times, it suffered the indignity of becoming an old clothes shop, a tailor's emporium, a newsroom and a library. Today though, its cramped interior has reverted to a more ecclesiastical purpose and visitors can pray here once more.

Directions: *Wakefield is easily accessible either off junction 40 (A638) or junction 42 (A650) of the M1. St Mary's Chantry Chapel, which is open to the public by arrangement, is on the old Wakefield Bridge (just east of the new bridge on Bridge Street) south of the city centre (use either Ings Road or Kirkgate). Map Landranger 104 – Grid Ref: 337202.*

86. WALTON: THE EXTRAORDINARY SQUIRE

Born in Walton Hall in 1782 into a distinguished Catholic family, Charles Waterton was an eccentric from an early age, his inspirational 260-acre home, on an island surrounded by animals and trees, spawning an interest in natural history and conservation that was to be his life's work.

At school, Waterton exhibited a passion for the outdoors and a fascination for climbing high buildings, his curiosity for the freakish and the bizarre developing a roguish bent for sensationalism in the years ahead.

After early adventures in Spain, Waterton visited Demerara in Guiana, subsequent 'wanderings' taking him to Barbados, Brazil, Venezuela, the United States and Canada. Oblivious to dangers and fevers, which frequently laid him low, he began collecting animals and birds, perfecting the art of taxidermy and bringing exotic exhibits back to England for study and display. A fearless specimen hunter who struck out into chartless territory with no shoes: '... in dry weather, they would have irritated my feet and retarded me in the chase of wild beasts', he set himself the task of discovering supplies of the fabled drug curare. He not only found the drug, but he learned the secrets of its manufacture, returning home to carry out experiments on donkeys.

Waterton's accounts of his confrontations with animals make hair-raising reading. One of his victims was an unsuspecting boa-constrictor, the squire binding its jaws with his braces! His most celebrated acquisition was a cayman: 'It was the first and last time I was ever on a cayman's back,' he admitted dryly. 'Should it be asked how I managed to keep my seat, I would answer – I hunted with Lord Darlington's fox hounds.'

In his personal habits, Waterton was no less unusual. He slept little, resting his head on a wooden pillow, and he performed regular self-venesection, describing the practice as 'tapping the claret.' 'If you desire to drink health's purest juices, shun care and wrath and drain your body's juices.' He gave lectures and taunted the establishment by creating a number of taxidermal curiosities and notwithstanding his advancing years, he continued to climb tall trees.

Waterton wrote a number of books describing his adventures, his *Wanderings in South America, the North-West of the United States and the Antilles in the Years 1812, 1816, 1820, and 1824* being an outstanding success. He died in 1865 in his 82nd year and was buried in the grounds of his beloved Walton Hall, which is today regarded as the world's first nature reserve. The Yorkshire Society of Anaesthetists honoured Waterton's pioneering work in 1982, when specialists attended an international symposium at his former home.

Directions: *Now a popular hotel, Walton Hall is in the village of Walton, around four miles south-east of Wakefield (A 61/B6378). There is a memorial to Waterton in* *the grounds. You can see many of the explorers amazing finds and specimens of taxidermy in Wakefield Museum in Wood Street. Waterton made his mark further afield. Named after him, the Waterton Park is in the province of Alberta, Canada. Map Landranger 111 – Grid Ref: 364165 (Walton Hall).*

87. FOULBY: TIME AND TIDES

For cussedness and determination against overwhelming odds, John Harrison, who was born in Foulby in 1693, has no equal. A lowly carpenter's son with little formal education who took on the biggest scientific challenge of the day, Harrison had to contend with bigotry, obfuscation, vacillation and professional jealousy on a monumental scale. Hindered at almost every turn by officialdom, he doggedly stuck to his task to produce a precision engineered instrument that fundamentally changed the world. Near the end of his life in 1775, this device was referred to as: '... our faithful guide through all the vicissitudes of climates', Captain James Cook thereby praising Harrison at the end of a three year voyage. The great explorer had proved beyond doubt that Harrison's invention worked, and that the fickle and unreliable calculation of longitude by primitive means was a thing of the past. After years of unrelenting toil and multiple setbacks, John Harrison realised his lifetime dream, his accurate marine timekeeper opening up a new chapter in global exploration.

In his sixth year, the infant Harrison became ill and was confined to bed. A pocket watch was placed on his pillow, 'that he might amuse himself by contemplating its movement.' The choice of plaything was inspirational indeed. After the family relocated to Barrow in Lincolnshire, the budding horologist produced his first longcase clock in 1713 at the age of 20. Made entirely of wood, this instrument was the precursor of a series of remarkable timekeepers that used pendulum rods made from alternate wires of brass and steel. This combination of materials prevented pendulum expansion during warm weather, greatly increasing accuracy. Having revolutionised the domestic market, Harrison turned his attention to an altogether more stirring goal.

Maritime trade was hampered by the lack of an accurate instrument for calculating longitude. Navigation in the middle of the eighteenth century was at best risky, and shipwrecks were frequent. Enter Parliament with a challenge, this assembly of eminent men offering the reward of a staggering £20,000 for a device that would defeat the motions of a ship and the vagaries of climatic change, to solve the problem of longitudinal calculation once and for all.

Harrison retired to his workshops and began his lengthy cogitations, producing a series of innovative and wonderfully engineered marine timekeepers with the prosaic nomenclatures H1, H2 and H3. The devices were tested on the Humber but none of them worked to the satisfaction of the adjudicating Board of Longitude. Harrison tried again, his radically redesigned H4 looking more like a pocket watch than its much bigger cousins.

On 18th November 1761, H4 was taken aboard the ship *Deptford* in the care of Harrison's son William. The vessel was outward bound for Jamaica, which she reached on 19th January 1762. In 63 days at sea, H4 lost 5.1 seconds! But the board was not sufficiently impressed to award the prize, William again putting H4 to the test on a second voyage to Madiera. The *Tartar* set sail from Barbados on 28th March 1764. During its 43-day-voyage, H4 lost 39.2 seconds, under the terms of the competition rules, Harrison qualifying for the £20,000 prize. It was not awarded, the board implying that the accuracy of H4 was a fluke. They were prepared to offer the inventor half the sum, provided he fully disclosed all his design secrets and agreed to the testing of similar time-pieces. Harrison refused to comply, a lengthy and militant stand off between the parties finally concluding with a conciliatory meeting in August 1765, when six experts examined H4 and accepted Harrison's designs. The £10,000 was paid over, but the payment of the balance depended on the manufacture of at least two identical watches. And still the experts prevaricated and dithered, the newly appointed Astronomer Royal, Nevil Maskelyne, insisting that the traditional lunar-distance method of calculating Greenwich Time was the best.

After another well-known watchmaker had been assigned to make a facsimile of H4, the septuagenarian again went back to his lathes, producing yet another masterpiece – H5. Surely this time the board would be satisfied? No! The board insisted that both watches had to be produced in the Harrison workshops and they were adamant that the outstanding £10,000 would not be paid.

The 79-year-old Harrison was outraged and he petitioned King George III to intervene. His highness met Harrison's son, allegedly remarking '... these people have been cruelly wronged ...' and 'By God Harrison, I will see you righted!' The king tested H5 himself and proved it to be wholly accurate but the Board of Longitude remained as implacable as ever. Finally, Harrison asked Parliament to adjudicate on the matter. Fully endorsing the supreme merits of the great man's work, the members voted him £8,750 in June 1773. Harrison had won the prize, and with it, immortality.

Directions: *Part of the Nostell parish, Foulby is a hamlet of houses on the A638 Doncaster Road between Crofton and Wragby, about five miles south-east of Wakefield. A blue plaque on a cottage, 100 yards south –east of the entrance to Nostell Priory Rose Gardens entrance (Wakefield side), records that Harrison was a resident of the hamlet. Three of Harrison's early wooden clocks survive. One of these treasures may be seen in Nostell Priory (a National Trust property open to the public) whose* *grounds abut Foulby to the east. Harrison's more famous chronometers are in the National Maritime Museum in Greenwich. Map Landranger 111 – Grid Refs: 399176 (plaque in Foulby); 404175 (Nostell Priory).* ☛ ***See also 54 (Whitby)***

88. ACKWORTH: A PLAGUE ON ALL THEIR HOUSES

All around, Roundhead and Royalist martyrs had perished for the cause, bloody civil conflict carrying off thousands of victims. But pike and musket were not the only cause of destruction in war-torn England between 1642 and 1646, flea – bearing rats bringing equal devastation. The pestilence had been endemic in England for three centuries, in one terrible outbreak alone, the Black Death carrying off around one third of the entire population. Now, as the domestic conflict reached its height at Naseby, Yorkshire was stalked by another visitation, the village of Ackworth, falling victim to another bout of the plague.

The villagers were woefully ignorant of the causes of the disease and were easy prey to the purveyors of quack remedies, wise women and self styled doctors who sold 'The Sovereign Cordial against the corruption of the Air,' 'Infallible preventive Pills against the Plague', and 'The only True Plague Water' amongst dozens of other antidotes. The inhabitants did realise, however, that the infection was highly contagious and was passed on from person to person by contact. Seeking to reduce the risks and contain the outbreak, they instructed that any infected person should remain within the village cordons. A hollowed out stone – the plague stone – was placed on the cordon boundary. Filled with water and disinfecting vinegar, it was used as a receptacle for money, diseased persons placing their coins in the bowl for collection by good Samaritans, who later left food at the same spot.

Most of the Great Plagues originated in London, a further infestation in the capital in June 1665 killing one in seven of the population. In the spring of the following year, the disease again reached Yorkshire, a notice issued by magistrates to the constable at Woolley (about ten miles south-west of Ackworth) making compelling reading:

> *... whereas it hath pleased God to visite the towne with a violent feavour whereas divers persons have lately dyed, and that as some of the inhabitants of the parish continue to resort to the houses in which the disease is or hath lately been and mingle with people that have been in them it is feared that the sickness may spread abroad....'* The constable was required: *'to sett one or more wardens at the door to prevent anyone going into an infected house, but to take care that the persons within may be accommodated with such necessary provisions and attendance as is requisite for them in their condition, and to advise the inhabitants not to intermingle themselves with any that have been in the houses visited by the plague.*

And there is a thought-provoking postscript, alluding to Woolley's lord of the manor. '*And you are to take care that ye effect and purport of this Warrant be as fully and duly executed upon the family or persons belonging to ye Hall or house of Mr. Wentworth as any other.*'

Directions: *High Ackworth is three miles south of Pontefract on the A628. The Plague Stone is north of the village on Pontefract Road, near the water tower. Map Landranger 111 – Grid Ref: 446187.*

89. PONTEFRACT: 'BLOODY POMFRET'

Shakespeare referred to this old fortress town in the most sanguinary terms, the allusion, in his play Richard II, highlighting the notorious Pontrefract Castle, an immense Norman structure that once occupied a spur of rock to the east of the town.

Built in the eleventh century, the castle was one of the strongest in Europe, its prisoners including the deposed Richard II who was axed to death with a dying scream: 'Mount, mount, my soul! thy seat is up on high, whilst my gross flesh sinks downward here to die.'

At the start of the Civil War, Pontefract Castle had become an impregnable stronghold of the Royalists, the third of three desperate sieges by the Roundheads only succeeding when the garrison succumbed to hunger after the ending of hostilities in March 1649. The defenders, who repelled fierce bombardment and numerous attempts at the undermining of the curtain walls, issued their own siege coins, finally surrendering some two months after the execution of Charles II. Within three days of submission, Parliament gave the orders for demolition.

Directions: *Pontefract is best reached via Junction 32 of the M62 going south on the A639. The castle is off South Baileygate. Fragments of the castle survive, notably parts of the walls, towers and an impressive powder magazine. The site is a municipal amenity area and is open every day. Much damaged by gunfire, is the nearby church of All Saints.' In Pontefract Museum (on Salter Row) you can inspect examples of the siege coins and other relics. Map Landranger 105 – Grid Ref: 461224.*

90. CASTLEFORD: 'NOBBUT A STONE WI' AN 'OLE BASHED THROUGH'

Castleford was coal. For countless generations, the black stuff dominated the town, spoil heaps and muck-down-to-the-finger-nails, signalling full employment and a jealously guarded mining solidarity and independence that brooked little individuality and even less change. So what did the pitmen make of the unconventional stranger in their midst? And what did they make of a man who spurned the shovel in favour of the maul and chisel?

There's an old saying in Castleford, which aptly describes the forthright personality of its citizens. 'I calls a spade a bloody shovel' you will hear one of the old colliers remark. 'And what does I think on Henry Moore?' he will add succinctly. 'Why, he was nobbut a lad who bashed bloody great 'oles in stone.'

A miner's son, the seventh of eight children, Henry Moore was born in Castleford in 1898, at No 30 Roundhill Road, a terraced property he later described as 'that awful little house.' From the age of 11 he lived at the equally unimpressive No 65 Smawthorne Lane, next to an old Victorian public house. He was a pupil at the Temple Street Elementary School – 'a mixed school and a rough one', and a regular churchgoer, his attendance at the Congregational Chapel Sunday School, where he was introduced to the art of Michelangelo, planting the seed of his career as a sculpture. A bright but introspective lad, Moore saw education as an escape from working class drudgery and he won a scholarship to Castleford Grammar School. He eventually became a teacher there but the war intervened and he was sent to France where he suffered the effects of a gas attack.

Returning home with a burning ambition to develop his talents, in 1919 he began a period of intensive study at the Leeds School of Art and at the Royal College of Art in London. In 1925, he married fellow student Irina Radetsky and settled in Hampstead, producing a succession of early sculptures that exhibit his fascination with pre-Columbian art and the masterpieces of the Italian Renaissance. By the 1930s, his work had undergone a metamorphosis, the familiar mother and child and family groups, vanquished warriors and voluptuous reclining human figures pierced by strange holes, dominating his considerable output.

Moore was never nostalgic for his native Castleford, having a cold ambivalence to the town. He did, however, return in December 1941. After producing a string of evocative pictures of Londoners sheltering from the Blitz in the underground, he was commissioned to sketch studies of reserved occupations. 'I had thought,' he said, 'of going to my home town … which has several coal mines.' He chose the pit at Wheldale where his father had been in charge of the lamp room. After his first morning down the pit, he wrote:

> *If one were asked to describe what Hell might be like, this would do. I have never had a tougher day in my life – of physical effort and exertion. But I wanted to show the Deputy that I could stand just as much as the miners.*

In 1948, Moore was awarded the International Prize for Sculpture at the Venice Biennale, exhibitions galore following on in future years. Today, galleries across the world are stuffed with his esoteric creations but there are only token sculptures in Castleford.

Directions: *Castleford is just north of junction 32 of the M62 (take the A639 into the town). Henry Moore's birthplace was demolished in 1974. 'It was just a run-of-the-mill miner's cottage', sniffed one town worthy, 'it was not worth preserving.' The site of 30 Roundhill Road has though, received some belated attention and is now the memorial Henry Moore Square. South of the railway line, Roundhill Road is best accessed via Bridge Street and Pontefract Road, going right 400 yards after the railway, down Smawthorne Lane and left down Beanland Road. The focus of the square, which is at the junction of Roundhill Road and Garden Street, is a trio of sandstone portals inscribed with quotational plaques.*

Unusually, there is an exhibition of Moore memorabilia including trowels, gouges, punches and files, in the Henry Moore Clinic on Smawthorne Lane.

Moore donated very little to his own town (he gave 400 pieces to a gallery in Ontario) but there is one of his works – a reclining figure – outside the Civic Centre on Ferrybridge Road. Use Bridge Street and go left 150 yards after the railway.

There are also other examples of the sculptor's art in Wakefield Art Gallery, the Yorkshire Sculpture Park in Bretton and in the City Art Gallery in Leeds. Map Landranger 105 –Grid Refs: 425253 (Henry Moor Square); 430254 (Henry Moor Clinic); 435256 (Civic Centre).

91. ALTOFTS: PIRATE KNIGHT

Many lesser-accomplished men have plaques and pedestals to their names, although in his native town of Altofts, Sir Martin Frobisher, privateer, explorer and outstanding patriot, is largely forgotten. One single, stained-glass window in Normanton Church is his only monument.

Born around 1535, Frobisher spent part of his childhood in London. His father died prematurely and Martin was despatched to a relative in the capital, his new guardian packing him off to sea. He voyaged to the Guinea coast of Africa in 1553 and 1554, obtaining his own command just a few years later. Emboldened by the granting of a privateering licence from the English Crown, he preyed upon French shipping in the Channel. This 'Martyne Furbisher of Normanton in the county of York, gentleman,' was arraigned in 1566 'on suspicion of having fitted out a vessel as a pirate.' The charge was unproved but within five years, he was involved in the plot to take the Earl of Desmond hostage.

Sir Martin Frobisher.

A professional seaman and a navigator of the highest calibre, Frobisher set out with three ships in 1576, on an expedition to discover the fabled North-West Passage, having suggested to a friend: 'That the discovery of the North-West Passage was the only thing that was left undone, whereby a notable mind could be made famous and fortunate.' As his little flotilla passed Greenwich, Queen Elizabeth 'commended them, and bade them farewell, with shaking her hand at them out of the window.' Frobisher succeeded in crossing the Atlantic that year, reaching Labrador, Baffin Island and the bay that now bears his name, although the fabled polar route to the Pacific remained a dream. In achieving its principle aim, the voyage was unsuccessful, but Frobisher returned with a captive, an Eskimo: 'A strange infidel, whose like was never seen, or heard of before.' This prize was exciting enough but what really animated the queen and the expedition's financial backers was the discovery of a pocket of seemingly worthless black ore. A crew-member brought the souvenir back to England, subsequent analysis setting off a gold rush and a bout of investment fever.

In 1577, again with three ships, Frobisher set sail, returning just four months later with 200 tons of precious ore, the whole of England rejoicing at the news. Most of the mineral was deposited in Bristol Castle, the rest passing into the safe keeping of the Tower of London. The delighted queen commanded that four stout locks be placed on the doors of the treasury, announcing that the newly discovered coast should henceforth be known as *Meta Incognita*. Heartily congratulating Frobisher, the queen presented him with gifts and a chain of gold, promptly asking him to mount a third, much larger expedition.

Fifteen vessels set out for the ore fields in 1578. Sailing up Hudson Bay the convoy anchored in Frobisher Bay, and, after unsuccessfully attempting to establish a colony there, it returned to England with its cargo of ore. Further assay inspections revealed that the cargo was worthless earth, Frobisher retiring to his Altofts estates, which the queen, despite her disappointments, appears to have presented as a gift. For a few years, the swashbuckling hero tended his roses until his country again called him to action.

In 1585, Frobisher served as vice admiral in Sir Francis Drake's expedition to the West Indies, his finest hour coming in 1588, during the battle to repulse the Spanish Armada. In that conflict, according to one commentator: 'He had the prudence of Hawkins with the resolution and quickness of Drake, while his dauntless courage was all his own. It was valour spiced with what can only be called devilry, acquired in his privateering days. His seamanship has perhaps never been surpassed.'

He was knighted during the action against the Spanish, over the next six years, commanding various naval squadrons, one of which unsuccessfully attempted to seize a Spanish treasure ship in 1591. Fighting as an ally of Henry IV of France in 1594, he led an assault on the Spanish fort of Croyzon, near Brest, receiving a superficial wound in his hip. Improperly treated, the wound festered and Frobisher died on 22nd November 1594 in Plymouth. His heart was laid in the port's St Andrew's Church.

Directions: *Altofts is about three miles north-east of Wakefield (A61 and a minor road east over the Stanley Ferry bridge). Save for the odd street name and the Martin Frobisher Infants School, there is nothing much left in the village that recalls the achievements of the famous man. He is said to have lived in the three-storey Frobisher Hall in Altofts. This imposing mansion once stood near the former Ship Inn and the old maypole. Sir Martin Frobisher owned a large house and 100 acres of land at Cantley near Doncaster. He also possessed other property at Heath and Whitwood Manor. The most significant memorial to Frobisher is in All Saints' Church in Normanton. It is contiguous with Altofts to the south-east. The window draws frequent visitors from the Frobisher Bay area of Canada. It is to the left of the porch entrance – church key available from the nearby parish centre. Map Landranger 104 – Grid Ref: 387225 (All Saints' Church, Normanton).*

92. GARFORTH: REACHING A MILESTONE

Milestones were Britain's first items of street furniture. An integral part of the logistics of empire, they were erected by the Romans, an impressive 110 specimens surviving in the UK. Some 1,200 years elapsed before we set up milestones of our own on the Dover to Canterbury road in 1633. Under a parliamentary act of 1767, milestones became compulsory on turnpike roads and by the mid-1830s, some 20,000 such stones were in place. Made gradually redundant by modern wooden and metal signs, these legacies of our communication heritage, soldiered on until 1940 when the government, as a security measure, ordered their removal. Miraculously, despite inevitable losses and breakages, and despite centuries of weathering, damage from vehicles, vandalism and theft, hundreds of milestones still survive, adding interest and not a little nostalgia to the travelling scene.

Communication and civilisation are mutually indispensable, milestones providing vital information for travellers. But they did much more. In a world without maps and satellite navigation, their very presence gave an assurance to long lost feet. 'Thank God. I'm on the right road at last!.' They were also used to time mail coaches and walking races and they were essential in calculating the cost of postage and horse hire. Some became status symbols for estate owners, others, made from cast iron, were essentially advertisements for iron foundries. And milestones often had a dual purpose, serving as mounting blocks, water pumps, boundary markers and memorials.

Perhaps, though, it is their hitherto unmentioned function that so evokes questions of time and place. In the featureless and often dangerous divides between towns and villages, they were obvious rendezvous points. Workers, eloping lovers, tramps, beggars and criminals would all meet at well-known milestones. Welcoming the backrest, weary pedestrians would sprawl out and take refreshment in their shadows, and, in states of near exhaustion, desperate fugitives would squint at the chiselled numbers and wince before taking deep breaths and rushing on.

Directions: *One good example of a surviving milestone is on the old Selby and Leeds Turnpike Road (now the A63) about three miles east of Garforth. Map Landranger 104 – Grid Ref: 443316.* ☛ ***See also 95 (Aberford)***

93. PARLINGTON: THE RUSSIAN PRINCE MYSTERY

In the spring of 1903, the dashing Crown Prince Ernestine Vladimir Zmronge of the Russian court paid a visit to Parlington Hall at the invitation of his great uncle Sir Cecil Gascoigne. The young man had a growing fascination for steam railways and was keen to inspect the recently completed mineral railway on his great uncle's estate. Crown Prince Zmronge spent several uneventful days inspecting the line and travelling on the rolling stock. On the sixth day he went out for a walk in the woods but never returned. Despite an exhaustive police search using bloodhounds, no body was ever found and his disappearance remained a total mystery until 1997 when the old hall was demolished.

A sheaf of papers belonging to Sir Cecil's bizarre wife Lady Constance Gascoigne was discovered in January of that year bricked up in the Orangery. The outlandish and previously dismissed mutterings of estate workers about the lady's fascination with the occult and witchcraft were suddenly given unquestionable veracity. Several manuscripts in Constance's own hand,

Parlington Woods: is this all that's left of the Crown Prince?

proved beyond doubt that she was a witch. But this was not the most sensational revelation.

In a long letter addressed to the Russian royal family, Lady Gascoigne finally revealed the fate of the crown prince. According to her own account, on the day of his disappearance he had inadvertently stumbled across a naked convention of witches in Parlington Wood. The cavorting ladies were angered at the interruption and charged their leader with striking the young man dumb. Before Constance could do so, however, the bewildered prince ran off towards the railway line. He sprinted only a few hundred yards before a spell took hold and he was rooted to the spot forever.

Directions: *Crown Prince Ernestine Vladimir Zmronge was transfixed in full flight on 1st April 1903 and his unmistakable aborescent form can be seen at Parlington, just off the track of the Fly Line to the east of the tunnel. The signposted Fly Line footpath runs from the Barwick – Garforth road to Aberford) Map Landranger 105 – Grid Ref: 422358*

94. BARWICK-IN-ELMET: A VIRILE POLE

Manly symbols come no bigger than the one in Barwick-in-Elmet near Leeds. At a height of nearly 100 feet it towers above Main Street, keeping up a ram-rod tradition of renewal and fertility that goes back nearly a thousand years. In a grand ceremony involving ropes, props, ladders and multiple muscle all under the direction of the pole-master, the decorated maypole is hoisted and hung with garlands and bells, remaining in position for three years. Custom dictates that the pole is taken down on Easter Monday for inspection, repair and repainting, followed by its triumphant replanting on Whit Tuesday. The whole process could be accomplished by two men and a JCB in under two hours ... but where's the fun in that? And where else in this modern age could you have the hands-on experiences of a pyramid slave without the whips?

Directions: *The maypole is in Main Street, Barwick-in-Elmet, eight miles north-east of Leeds. Triennial festivities involving the whole village and thousands of visitors take place in Hall Tower Field, the site of an ancient motte and bailey castle, 100 yards west of the Gascoigne Arms. Map Landranger 104 – Grid Ref: 399375.*

95. ABERFORD: MEN ON TOP BOUNCING

In this third millennium, we can whizz by road from Wetherby to London in under three hours. Imprisoned in steel and glass, with little interaction with the world outside, we can fly, the speed of the modern car saving precious hours, to be squandered in pursuit of the trivial and the themed. Give me the adventure of the open road every time. Give me an outside seat on a stagecoach, for a bouncing, roller-coaster ride of yesteryear.

The Swan at Aberford.

The passing of the Turnpike Acts in the eighteenth century, spurred widespread road improvements and a tremendous increase in the volume of wheeled traffic and inn building. In just 30 years, between 1720 and 1750, the average speed of coach travel between London and York increased from five miles to an impressive seven miles an hour, the majority of coaches averaging between fifty and sixty miles per day. By 1775, coaches were carrying eight passengers inside and 10 up top, the annually published coaching register for that year informing us that the 'number of public coaches, flys, machines and diligences is 400 … the number of four-wheeled carriages is 17,000.' Inns, offering every equestrian facility and modern amenity, sprang up to cater for the new trade, the best establishments providing lavish meals, plated cutlery, spotless table linen and curtained four-poster beds.

The White Swan on the Great North Road in Aberford, was typical of the hostelries of the period. Built expressly for the coach trade, it had a handsome arched entrance to accommodate the largest vehicles, stabling for dozens of horses and, above the nags' quarters, rooms for the so-called post boys. These were responsible for riding postillion, for assisting passengers, paying toll fees and returning horses to their own stables.

With its 'quaint settles and picturesque interior', the White Swan entertained a vast range of customers who plied one of the busiest routes in England. In a single day, the old inn with its tumult of coachmen, passengers, farmers, tradesmen, travelling rogues vagabonds and ladies of easy virtue, chimney-corner story tellers and anxious chamber maids, all supervised by a landlord of dubious reputation, must have witnessed relief, exhaustion, jollity, drunkenness, gluttony, exasperation, astonishment, disappointment, licentiousness, debauchery and crime galore. If only walls could talk!

HULL, JULY 17

HULL AND YOR

ROYAL MAIL-COACH,

WITH A GUARD

WELL ARMED.

SETS out every Day about *Half-past Three* in the Afternoon, Mr. *BAKER's*, the *Cross-Keys*, in the *Market-Place*, *HULL*, arrives at Mr. *PULLEINE's*, the Tavern in *YORK*, in SIX HOU returns from thence about *Half-past Twelve* at Night, or immedi after the Receipt of the LONDON MAIL, and arrives at *HULL* in the Morning.

No more than *Four Inside* and *Two Outside* Passengers will be taken.

Fare, 10 s. 6d. INSIDE; OUTSIDE 5 s. 3 d.

Short Passengers Threepence-halfpenny *per* Mile.

Parcels from 3 d. to 6 d. if above a Stone Weight One Ha penny *per* Pound.

For Places or Entry of Parcels, apply to *Henry Cawood*, at the Po Office, *Hull*, Mr. *Pulleine*, *York*; Mr. *Bland*, *Beverley*, and to Mr. G King's Arms, *Market-Weighton*, from those Towns respectfully *Hull*, *York*, *London*, *or Edinburgh*.

Conveyance may be secured for Passengers and Parcels from *Hull* *London* (Fare 3l. 13s. 6d.) by the MAIL COACH, the whole Way, e cept the Places be previously disposed of at *York*, in which Case M *Pulleine* engages to send the Passengers forward in a Post-Chaise at t same Expence and accompanying the MAIL COACH; the same fro *Hull* to *Edinburgh*, 3l. 13 s. 6 d. or any intermediate Places at Fares the Proportion of Distance.

*** The Proprietors give Notice, that they will not be accountable for any Parcel exceed the Value of Five Pounds.

A Mail coach handbill of 1787.

Directions: *Aberford is contiguous with the A1 (the village was by-passed some years ago) about 10 miles north-east of Leeds (A64 and a minor road through Barwick-in-Elmet). The White Swan is in the centre of the village, south of the Cock Beck. The inn preserves its archway and rear stables together with an old sign and a coaching bell. A few hundred yards north of the inn on the left-hand side of the road (over the Cock Beck and up the hill) is a surviving Toll Bar House. Map Landranger 105 – Grid Refs: 433373 (the White Swan); 433386 (Toll Bar House).* ☛ ***See also 92 (Garforth)***

96. LEEDS: THE GOLDEN FLEECE

It's no coincidence that the arms of Leeds bear the emblems of twin lambs, the fortunes of the founding city relying heavily on wool. The monks of nearby Kirkstall Abbey had some of the largest flocks of sheep in England, Edward the Third inviting Flemish weavers to plant the seeds of an industry that was to clothe the world.

In the Tudor period, Leeds became notable for its 'art or mystery of making and working woollen cloths, commonly called in English "Northern Dozens"', production in cottages and small workshops giving way to a factory system propelled by the Industrial Revolution and steam powered machinery. Famous for its cloth halls and immense factories in Hunslet, Armley and Holbeck, Leeds produced a dazzling variety of cloth for domestic and international markets, the sale of linens, worsteds, serges, tweeds, cords, moreens, damasks, shalloons, crapes, coburgs, tammies, merinos, salteens, paramattas and camlet yarns funding unprecedented urban expansion and a lavish civic building programme that has left us with some of the finest architecture in the north.

Local inventors and entrepreneurs were every bit as catalytic as the new machines, men like engineers Matthew Murray and Peter Fairbairn, and business pioneer John Barran – who in 1855 opened the first ever machine-made clothing factory – paving the way for a former refugee from Lithuania, Sir Montague Burton, who set up his clothing workshops in Leeds in 1909. By 1925 his massive factory had become the largest in the world, employing 10,500 people on its Hudson Road site. Cleverly promoted to a mass market as the 'Tailor of Taste', Burton's manufactured made to measure suits 'for a week's wages', at one time, clothing one in five of British men.

Directions: *Leeds has a range of access options (M1, M62, A1 etc). A number of grandly eccentric buildings reflect the former importance of the Leeds textile trade. Finished in 1879, John Barran's warehouse on St Paul's Street (St Paul's House) is built in brick and terracotta with Moorish arches and striking minarets. In Crown Street (at the rear of the Corn Exchange) are the remains of the White Cloth Hall built in 1775 as a centre for cloth sales.*

Within walking distance of the city centre on Marshall Street (go south from the railway station and cross the river on Neville Street, going next right on Water Lane) are the amazing Marshall Mills, a flamboyant creation of 1840 in an Egyptian style. Its lotus columns, arches and an obelisk shaped chimney were inspired by Napoleon's campaign of 1798. This former flax mill had a thousand strong workforce producing 70 million yards of linen ever day. Over its 400 feet long principal workroom, it had a most ingenious system for venting hot air and maintaining an equable temperature for the workers. Rising to nine feet above the roof, with a diameter of 14 feet, were 66 circular lanterns. The flat space between was covered with a mixture of coal tar and lime with a top dressing of mould sown with grass. 'Not infrequently, the singular sight of sheep grazing on the roof may be witnessed.'

Sir Montague Burton's factory in the Burmantofts district (two miles east of the city centre – take the A64 York Road and go left on Lupton Avenue and third left on Hudson Road) is no longer in existence, but a plaque marks its site. Map Landranger 104 – Grid Refs: 295337 (St Paul's House); 305334 (White Cloth Hall); 295325 (Marshall Mills) and 325344 (Sir Montague Burton's Factory).

97. LEEDS: MOVIE STAR

A lady in a ridiculous feathered hat rushes to an appointment with a parcel beneath her arm, and a man nonchalantly wipes a sleeve across his nose. Frozen in time, these unknowing stars occupy the unlikely stage of Leeds Bridge. Just twenty staccato frames occupy a running time of three seconds tops. Blink and you'll miss the action in the world's first ever movie.

The pioneering camera-man on that sunny October day in 1888 was Frenchman Louis Aime Augustine Le Prince. A graduate of the University of Leipzig where he studied physics and chemistry, Le Prince initially worked as a photographer and painter, coming to Leeds in 1866 at the invitation of his friend John Whitley. Le Prince became a designer in the Whitley Partners Brass Foundry in Hunslet. He soon settled in his Yorkshire home, marrying his employer's daughter Elizabeth Whitley in 1869. Elizabeth had a flair for art, and together, the couple opened a school of applied art in Park Square, Leeds, in 1870.

In Victorian Leeds, which was a vibrant focus of artistic, cultural and scientific expansion, Le Prince became interested in the possibilities of creating moving pictures. He read widely and recognised a fundamental fact. Pictorial animation demanded the production of at least sixteen images per second.

In 1881, Le Prince left Leeds with his wife for New York. Here, he took a job as a specialist working on the Lincrusta wallpaper process, devoting his spare time to the development of a camera. To deliver the holy grail of image sequences, he manufactured a sixteen-lens camera, filing an American pattern for his device in November 1886. Soon afterwards, he returned to Leeds alone to refine his ideas. Collaborating with mechanic James W Longley and cabinet-maker Frederick Mason, Le Prince constructed a second experimental camera. This improved instrument had a single lens, and unlike its predecessor, it used only one roll of paper film. It was all in the testing.

On location in Leeds, Le Prince shot his remarkable images in October 1888, moving images of figures in his father-in-law's garden in Oakwood Grange Road, Roundhay, and on the busy thoroughfare of Leeds Bridge, proving the new technology beyond doubt. Some sceptics of the day, dismissed the achievement as a vacuous amusement, with little hope of commercial success. Undaunted, Le Prince persevered, adding further refinements to his camera and developing a projector.

In 1890, he left Leeds for the final time, travelling to meet his brother in Dijon where he collected part of an inheritance left to him by a relative. Having made further arrangements to meet friends in Paris, he boarded a train at precisely 2.42 pm on the afternoon of 16th September 1890. He was never seen again. Detectives carried out an exhaustive search, but no trace of either Louis Le Prince or his bags was ever found.

Directions: *Leeds has a range of access options (M1, M62, A1 etc). Leeds Bridge, the spot where cinematographic history was made, is a few hundred yards east of Leeds City Railway Station. It spans the River Aire, linking Briggate with Bridge End. Using the second of his single lens cameras, Le Prince shot his footage from a window in the premises of Hick Brothers, at the south-east corner of the bridge looking back towards Briggate. Remarkably his blockbusting images can now be seen on the internet at* www.web.inter.nl.net/users/anima/pre-cinema/leprince/leprince.htm. *The* *carts and carriages in the three seconds sequence have since been replaced by motorised transport, but the Leeds Bridge, which was opened in 1873, has hardly changed. The work of Louis Le Prince is well represented in archives and exhibits in the National Museum of Photography, Film and Television in Bradford. Map Landranger 104 – Grid Ref: 303333 (Leeds Bridge).*

98. LEEDS: THE MARY CELESTE

Mount St Mary's Church, the brightest flower of Roman Catholic pride and fervour in Victorian Leeds, took root on one of the city's most prominent hills in 1867. Designed by Joseph Hansom in the Decorated Gothic style with chancel and transepts by Pugin, it was part of a family of buildings including a convent and an orphanage capable of accommodating up to a hundred inmates. In later years, schooling was provided for local children.

Serving a large, tightly knit, God fearing, predominantly Irish community that had settled on the east bank of the Aire, it soared above serried rows of cheap housing, cobbled, back-to-back streets with names like Bertha Street, Ada View and Nellie Crescent, providing congregations that on Sundays and holy days thronged the aisles.

Like many other religious enclaves across the country, Mount St Mary's was an ethical powerhouse, its influence, backed-up by a group of robust peripatetic priests who acted as confidants, counsellors, mediators and unofficial bobbies-on-the-beat. On occasions they rolled up their sleeves and thumped offenders! These pioneers built a community of rare solidarity and cohesion, but the radical slum clearance programme of the 1970s swept the streets away, their lone, decaying and vandalised church serving as a metaphor for urban disintegration everywhere.

Directions: *Clearly visible from the city centre, the ruined Mount St Mary's Church is on Church Road, Richmond Hill and is best reached from East Street, going via Cavalier Street and Ellerby Road. Its curtilage, through which priests and altar boys paraded in solemn procession on feast days such as Corpus Christi, was closed off once a year to underline its private ownership. Map Landranger 104 – Grid Ref: 313333.*

Leeds: Mount St Mary's Church.

99. LEEDS: THE CONCRETE BUNGLE

When they were completed in 1941, the Quarry Hill Flats were hailed as the bright new future for urban housing, municipal delegations coming to Leeds from all over the world. Designed by architect R. A. .H. Livett in 1935 and influenced by other pre-war schemes such those in Berlin and Vienna, the flats, which formed the largest such complex in Europe, occupied a prominent hill east of the city centre, their position, on a broad axis that arrowed to the steps of the magnificent Town Hall, echoing the imperialist sentiments of Rome.

Covering a site of 28 acres, the impressive if somewhat austere flats, were built in the fashion of a girding wall pierced by semi – circular and parabolic arches. Between two and eight storeys in height and named Jackson, Moynihan, Priestley, Savile, Victoria, York, Lupton, Oastler, Rhodes, Thoresby and Wright Houses, these ultra – modern homes were constructed from light steel frames and vibrated concrete slabs, a total of 938 dwellings accommodating 3,280 people. Several lower ranges provided a day nursery, a communal hall for 500 and a row of shops.

At a time when nearby residents were living in back-to-back houses with single open fires and outside lavatories, Quarry Hill Flats were seen as the height of luxury, but a combination of factors spelt their doom. Inferior construction materials and high maintenance costs, poor insulation and acoustic qualities, vandalism and social rejection from tenants who felt increasingly cut off and isolated, resulted in a radical reassessment of housing needs. In less than one generation, the grand plan had been shattered and by 1976 the flats were empty, demolition sweeping away a municipal dream.

Directions: *The site of Quarry Hill Flats is prominently located east of the city centre overlooking the Eastgate roundabout near the Bus Station (the best access is from the A64 – York Road). Nothing remains of the flats except their site, now part-occupied by another futuristic building – the West Yorkshire Playhouse. Map Landranger 104 – Grid Ref: 308338.*

Leeds: Quarry Hill flats.

100. LEEDS: THE WORLD'S OLDEST RAILWAY

There is not a country in the world without its railway, the town of Leeds sowing the seeds of global locomotion in 1758. In that year, an act was passed to permit the construction of a wooden railway track linking the Middleton collieries with Leeds and by 1812 the line was open. To the astonishment of the crowd on the inaugural day of 24th June, the steam locomotive 'Salamanca' transported coal in 38 wagons, moving at a breakneck speed of three miles per hour between Middleton and Casson Close near Leeds Bridge.

The partners in the ambitious enterprise were pit manager John Blenkinsop and engineer Matthew Murray, the pair rejecting the idea of an engine with smooth wheels in favour of a vehicle with cogwheels operating on a toothed track. Three more engines were produced and although the driving gears of the locomotives and the horizontal tracks suffered adverse wear, the operation was a commercial success, paving the way for more sophisticated projects elsewhere.

Directions: *The Middleton Railway is at Moor Road Station, Hunslet, two miles south of Leeds city centre and adjacent to junction 5 of the M621. The railway was saved from oblivion by a preservation society in 1960. The direct descendent of the original wagon-way now extends for one mile between the railhead and Park Holt on the outskirts of Middleton Park. Using restored steam engines – some were originally produced in the local Hunslet Works – 25 minute trips are offered at weekends throughout the year. Telephone 0113 2710320. Map Landranger 104 – Grid Ref: 304310.*

101. WHITKIRK: LEADING LIGHT

John Smeaton, the famous engineer, came into the world with a hammer in his hands in 1724. 'His playthings were not the baubles of children, but the tools with which men could work.' Little John was an inquisitive and inventive child with a remarkable genius for engineering, and by the time he was six, he had made for himself a windmill and a pump that raised water. At fifteen years of age, he manufactured a lathe, his formal education taking him to Leeds Grammar School, after which, he joined his father's law firm.

Smeaton learned mathematical instrument making in York and London and set up business in the capital, producing a number of scientific papers that led to his election to the Royal Society in 1753. Keen to study the accomplishments of Dutch engineers, he visited the Low Countries in 1754, his keen analysis of the materials and techniques involved in constructing canals, harbours and mills taking him to the climax of his career. Between 1756 and 1759, he built the third Eddystone Lighthouse employing precisely cut, dovetailed blocks of Portland stone to withstand wave action, his design becoming standard for all such structures. And in experimenting with mortar

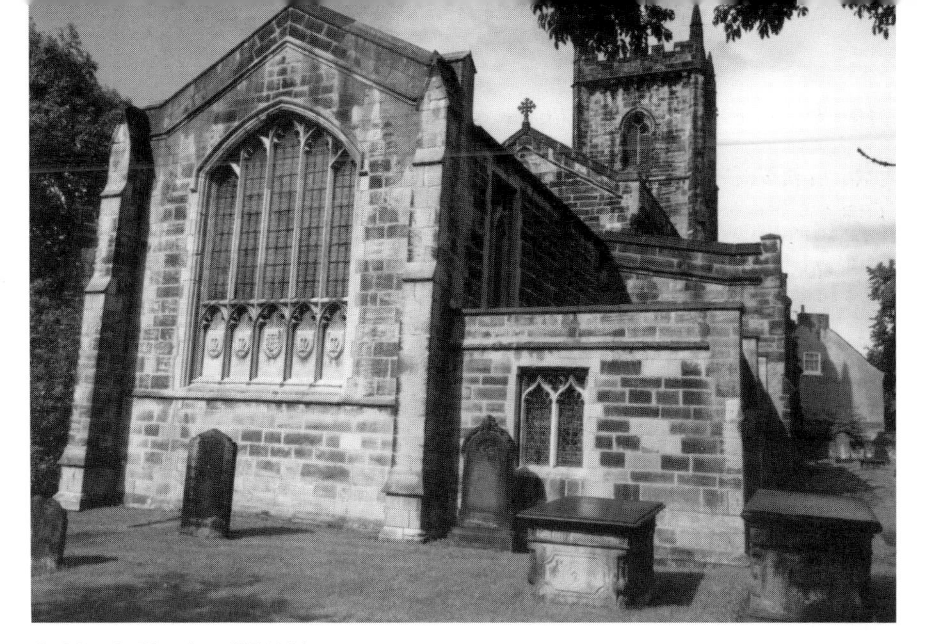

St Mary's Church at Whitkirk.

for the light's submerged foundations, he became the first engineer to identify the over riding merits of hydraulic lime – an admixture of limestone and high proportions of clay.

Smeaton's other commissions were equally impressive. He supervised the construction of the Forth and Clyde Canal in Scotland and he erected the bridges at Perth, Banff and Coldstream. In Yorkshire he was the resident engineer on the Calder Navigation project and he built a lighthouse at Spurn Point.

At the forefront of innovative research and experimentation, Smeaton took a leading role in the Industrial Revolution, developing the new technologies of steam power. He pioneered the introduction of cast –iron shafts and gearing in mills and he improved the performance of the Newcomen atmospheric steam engine, designing pumping engines for Long Benton colliery in Northumberland, Chacewater mine in Cornwall and Kronshtadt docks in Russia. Ever fascinated by pumps, he also made modifications to the deep-sea diving bell, installing an air pump to improve safety.

In 1771 John Smeaton founded the Society of Civil Engineers.

Directions: *Whitkirk is four miles east of Leeds centre (A64 and A63). John Smeaton was born and died (in 1792) at the family home. Built in 1698 by John Smeaton (the engineer's grandfather) Austhorpe Lodge is on Austhorpe Road (east off the roundabout in Crossgates for 750 yards and south over the narrow railway bridge; the lodge is on the hill on the left). John Smeaton is buried beneath the chancel in St Mary's Church. Whitkirk (half a mile west of Austhorpe on A63). Nearby is a commemorative tablet bearing an image of the Eddystone Lighthouse. Map Landranger 104 – Grid Ref: 371340 (Austhorpe Lodge); 364336 (St Mary's*

Church, Whitkirk). ☛ ***See also 165 (Spurn)***

102. CARLTON: FORCE MAJEURE

Rhubarb is the most flavoursome, useful, under-rated, love-it-or-loathe it fruit in the world. And like our famous pudding, the forced variety hails from Yorkshire, thriving on rich soil, horse muck and nitrogen-rich shoddy from the local woollen industry providing the ideal medium for fast growth.

Rhubarb is said to have originated in Tibet and Russia, its name deriving from the word *Rha*, the ancient name for the River Volga. The plant has long been known for its medicinal use, knowledge of its purgative and astringent properties coming to Europe via the Silk Road and the Levant.

Visually, and on the palate, rhubarb is unmistakable. Varying from pink to deep red, its long, fleshy stalks radiate like the spokes of a parasol from a central crown, deeply-veined, massive, emerald green leaves casting their shadows all around. Some of the older varieties have delicious names such as Baldry's Scarlet Defiance, Crimson Emperor and Hawke's Champagne. But it's on the tongue that tusky, as it is known in the West Riding, makes it reputation. There is not another comparable taste in the world.

As aggressive in the mouth as a vindaloo- filled flame-thrower (use plenty of sugar) with an acidic second phase that storms the taste buds and overwhelms the teeth in plaque, rhubarb has a singular taste that defies description.

Yorkshire continues to make a sizeable return on its production of the more delicately flavoured forced rhubarb, the area known as the 'Rhubarb Triangle' between Leeds, Bradford and Wakefield, growing hundreds of tonnes each year.

Four generations of the same family have forced rhubarb in their heated, irrigated sheds at Carlton. Plants spend three years outdoors prior to lifting and transfer into the light-tight sheds, the absence of illumination denying the crowns the opportunity of producing chlorophyll and inhibiting the growth of leaves. As highly prized as the first truffles, rhubarb stalks have recently become a gourmet dish, forcing between January and February each year, attracting parties of visitors to the so-called 'Rhubarb Trail.'

Directions: *Carlton is about four miles north of Wakefield (A61 to A654 crossroads and right). The fields around Carlton grow acres of rhubarb ready for forcing. Guided walks, that include visits to the forcing sheds, are arranged annually in early February by Wakefield District Council. Other events feature themed rhubarb dinners and cookery demonstrations. The National Collection of Rhubarb is in the Harlow Carr Botanical Gardens in Harrogate. Map Landranger 104 – Grid Refs: 335273 (Carlton); 280543 (Harlow Carr Botanical Gardens, Harrogate).*

103. PUDSEY: LEN'S TUESDAY

Only once in their entire history have the bells of Pudsey's church of St Laurence peeled exactly 364 times, the joyful campanological spree taking place on Tuesday 23rd August 1938 after one of the most exciting moments in sporting history.

Begun on Saturday 20th August before a crowd of 30,000 spectators, the Test Match between England and Australia had reached an exciting stage. In hot sun, Len Hutton, the pride of Pudsey, had battled to a memorable 160 runs before stumps were drawn for the weekend. Monday dawned and the innings resumed, Hutton putting on another 140 runs by close of play. He had already broken the record for the highest individual Test Match score against Australia and had claimed a tally only 34 tantalising runs short of Don Bradman's all time record made at Headingley in 1930. On that sultry Tuesday, the scene was set for a cliff-hanger and the whole of Pudsey held its breath.

Shopkeepers left their counters, employees skived off work and children stopped playing, nearly everybody in the town gravitating towards their red-hot wirelesses. Clamouring round the dials, fans of the great cricketer ran every run, screaming and lunging for the crease and lashing out at the projectile that stood between Len Hutton and immortality. As the innings progressed towards the magic 335, a quiet descended on Pudsey. 'On'y fower runs wanted,' whispered a myriad hoarse voices. 'He'll never risk it will he?'

At the moment Hutton went for glory, there was a deadly quiet. For some seconds, the announcer fell silent, listeners biting on their fingers and praying. Then the confirmation came in one glorious shriek of delight and you could have heard the delirious howls of approval in Huddersfield. 'He's done it! yelled the town to a man. Our Len's gone and done it. Risked ivverything and 'it a boundary!'

After an innings lasting a marathon 13 hours and 20 minutes, Hutton was finally out for a record breaking 364, the 26,000 inhabitants of his native town going wild. That night, there was many a long toast to Len Hutton in the local hostelries, every drinker raising a glass and toasting their hero as eight ringers rang a peal of 364 chimes on the parish bells.

Directions: *Pudsey is five miles west of Leeds City Centre on the A647. St Laurence's Church is on Church Lane (next to Pudsey Park) about half a mile south-west of the town centre. The famous bells have been rung to celebrate other momentous events in the town's history and records of the occasions are permanently etched on the belltower walls. In 2001, the home of Yorkshire County Cricket commemorated the sporting life of Len Hutton by erecting a pair of decorative iron entrance gates showing the hero at the crease. Map Landranger 104 – Grid Refs: 221331 (St Laurence's Church); 276357 (entrance gates at Headingley Cricket Ground).*

104. BIRSTALL: GAS LIGHT

Statue of Joseph Priestley.

Joseph Priestley, the son of a Birstall cloth dresser, was born into an epoch making age in 1733. At a time of great philosophical and political change, and in an era that witnessed the French Revolution and an international debate on the fundamental rights of man, he became a leading intellectual and an internationally famous scientist, his list of associates reading like a *Who's Who* of the eighteenth century. He knew Richard Price, Mary Wollstonecraft, Matthew Boulton, James Watt and Erasmus Darwin and he became close friends with the American patriots Benjamin Franklin, John Adams and Thomas Jefferson. Priestley's contributions to science were recognised in his elections to the Royal Society, the French Academy of Sciences and the St Petersburg Academy, the University of Edinburgh also acknowledging his more theoretical accomplishments in the award of a doctorate of laws.

But this radical thinking luminary experienced darker days. He was an ordained minister of religion but was condemned as an atheist. He did much for the advancement of science in his work on electricity and gases, but his radical views on civil and religious liberties brought opposition and derision. On one occasion his house and laboratory were ransacked by a mob incensed at his outrageous views. Eventually, by degrees, he became increasingly disillusioned and ostracized, and he left England for America in 1794.

Priestley firmly believed that science and human advancement were intertwined, the advancement of one enriching the other. He expostulated his theories in a series of books, *The History of the Present State of the Discoveries relating to Vision, Light and Colour,* which was intended to be the first volume of a series delineating the history of experimental philosophy, bringing his work to the attention of Captain James Cook. The great explorer was about to embark on his second world voyage of discovery and Priestley was invited to serve as the official astronomer onboard the *Resolution.* Interestingly though, the invitation was withdrawn as a consequence of Priestley's growing reputation as a political radical.

Practically, Priestley is best remembered for his work on analysing the chemical properties of gases. He discovered several gases unknown to science and he isolated oxygen, his 'dephlogisticated' air, shattering the notion that air was an element. He demonstrated that the red colour of blood is derived from its combination with atmospheric oxygen and he identified the respiratory processes of plants. When awarding the prestigious Royal Society's Copley Medal to Priestley in 1773, the president eloquently said:

> *From these discoveries we are assured that no vegetable grows in vain; but from the oak of the forest to the grass in the field, every individual plant is serviceable to mankind, if not always distinguished by some private virtue, yet making a part of the whole which cleans and purifies our atmosphere.*

In Yorkshire, Priestley spent six years between 1767 and 1773 as the minister of Mill Hill Chapel in Leeds. Here, with no formal training and with only the simplest equipment, he embarked on the scientific studies that were to bring him fame. According to one old tome, '... the vicinity of his dwelling to a public brewery was the occasion of his attention being directed to pneumatic chemistry. When visiting the place one day, he noted the peculiar appearances attending the extinction of lighted chips in the gas floating over the fermented liquor.'

Priestley was a highly controversial man. The Bishop of Durham of his day, who publicly criticised such staunchly defended tenets of faith as the virgin birth and the atonement, objected to Priestley and he had to leave his home for America. In this land of the free, he spent his last 10 years, going to rest in a Quaker burial ground in Northumberland, Pennsylvania. Thomas Jefferson, who was elected President of the United States in 1801, spoke for many when he referred to Priestley as: '... one of the few lives precious to mankind.'

Directions: *Birstall is on the B6125, about six miles south-west of Leeds, just north of Birstall Smithies. There is a statute of Priestley in Birstall centre. The best access is from junction 27 of the M62 (A62 and A643). Joseph Priestley was born in a cottage at Fieldhead (see plaque on a cottage to the right of the road immediately south of the motorway on the road signposted from Birstall to Drighlington. Going west from Birstall centre, take the first right uphill for about three quarters of a mile. Mill Hill Chapel (see plaque to the right of the entrance) is in the centre of Leeds on the east side of City Square opposite Leeds City Station. Across from the chapel, on the pedestrianised and landscaped roundabout (it has a massive monument of the Black Prince as its centrepiece) is a statue of Joseph Priestley. Map Landranger 104 – Grid Refs: 225263 (statue of Priestley in Birstall); 223274 (plaque at Fieldhead); 311334 (statue of Priestley in City Square); (303334 Mill Hill Chapel).* ☛ ***See also 54 (Whitby)***

105. BRADFORD: DEAD CENTRE

One hundred and twenty three thousand bodies inhabit the quietest 26 acres in Bradford, its Undercliffe Cemetery being the only such repository in Yorkshire that flaunts itself as a tourist attraction. Alongside the name, rank and serial number mounds of the mill workers, are the graves of the city's businessmen, politicians and wool barons who are remembered in expensive splendour. With an eye for status and ostentation, even in death, these grandees occupy the millionaire rows, as if somehow the marble and stone of their lavishly ornamented tombs and mausoleums might outlast their bones.

Privately owned by the Bradford Cemetery Company, the graveyard was opened in 1854, its dramatic position overlooking the industrial heartland making it a popular final destination for all classes. A walk among the carefully demarcated rows, is a social history lesson, the generally mean plots of the labourers, street sweepers, factory operatives, masons, carpenters, fellmongers, and victims from the Crimean War surrounding the grandest graves of all. These are centrally located on the so-called Boulevard, an in-your-face Valley of the Kings stuffed with weeping angels, spires, mock towers, obelisks and one incredible mini Temple of Giza complete with a pair of guarding sphinxes.

Closed to further interments in the mid-1970s, Undercliffe Cemetery, which is frequently used as a film set, is today more theatre than theosophy. Easy to explore along smoothed and levelled paths, it has an interpretation centre in the New Lodge … but the place is spooky. There's not a flower in sight.

Directions: *Bradford is 10 miles west of Leeds. The best access is via the M62 (junction 26), going north towards the city centre on the M606. Undercliffe Cemetery is north-east of the city centre between Undercliffe Lane and Otley Road (A658). Map Landranger 104 Grid Ref: 175343.*

South Yorkshire

106 to 120

Think of South Yorkshire and you immediately think of steel and heavy engineering, this metallic forge that clothed the ironclads and the leviathans of the railway age, pulsating with the roar of blast furnaces and steam hammers. Despite the transformation of the local economy and the disappearance of the dark galvanic rolling mills, this densely populated area is proud of its industrial past, Sheffield and Templeborough banging the drum of tradition in two popular museums – Kelham Island and Magna. But South Yorkshire is more than a museum to cold steel. It made parts for revolvers and rifles but it also manufactured two of the most enduring legends in England and was the scene of a remarkable medical experiment that transformed the health of the nation. Spit-in-your-eye South Yorkshire is as warming and welcoming as a shower of sparks, although it is not totally divest of humour. Let me take you to the site of a hilarious hoax that fooled thousands and a sardine packed pub-bar where you will need to sing for your supper and practise the art of communal breathing ... in unison.

DUNGWORTH DAILY – 24th DECEMBER 1883

RECORD CROWD OF CHORISTERS RAISE RAFTERS

Crowds spilled out onto the streets this week during the best-attended communal carol singing event ever held in the Royal Hotel. Such was the press of bodies and the lack of room for the traditional raising of glasses that a system of overhead tubing was installed to ensure that every man got his share of tonsil lubrication.

BARNSLEY CLARION – 16th OCTOBER 1837

MAN WILL WALK ON WATER!

In his interview with Barnsley Clarion staff today, the German dare-devil Herr Von de Hom Bugie soberly assures all our readers that he really will walk on water this evening. Science and technique, he maintains, will provide a spectacle unsurpassed in the history of the borough. His advice is to get to the canal early.

---

106. DORE: 'BRIGHT SWORD'

The Golden Dragon of Wessex should be an international symbol of tribal integration and ethnic harmony. The reason? At a stroke, without raising his sword in anger, Ecgbert, the leader of the West Saxons, united three warring factions into one country.

In a familiar sounding ninth century, England was a land riven by military struggles and political ambitions, the rival houses of Northumbria, Mercia and Wessex struggling for supremacy. Elected to the throne in 802 by the *witenagemote* – the assembly of wise men – Ecgbert, who became known as the 'Wealder of Britain', ruled through a combination of war and diplomacy. In the first nine years of his reign, the southern kingdoms capitulated without a fight and in 823, the Mercians were defeated at the Battle of Ellandune. Turning his attention to the Northumbrians, Ecgbert led his army north.

The Dore Stone.

In 829, on the Mercian-Northumbrian border, Ecgbert confronted the forces of Eanred, a decisive battle threatening to topple the northern king. Ravaged by internal dissensions and threatened by Scandinavian invaders, however, the Northumbrians realised the folly of an all out confrontation, the ancient *Anglo Saxon Chronicle* recording Ecgbert's diplomatic triumph: '... he led an army into Dore against the Northumbrians and they submitted to him and peace was declared.' Ecgbert had become overlord of all England.

At the time of his death in 839, Ecgbert the Great, whose name means 'Bright Sword', ruled over the whole country south of the Forth, with the exception of Cornwall and the south –west of Scotland and the north-west corner of England. Sixty sovereigns and nearly 1,200 years later, we can still rejoice in England's first king.

Directions: *Dore is a village five miles south-west of Sheffield on the A621. A sandstone memorial stone on the village green (Vicarage Lane off Dore Road) commemorates Ecgbert's bloodless victory. An affixed plaque is shaped in the fashion of a Saxon shield and emblazoned with the Golden Dragon of Wessex. Map Landranger 111 – Grid Ref: 309811.*

107. SHEFFIELD: PROSPERITY ON A KNIFE EDGE

Diverted and dammed, the picturesque little rivers Don, Sheaf, Loxley, Blackburn and Rivelin together with the streams of Moss Beck, Porter Brook and Shire Brook, became powerhouses that helped create Sheffield, the exploitation of their power using giant water-wheels, creating a template for mechanisation and industrialisation that spawned one of great industrial expansions of modern times.

Even by the early years of the seventeenth century, water-grinding-wheels were present on some flows, the later construction of storage dams and head and tail goits in places like the Rivelin Valley helping drive stones for the grinding of scythes, cutlery and tools.

This great Yorkshire city was to become synonymous with quality steel making, the imprint 'Made in Sheffield' still beaming out from the finest cutlery in the world.

Directions: *Sheffield is easily accessible from the M1. The Rivelin Valley – now a nature reserve – is west of the city centre on the A6101. Follow the A57 signposted to 'Glossop' for about four miles leaving the built up area and go sharp right at Rivelin Mill Bridge onto the A6101 for a further two miles north –east. Signposted valley trails lead past a succession of dams, goits, sluices and the named sites of successive water wheels. On the Porter Brook, a restored so called 'Little Mester's' cutlery grinding mill dating from the sixteenth century can be found south of the Rivelin Valley off Hangingwater Road in Whiteley Woods in the city's Nether Green district. The Kelham Island Industrial Museum on Alma Street, north of the city centre, tells the full story of Sheffield's industrial past. Map Landranger 110 – Grid Refs: 324888 (Rivelin Valley Nature Trail); 317854 ('Little Mester's Mill); 353883 (Kelham Island Industrial Museum).*

108. SHEFFIELD: OCEANS APART

A vast ocean separates two records of human endeavour. One, held in the Buenos Aires archives of the Argentine military, is terse and chillingly matter-of-fact. The other, housed in Sheffield Cathedral, is equally brief and unemotional but it belies a dreadful pathos. The records read:

TOP SECRET
AM 39 Mission Report (*Sheffield*)
Date: May 4th, 1982
Aircraft: 3-A-202 – Lt Cdr Bedacarratz, Augusto
3- A-203 – Lt Mayora, Armando
Take Off Time: 0945
Initial Position of Target
Lat: 52 41 0 S
Long: 57 41 0 W
Time: 0845
Distance to target at the ending of the refuel: 245 NM

HMS SHEFFIELD
1971–1982
LAUNCHED BY HM QUEEN ELIZABETH II

AT BARROW-IN-FURNESS 10TH JUNE 1971
COMMISSIONED ON 28TH FEBRUARY 1975
DESTROYED BY AN ENEMY ATTACK
DURING THE LIBERATION OF THE FALKLAND ISLANDS
ON 4TH MAY 1982
WITH THE LOSS OF 20 LIVES

HMS *Sheffield*, a 3,500-ton Type 42 destroyer, was part of a naval task force that embarked for the South Atlantic on 5th April 1982. Its task was to liberate the Falkland Islands from occupation by Argentine forces. With patriotic passions running high, the convoy completed the 7,500 miles voyage in record time, engaging the enemy forces in the biggest naval action of the war on 1st May, when over 1,000 men lost their lives. Just three days later, two Argentine pilots, flying Super Etendard fighter planes, pierced the inadequate radar cover of the *Sheffield* to launch an Exocet missile attack. The ship suffered direct hits and sank in a mass of flames.

Directions: *There are a number of tributes to the Sheffield (and an earlier similarly named cruiser) in Sheffield Cathedral. The quoted epitaph is in the St George's Chapel (the regimental chapel of The York and Lancaster Regiment). To the right of the chapel is a memorial 'to commemorative the special relationship between the City of Sheffield and ships of the Royal Navy bearing the city's name …' Left of the main cathedral entrance is a print showing the destroyer Sheffield. Map Landranger 111 – Grid Ref: 353876.*

109. SHEFFIELD: HOT STEEL

It's impossible to enunciate the word without sounding like Clint Eastwood before he pulled the trigger. Steel. Seering hot, the word rasps from the lips, images of molten metal, sparks and steam surrounding a product that is the backbone of the modern world. Sheffield and its satellite towns have long been associated with steel production, south Yorkshire once supplying everything from nappy pins to navel guns.

Men such as the pioneering Benjamin Huntsman, who invented the 'crucible' or 'cast' steel process in the 1740's, kick started the Industrial Revolution, other entrepreneurs – Mark Firth, Albert Vickers, Thomas Jessop, Sir Robert Hadfield, Sir John Brown, Harry Brearley and Charles Cammell – making Sheffield the centre of the world's steel industry.

In the war years, Sheffield was Britain's arsenal, the manufacture of steel tubes, crankshafts, hydraulic presses, steam hammers, boilers, armour plate, torpedo parts, milling machines, turbine forgings and myriads of shells all helping the war effort. During the second of the great conflicts, the town was, for a time, the only centre producing Rolls Royce Merlin crankshafts for the

Spitfire, its strategic importance drawing the might of the Luftwaffe on the nights of the 12th, 13th and 15th December 1940. Ironically, what the bombers failed to achieve in 1940, was accomplished in latter years by international competition and a glut of steel in world markets, recession and subsequent factory demolition accounting for much of Sheffield's industrial heritage.

Directions: *Two surviving centres of steel production have been partly preserved and adapted to tell the story of Sheffield steel. The Kelham Island Industrial Museum occupies what was the Green Lane Works of Messrs A. Scott built in 1860. Its gatehouse is regarded as the most spectacular survival of factory architecture in the city. The triumphal arch over the central entrance with its relief panel of Vulcan sets the mighty scene for a museum whose exhibits include reconstructed workshops and the most powerful working steam engine in Europe. The museum is on Green Lane (entrance off Alma Street) about half a mile north of the city centre (go towards the River Don on Corporation Street).*

North-east of the city centre, occupying the former Templeborough Steel Works in Rotherham is MAGNA, the UK's first Science Adventure Centre. Providing an elemental 'hands on' experience in a 'Star Wars' setting, the centre cracks and sparks to the themes of earth, fire, air and water, and features an original arc furnace amazingly 'brought to life' to reveal all the drama of the steel making process. In one of its four 'adventure' pavilions, you come 'face to face with the people whose lives were shaped by steel' in the UK's biggest multi-storey, multi-media exhibition. MAGNA is just off junction 33/34 of the M1, one mile from the Meadowhall Shopping Centre. Map Landranger 111- Grid Refs: 353882 (Kelham Island Industrial Museum); 405915 (MAGNA).

110. DUNGWORTH: CHORISTERS WITH MUCKY BOOTS

The Royal Hotel is as an appropriate a venue for carol singing as a Bethlehem inn. Every Christmas time for the last 200 years, from 'the first Sunday after Armistice' until Boxing Day, the singers have gathered in its bar like sardines in the spawning season, straining to take a swig, and praising the Lord in a uniquely genuine and robust Yorkshire way. Here in the Royal, and in a cluster of half a dozen or so other similar pubs in Worrall, Ecclesfield, Oughtibridge and elsewhere in north-west Sheffield, the choirs belt out some unfamiliar verses for two rafter-raising hours each Sunday. Men with muddy boots and pints in their hands, some of who can't sing a blessed note, creating a raw and earthy cavalry charge of sound to the accompaniment of the organ. Unadorned, unabashed and untainted by the glitzy seasonal commerciality that has debased the rest of the festive season, this annual eisteddfod has the power of any Welsh assembly but with a grittier edge.

Some of the carols, sung by generations of farmers, steel workers, file makers, cutlers and the rest, were composed in the area, angelic hosts, mangers and other over sentimentalised references to Christmas giving way to more robust and locally relevant lyrics in carols with titles such as *Fern Bank, Malin Bridge, Tyre Mill, Mount Zion* and *Spout Cottage.*

Rare, spontaneous and un-orchestrated examples of continuity and community spirit enjoyed by Christians and non-Christians alike, the choral services draw hundreds of people, some from abroad, who make annual pilgrimages to Sheffield just for the purpose.

These carol festivals have less of the raw passions of pint-clutching football fans on FA Cup day – but only just. The advice is to get there early, to breathe out when you can and to wear something that tones with ale.

Directions: *Dungworth is about six miles north-west of Sheffield (A61 and A6101 to Malin Bridge) on the B6076. The Royal Hotel is in the centre of the village. Map Landranger 110 – Grid Ref: 851213.*

111. UPPER BRADFIELD: 'YOU'D MAKE A LOVELY CORPSE'

'Shake a bridle over a Yorkshireman's grave', goes the old adage, 'and he will arise and steal a horse.' The saying alludes, of course, to the Tykes' insistence on wasting nothing and utilising everything, the talent for squeezing blood out of a stone, even extending to dead bodies.

In the eighteenth century, the developing science of human anatomy made great strides, eminent doctors using a steady supply of cadavers in their studies and lectures. Donated corpses were increasingly harder to come by, so some unscrupulous surgeons consorted with criminals, who exhumed newly buried bodies and sold them on. The first recorded case of body snatching by gangs, euphemistically called resurrectionists or resurrection men, was in 1742, the spreading practice causing great alarm throughout Yorkshire.

The resurrectionists preferred to target isolated graveyards at night,

The watchtower at Upper Bradfield.

the burial ground in the lofty village of Upper Bradfield being ideal for the purpose. Alarmed at the prospect of loosing newly buried loved ones (had a body already been lost to the snatchers?) the parishioners of St Nicholas decided to build a watchtower, occupants taking it in turn to keep their spooky vigils at night. The light of a lamp for a week or so was all that was needed to deter the thieves, decomposition and putrefaction doing the rest. Anatomists would only accept fresh corpses.

The best-known anatomist of the period was Dr Robert Knox of Edinburgh University Medical School. This distinguished doctor who became the conservator at the Museum of the Royal College of Surgeons in 1824, used the infamous Burke and Hare to satisfy his demand for corpses. They, of course, identified suitable material for dissection before it had died!

The vile practice dwindled after the passing of the Anatomy Act of 1832.

Directions: *Upper Bradfield is about seven miles north-west of Sheffield (A61/A6101 and the B6077). Upper Bradfield and Lower Bradfield are twin villages in the Loxley Valley. Built in 1745, the watchtower, in St Nicholas's churchyard, looks purposeful with its embattled top and beady-eyed windows. Burke and his sidekick had all-appraising eyes and were catholic in their choice of specimens. Would you have fancied spending the night here alone? Map Landranger 110 – Grid Ref: 266926.*

112. WORTLEY: NEEDLE WOMAN

Born in 1690, Lady Mary Wortley Montagu was a woman before her time. An astounding beauty and a famous and prodigious letter writer, she alone is credited with the introduction into Europe of a boon to mankind, her careful observation, perspicacity and dogged determination in the face of ridicule and scientific censure, bringing the benefits of inoculation for smallpox to an initially sceptical public.

Married to Edward Wortley Montagu in 1712, she accompanied her husband on his ambassadorial posting to Constantinople where she witnessed the efficacy of inoculation at first hand. This preventive intervention against smallpox was widespread throughout Turkey, its success persauding Lady Mary to inoculate her own young son. Buoyed on by the child's continuing good health, she promoted a successful experiment on criminals in 1721, going on to inoculate a second child, a six year old daughter who eventually became the Countess of Bute.

Despite the obvious medical benefits conferred by inoculation, there were still many strong prejudices against the revolutionary treatment, and it was not until the children of the Royal Family and other aristocratic families were inoculated, that the practice was embraced by the general population.

Directions: *Wortley is two miles north-west of Stocksbridge (A61/A629 from Sheffield). Wortley Hall, whose drive is opposite the church, was the family home of Lady Mary Wortley Montagu. Sold in the 1950s, it is today used as a holiday home and conference centre.*

In Wortley Woods is a terrace of railway houses known as Chemistry Cottages because of their association with Lady Mary and her work on inoculation. From Wortley, go south-east towards Sheffield on the A629 for about a quarter of a mile and turn right down Finkle Street Lane, dropping down to the bottom. Three hundred yards before the railway bridge, go right on the Upper Don Trail public footpath and pass the farm, swinging left to a bridge over the redundant railway line. Cross the bridge, and swing right on a fieldside footpath for about 600 yards to the cottages. The cottages take their name from a building in the woods where Lady Mary carried out some of her pioneering work. Sadly neglected and almost unrecognisable save for a few surviving fragments of stone, The Chemistry was apparently sited over a spring line, well away from habitation to reduce the risk of contagion. To view the ruins, walk north-east from Chemistry Cottages for about 250 yards, dropping down on a riverside footpath upstream. The ruins are at the foot of the bluff.

St Leonard's Church in the centre of the village has many memorials to the Wortley Montagu family and their descendants. Map Landranger 110 – Grid Refs: 313995 (Wortley Hall); 297999 (The Chemistry, Wortley Woods): 307994 (St Leonard's Church).

113. THURLSTONE: READY RECKONER

Genius will find a way. Denied expression through one outlet, it will find another, the mental gifts and the determination of a Thurlstone child cruelly blinded by smallpox, showing the remarkable capabilities of the human mind.

The son of an excise officer, Nicholas Saunderson was born in 1682, a terrible infection at the age of two seemingly blighting his entire life. But he was a boy with a surfeit of Yorkshire grit. Determined to learn, he won a place at Penistone Free School, teaching himself to read by tracing his fingers over the carved words on tombstones in the nearby churchyard. At school, he was taught the rudiments of the Latin and Greek languages but it was his astounding facility for mathematical thought and problem solving that marked him out as an exceptional scholar. Saunderson progressed to an academy at Attercliffe, near Sheffield, going on to establish himself as a teacher in Cambridge University in 1707. A resident of Christ's College, he immediately embarked on a series of lectures on what were described as '*Universal Arithmetic, the Optics and the Principia of Newton.*' In 1711, he became Professor of Mathematics, the climax of his incredible career coming in 1728 when he was created Doctor of Laws.

Directions: *Contiguous with Penistone, the village of Thurlstone is about eight miles south-east of Barnsley on the A628. Saunderson lived in a house on Towngate (now demolished). An inscribed stone in the centre of the village (on a wall near the seating area at the main road end of Towngate) commemorates its most famous son. The building opposite was Saunderson's former school. Close your eyes in Penistone churchyard and read the inscriptions by touch. It's more difficult than it seems. Map Landranger 110 – Grid Refs: 234035 (inscribed stone); 246034 (Penistone churchyard).*

114. SILKSTONE: ANGELS WITH DIRTY FACES

On the 4th July 1838, an accident happened underground that stunned the nation. Caught terrified and screaming by a summer flood that poured into a drift of the Huskar Pit, thirty two children were drowned like rats, the roll call of death including the names of Catherine Garnett aged eight, Eli Hutchinson aged nine and George Burkinshaw aged 10 who died clinging to his younger brother, seven-year-old James.

Young children had worked routinely in local pits for generations, their meagre wages contributing vital pennies to family incomes. Employed as hurriers, both sexes were tasked with pushing up to seven-hundredweight tubs of coal from the coal-face to the pit shaft. Working alongside their older brothers and sisters, the very young children were designated trappers whose essential job was to ensure that the air doors were closed as the hurriers passed by. Underground up to 14 hours a day in total darkness, these minions often worked by touch. Candles were expensive.

During that intensely hot summer's afternoon, a thunderstorm erupted over Silkstone, heavy rain and hailstones persisting for over two hours. The downpour extinguished the fire in the steam engine used for raising coal and miners to the surface, 40 children who, by four o'clock had already spent nine hours underground, deciding to make their escape via a drift to Nabbs Wood. It was a fateful mistake. A bloated stream poured into the drift overwhelming nearly all the children, only six young mites managing to escape the flood by fleeing into a side roadway.

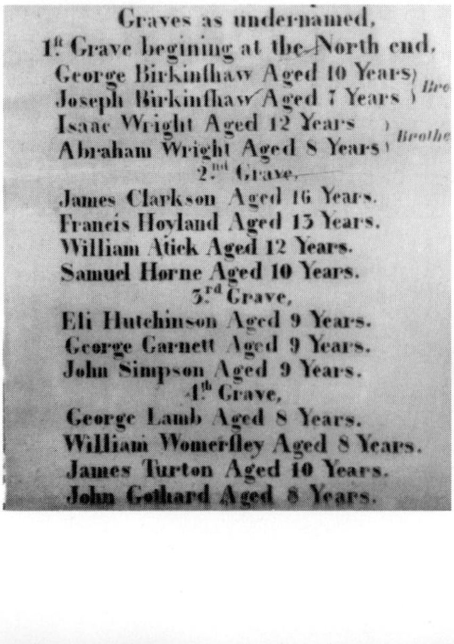

Graves as undernamed,
1st Grave begining at the North end.
George Birkinſhaw Aged 10 Years } Bro
Joseph Birkinſhaw Aged 7 Years }
Isaac Wright Aged 12 Years } Brothe
Abraham Wright Aged 8 Years }
2nd Grave,
James Clarkson Aged 16 Years.
Francis Hoyland Aged 13 Years.
William Atick Aged 12 Years.
Samuel Horne Aged 10 Years.
3rd Grave,
Eli Hutchinson Aged 9 Years.
George Garnett Aged 9 Years.
John Simpson Aged 9 Years.
4th Grave,
George Lamb Aged 8 Years.
William Womerſley Aged 8 Years.
James Turton Aged 10 Years.
John Gothard Aged 8 Years.

Memorial in Silkstone to the dead children (photo courtesy of Roy Hartley).

When the water had subsided, the mound of bodies was disentangled and the corpses were removed to Throstle Hall, two men washing the victims faces before each was delivered home by cart. Most of the children were from Silkstone but three apiece came from Dodworth and Thurgoland. The solemn procession was the most pitiful sight imaginable. 'Mothers were in a state of distraction,' reported one observer, 'and some tore the hair from their heads.'

An inquest was held in the Red Lion Inn in Silkstone on the 6th July, the surviving children giving evidence of the calamity. Joseph Huskar said: 'Eleven of us were together, and they all drown but me. If we had stopped at the pit bottom, we should have all been saved.' Uriah Jubb, another boy who managed to avoid death, testified: 'We heard the water coming and me and Elizabeth Taylor got into a slit in the day hole and we stopped till we could get out. The water met the others as they were coming up and drove them against the door, where they were drowned.'

The coroner recorded a verdict of accidental death but the story did not end there. Queen Victoria intervened and in 1838 pressed for an enquiry into the employment of young children in the mines of the Yorkshire coalfield. The unstoppable move to end the appalling exploitation of children had begun. In 1842, despite stout opposition from mine owners, Peel's government passed the Mines Act forbidding the employment of women and children underground in mines.

Directions: *Silkstone is three miles west of junction 37 of the M1. In 1988, two child sculptures, together with a memorial tablet, were erected at the entrance to the drift where the children drowned. The monument is in Nabs Wood (in the care of the Woodland Trust) at Silkstone Common. Silkstone Common is about one mile south of Silkstone. Take the A628 and fork left after 1/3 mile to the junction with the B 6449 in Silkstone Common. Go straight across the junction passing the 'Bonny Bunch of Roses' on the right and proceed down Moorend Lane for about a a quarter of a mile, passing under a railway bridge. The entrance to the wood is immediately on the right. About 100 yards left of the entrance is the monument. A second monument to the dead children stands in All Saints' churchyard in Silkstone. The Red Lion (an external notice board gives details of the tragedy) is on High Street, Silkstone. Map Landranger 110 – Grid Refs: 295039 (Nabs Wood sculptures); 292058 (All Saints' churchyard monument); 291055 (Red Lion).* ☛ ***See also 82 (Overton)***

115. WORSBROUGH: 'IN THE MIDST OF LIFE ...'

Dracula could have no more gruesome a sepulchre. So what prompted the god-fearing family of Sir Roger Rockley to erect a macabre monument to his name in St Mary's Church?

Roger Rockley's tomb at Worsbrough.

The two-tier tomb of Sir Roger who died in 1533 aged 35, shows two utterly contrasting figures, one of a resplendent knight gazing heavenwards, the other of a skeleton laying on a shroud. No pulpit oratory could ever compare with this lightning strike image of death.

The rare memorial is amongst a collection of only seven wooden military effigies in Yorkshire. Made of oak, the carvings are said to have been covered with fine linen prior to painting. The armorial shields of Sir Roger and his wife Isabel Mounteney are carved on the base of the tomb and although its inscription has long since disappeared, records show it once read: 'Here lies Roger Rockley, Knight, son of Thomas Rockley, Knight …'

Why then, was Worsbrough's wood carver given the most unusual commission of his entire life? Was Roger Rockley a cocky, dissolute roué who scoffed at life? Was this a powerful message to his friends to mend their ways? Or, in a post Dissolution age, when thousands of hungry and destitute people could no longer rely on the monasteries for succour, was it a visual interpretation of the oft-recited verse: 'In the midst of life we are in death?'

Directions: *Worsbrough Village (not to be confused with Worsbrough Bridge to the north-east) is three miles south of Doncaster on a minor road off the A61. St Mary's Church is in the village centre. Map Landranger 111 – Grid Ref: 350026.*

116. BIRDWELL: BURNING SENSATION

Before the widespread availability of coal, charcoal was the fuel of life. Burning at a high temperature with little smoke, it was used in vast quantities for domestic purposes and by the pioneers of industry, consuming, in the process, vast tracts of England's woodlands. Charcoal production necessitated controlled burning under straw or turf covered pyres, the restriction of oxygen in the combustion process carbonising the wood. This versatile fuel was burnt extensively in Yorkshire's original blast furnaces, the hearth at Rockley surviving, but only just, as the oldest such industrial facility in Europe.

Dating from 1652, it was built by Lionel Copley from Rotherham. At the height of production, it is estimated to have smelted some 400 tons of pig iron every year, the charcoal burners in the surrounding forests up to 15 miles distant, providing at least three carts loads of fuel per day. Some burn! For almost a hundred years, the furnace was hardly extinguished, a forest the size of Sherwood disappearing up its flue. But the trees are having the last laugh. Encroaching on the old masonry, they now encircle the furnace completely and given the penetration of a few stout seeds, its bosky end is nigh.

Directions: *Birdwell is on the A61 adjacent to junction 36 of the M1. Rockley Blast Furnace is on the opposite side of the motorway from the village, so go north through Birdwell and turn left in Worsbrough, passing the Country Park and going under the motorway. Turn left on Rockley Lane for about three quarters of a mile. The furnace is on the left down a signposted track (turn right at the gate). A little exploration will reveal the sites of the wheel pit and the bellows building. There are traces of several dams in the surrounding woodland. Map Landranger 110 – Grid Ref: 338022.*

117. BARNSLEY: WET FEAT

The entire town was agog with anticipation, people reading the handbills and shaking their heads in some disbelief. Bluff, unflappable and not easily fooled, Yorkshire folk are always sceptical of boastful claims and yet here was a fellow, and a sober German at that, who had spent good money on printing hundreds of flyers. That proved it. It must be genuine!

The unique performance was set for half past four in the afternoon on Monday 16th October 1837. The venue? Barnsley Canal. The entertainment? A man, walking on water.

According to the widely circulated handbill: 'Her Von de Hom Bughie begs to inform ladies and gentlemen that he intends displaying his wonderful and novel feat of walking upright on the surface of the water from Old Mill to the aqueduct and back with no other assistance than a pair of cork shoes. He earnestly invites every admirer of genuine science and agility to witness the above unparalleled exhibition, which has already excited the astonishment of assembled thousands in England and the Continent.'

Some distrustful people in the town scoffed at the idea of a man emulating the miraculous feat of Jesus, other pointing out that the miracles of modern science had delivered unto them a canal, an aqueduct, flushing lavatories and other watery wonders of engineering that would have left their grandfathers gasping in astonishment.

'It can be done tha knows,' said one enthusiastic disciple. 'And ant tha heard t'rumours? Bugger, or what ever is name is, has written a book with a philosophysing chap called Dontsapie. They've proved it's possible. I'd get there early if I was you. What's tha to lose? He's probably banking on a collection or summat. Take odd washer or two. That's what I alus does.'

From mid-day the whole of Barnsley began to shut down. Tools were put aside, shops were closed and barges were tied up, a mass exodus of excited people converging on the canal hours before the performance was due to begin. As the appointed hour approached, the crowd swelled, vast numbers of black-faced miners, who had just come off shift, pushing forward, spectators on the edge of the water struggling to prevent an early bath. The town clock struck half past four and a cheer went up. Someone had spotted Herr Von de Hom Bughie and the fun was about to begin!

Not a ripple stirred the water's surface. Everyone craned their necks in the direction of the Old Mill to see the first tentative steps of the magic man. But nobody came. There were shouts and cries of derision. By five o'clock, the light began to fade and the increasingly dubious and restless crowd began to disperse, only a few dozen eternally gullible fools lingering until dark.

The event, of course, had been an elaborate masquerade, a hoax, a wind-up that had fooled thousands. Herr Von de Hom Bughie was a fiction, some in the town suggesting Charles Rogers, a Manchester man who had been a Barnsley apprentice, as his creator.

With his sides splitting in mirth, did this wag watch the proceedings from some concealed window? What a double glazing salesman he would have made.

Directions: *Barnsley is one and three quarters of a mile east of junction 37 of the M1. The Barnsley burghers were anxious to expunge the most embarrassing chapter in their history from the official records, in a fit of denial, even the line of the canal being wiped clean. There is no annual re-enactment of the deception, only copies of the famous handbill, in a local museum and in private collections, remembering the town's 'clownest' hour. Map Landranger 111 – Grid Ref: 000000 (still classified).*

118. CONISBROUGH: THE CASTLE OF IVANHOE

'Their grey locks and long full beards, together with their antique tunics and loose black mantles, suited well with the singular and rude apartment in which they were seated, and gave the appearance of a band of ancient worshippers of Woden, recalled to life to mourn over the decay of their national glory.'

In this passage from the novel *Ivanhoe*, Sir Walter Scott describes a solemn convocation, King Richard and the knight Ivanhoe joining with a group of Saxon elders to prematurely mourn the death of Athelstane, who, a few pages on, '... arrayed in the garments of the grave, stood before them, pale, haggard and like something arisen from the dead!.'

The scene is set in the third floor apartment of the 'great tower of Coningsburgh Castle.' Built in the twelfth century, this central keep survives, its geometrical simplicity, ashlar facing and six mighty buttresses soaring to a height of nearly 100 feet, still presenting a vision of impregnability unsurpassed in England.

In gathering material for his book, Sir Walter Scott came to the district in 1865. He visited Conisbrough Castle and wrote part of his novel in a house in nearby Lower Sprotbrough. Built in 1653, that house is now the Boat Inn.

Directions: *Conisbrough is four miles south-west of Doncaster on the A630 (junction 36 of the A1(M)). Conisbrough Castle is on the east of the town. After years of neglect, the keep was restored in 1994 and opened to the public. Map Landranger 111 – Grid Refs: 515989 (Conisbrough Castle); 537015 (Boat Inn).*

119. BRODSWORTH: WARTS AND HALL

This time-capsule of Victorian life is unlike any other mansion in the county. An Italianate-style home originally erected in 1863, it was purchased by English Heritage in 1990 and rescued from years of decay. But it was a rescue with a difference, a policy of 'arresting decline' preserving generations of family living, warts and all.

The hall was bought by Charles Thelusson in 1863, his family continuing to live in the fast deteriorating pile until 1988, when incessant rain penetration and structural damage forced them to sell. English Heritage set about the gargantuan task of repairing the roof in 1992, some limited remedial cleaning and repair of carpets, curtains and other furnishings taking place at the same time. The hall opened to the public in 1995, the new owners describing their charge as: 'A sleeping beauty of a Victorian country house which has awoken after many years to find herself a well-preserved elderly lady.'

The contents of the hall – some a little dog-eared and timeworn – have survived almost completely intact since the 1860s. So personal and intimate are its treasures, that some visitors feel a little intrusive, gingerly poking their heads round doorways, half expecting to meet old Thelusson with his shotgun!

Directions: *Brodsworth Hall is on the B6422, six miles north-west of Doncaster. Map Landranger 111 – Grid Ref: 507071.*

120. CAMPSALL: ROBIN SAYS 'I DO.'

If the legend of Robin Hood fails to stir your passions, you've water in your veins. Despite all the Nottinghamshire bluster, the hero was indubitably a Tyke, numerous allusions to his exploits throughout the county confirming his Yorkshire blood. One of his main stomping grounds was Barnsdale Forest near modern Wentbridge, the steep and thickly wooded valley of the River Went proving ideal for the outlaws' trade. But Robin had other interests, one old ballad suggesting that 'next to the ladies, he loved the yeomanry of England …' His real love, of course, was the lady Marion, the couple plighting their troth, or so the story goes, in the early Norman village church of St Mary Magdalene at Campsall, just east of Barsdale Bar.

Directions: *On a minor road, the village of Campsall is two miles east of the A1 at Barnsdale Bar. The church is in the village centre. Not far from Campsall, in a lay-by off the southbound carriageway of the A1 just over a mile from Barnsdale Bar, is Robin Hood's Well. Originally erected over a well that was a popular refreshment stop for travellers on the ancient route between York and London, the stone structure was moved to its present position after road widening. The Robin Hood Inn once stood close by. Its prized possession was a three-pint capacity leather bottle reputed to have belonged to the outlaw himself. Map Landranger 111 – Grid Refs: 141545 (Campsall Church) and 519119 (Robin Hood's Well).*

York

121 to 125

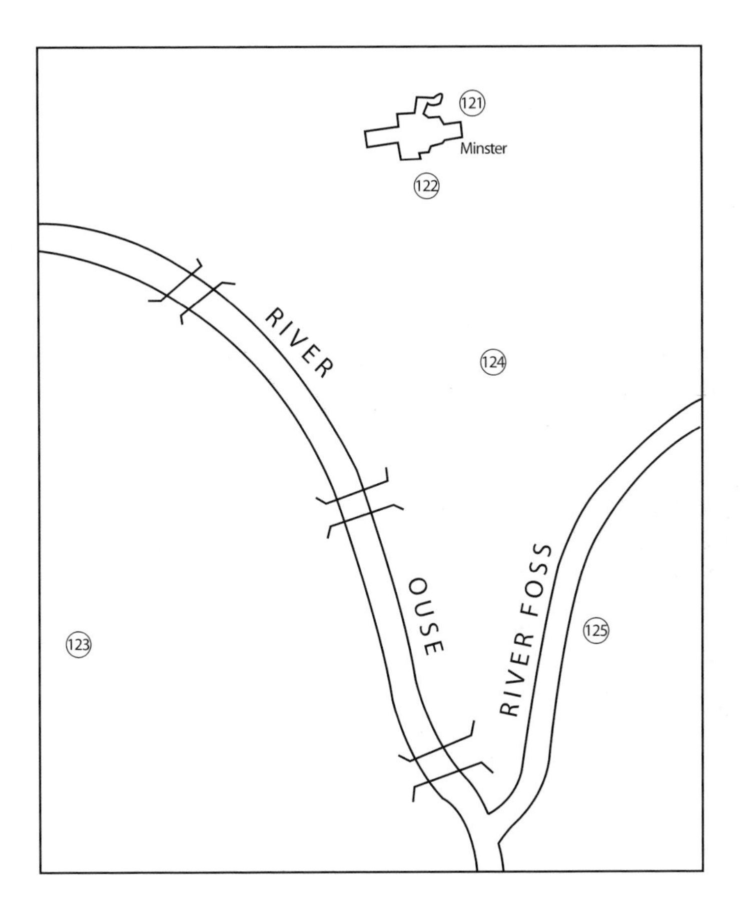

So good, they named it thrice – Eboracum, Yorkvic and York. In its encircling walls, this regional capital has seen more history than some countries, its impressive archaeological and architectural legacy drawing visitors from all over the world. At the cusp of national events, York has hosted emperors, kings and queens, many without their heads, together with archbishops, novelists and artists by the score, almost every house in the old medieval web of snickleways and alleys having its own full blooded past. So beware! Mind the splashes and wear a rubber smock for the next few pages.

EBORACUM HERALD – 26th JUNE 306

CONSTANTINE TO BE PROCLAIMED EMPEROR TODAY

The Porta Praetoria was thronged yesterday for the cremation of Constantius Clorus. After the ceremony, a symbolic eagle was released into the sky, the multitude following its flight with shouts and prayers supposing therewith that the emperor was mounted into heaven. His son and heir Constantine is to be sworn in as ruler of the Western Empire today.

YORK MESSENGER – 17th MARCH 1190

MOUND OF DEATH HAUNTS CITY

In a dreadful orgy of slaughter, 150 Jews are thought to have committed suicide last night in Clifford's Tower. The pall of death over the city today is palpable, fires in the Minster only adding to the gloom and desolation. As the dreadful task of identification and burial gathers place, volunteers are asked to help dig pits.

---

121. YORK: 'WHERE'S THE FIRE? IN DEANGATE! THE MINSTER'S BLAZING!'

The Fire Brigade responded to the initial 999 call on the 9th July 1984 with typical efficiency but by the time their appliances were in place just after 2.30 am, molten lead was already pouring from one of the most famous roofs in the world. The spectacular prelude to the lightning strike on York Minster was a fiery display of corona – a low – powered electrical discharge – followed by two devastating bolts of lightning, one of which melted the lightning conductor.

The Minster's south transept was soon wreathed in flames and it took fire fighters three hours, using turntable ladders and dozens of high-powered hoses, to bring the blaze under control. As dawn broke the true extent of the damage could be seen. Dating from the 1770s, the south transept roof lay in a tangle of charred timbers and the priceless Rose Window was in a myriad scattered pieces.

The south transept of the Minster after the fire. A scene surveyed by Dr Robert Runcie.

The work of reconstruction took four years to complete. The roof was restored using traditional English oak, much of it donated from private estates. The massive timbers, some weighing half a ton or more, were deliberately oversized to allow for – God forbid! – up to one hour's exposure to full flame without collapsing. Sixty-eight bosses inspired by the theme of the *Benedcite,* a canticle celebrating the earth's physical wonders, were carved to adorn the rib intersections and work on one of the biggest jigsaw puzzles ever attempted saw the salvation and reinstallation of the Rose Window.

Directions: *In Deangate, York, the Minster is open to visitors every day. The south transept is to the right of the crossing tower. A large flat table mirror allows inspection of the roof without neck strain. A scale, cut –away model shows the constructional techniques employed. York Minster has suffered from the scourge of fire before. One of the most notable incidents last century was an arson attack in 1829 by madman Jonathan Martin who deliberately set fire to the choir. The extensively damaged choir stalls, archbishop's throne and pulpit were replaced in 1832 to designs by Smirke. Map Landranger 105 – Grid Ref: 603522.* ☛ ***See also 146 (Goodmanham)***

122. YORK: 'HAIL CAESAR!'

Of immense strategic and cultural importance, York became the capital of the Roman province of *Britannia Inferior* and the largest town in the north. Named *Eboracum,* it was used by Emperor Septimius Severus as a base for

The Emperor Constantine at York.

his campaigns in Scotland, the town achieving *colonia* status – the highest legal entity a Roman settlement could attain. Centred around its legionary fortress, the town became a cosmopolitan centre for trade, luxury goods such as pottery, jewellery, figs, dates, wine and even edible dormice coming from all over the empire. In the rearguard of conquest, the Romans planted the rootstocks of civilisation all across Europe, their literature and art, architecture and industry bringing order, sophistication and pleasure to an astonished world.

With its imposing fortress, barracks, granaries, wharfs, temples, baths, and properly engineered roads and pavements, imperial York must have been a sight to behold, the lavishly dressed tribunes and legionnaires strutting round their creation like peacocks.

Far from being a forgotten outpost of the empire, York was at the hub of the drive for expansion in the west, the presence of crack troops – initially the IX *Hispana* Legion followed by the VI *Victrix* – ensuring rapid development and the establishment of a flourishing civilian population on both banks of the Ouse. Underlying its importance was the presence of Romans of the highest rank, York witnessing the deaths of two emperors and the crowning of another.

Worn out by three years of defending Hadrian's Wall against guerrilla attack, Septimius Severus died in York in 211. In the year 306, Constantius I also perished in the town, the garrison immediately proclaiming his son Constantine as ruler of the Western Empire, the shouts of 'Hail Caesar' echoing down the centuries.

Directions: *Reclining on a plinth outside York Minister, near the legionary fortresses main access road – the Via Principalis – is a wonderfully evocative statue of Constantine who eventually became emperor. Opposite is a surviving Roman column. Under the Minster itself can be seen the foundations of the garrison's headquarters building. To get some idea of the size of the 50-acre fortress, take a five minute walk from the Minster down Duncombe Place and turn right just past the Library through the Museum Gardens, following the path right to the Multangular Tower. This 10-sided bastion marked the western corner of the fortress and is one of the most impressive structures in the whole of Britain. At 17 feet high, it is capped by a further 11 feet of thirteenth-century masonry. The* caldarium *or hot-bath, another compelling fragment of the old town, can be found in the aptly named Roman Baths Inn facing St Sampson's Square, off Davygate and Parliament Street. But unlike other facets of Roman life, personal hygiene was not something that our wode-smeared ancestors took to readily. Map Landranger 105 – Grid Ref: 603522 (Statue of Constantine).*

123. YORK: DRIPPING HEADS

At two and three-quarters of a mile long, the walls of York are the most extensive and best preserved in England. Protected by watchtowers, bartizans and arrow-slits, the defences are breached by a series of gates or bars, the ancient portals known as Bootham Bar, Monk Bar and Micklegate Bar controlling access into the city. Both practical and symbolic, these medieval 'Checkpoint Charlies' were stoutly built and lavishly decorated to reflect the strategic and political importance of York, the barbican and the portcullis proclaiming the power of York alongside the gorgeous imagery of the shield and the statue. But these bars had another, more sinister purpose. Their battlements were used as bloody flagstaffs, the spiked heads of traitors and transgressors winking out their warnings for years on end. Guarding the principal route into the city from London and the south, lofty Micklegate was the most decorated bar of all.

Had you visited Micklegate in July 1403, you would have been confronted by

Micklegate Bar. York: Dripping Heads.

the most famous of its trophies, the dripping head of Hotspur, Sir Henry Percy, staring down after his defeat at the Battle of Shrewsbury. Killed during the melee after an arrow pierced his visor and lodged in his brain, Hotspur was hauled off to York for dismemberment, dozens of other so-called traitors facing a similar fate in the years ahead. After the Battle of Wakefield Green at the end of December 1460, the head of Richard Duke of York was cruelly displayed on Micklegate Bar. Wearing a paper crown, its pallid face was turned towards the city with the taunt 'So York may overlook the town of York.'

Just three months later, the Yorkists were triumphant at the Battle of Towton. They repaid the barbarism of their enemies in equal measure, the Duke of York's head making room for that of the Earl of Devon.

The grisly practice of impaling body parts persisted until 1746 when the remains of two Jacobite rebels were hauled up after the Battle of Culloden. In 1754, after eight years of decay and predation by birds, the eye-less scraps were stolen by a Jacobite sympathiser, much to the consternation of the Government.

Directions: *Built of magnesian limestone, the splendidly decorated and preserved Micklegate Bar dates from the twelfth century with many later alterations and additions. It should be viewed as part of a perambulation of the city walls, the tour to include a visit (entrance fee) to Monk Bar which is preserved as a museum. Map Landranger 105 – Grid Ref: 597514.* ☛ ***See also 33 (Towton)***

124. YORK: BUTCHER'S WIFE EXECUTED BY CRUSHING

In God's league of sinfulness, the crime of religious persecution must rank high, the horrors that were perpetrated in his name leaving an indelible blot on England's Christian past. The 1679 martyrdom in York of the 82-year-old Catholic priest Nicholas Postgate was heinous enough, but for sheer evil, nothing can surpass the pitiless execution of seemingly ordinary housewife Margaret Clitherow nearly a century earlier.

In 1571, the fifteen-year-old Margaret married prosperous butcher John Clitherow who had extensive pasturage near York. The couple moved into the Shambles, a street dominated by the butchering trade. The ground floor of the house was a shop decked out with racks, hooks and slabs for the display of fresh meat. Margaret was keenly involved in the business, especially during her husband's long absences from home. Although profitable, the butchering business was, in Yorkshire parlance, a mucky one. Ankle deep in droppings, sheep on the way to slaughter would clog the narrow Shambles, and in a street rarely blessed by sunlight Margaret would have picked her way through sticky piles of excrement, sawdust and blood.

Margaret was gradually attracted to Catholicism and clandestinely practised her faith, eventually constructing a secret room for the celebration

The Shambles, a pre-tourist photograph.

of mass. It was described in a report of 1619 thus: '... she ever kept her priest within a chamber of her neighbour's house (which she had hired for the purpose) and had made not only a passage from her own house unto that chamber, but means for the priest to escape ...'

The maturing Margaret become bolder in her convictions and her allegiance to the old faith came to the attention of the authorities. For the next 12 years she defied the constant inquiries and interrogations of the establishment and the exhortations and protestations of her friends and relatives. She suffered three long periods of imprisonment in York Castle and was finally condemned to death. At eight o'clock on the cold spring morning of 25th March 1586, Margaret was led barefoot and bare-legged to the Tollbooth. Here she was stripped, wrapped in a white shroud and lain down on the ground with a handkerchief covering her face. A specially recruited party of beggars then placed a heavy door on top of her. An old chronicle records: 'She was in dying one quarter of an hour. A sharp stone, as much as a man's fist, was put under her back; upon her was laid to the quantity of seven or eight hundredweight at the least, which, breaking her ribs, caused them to burst forth of the skin. This was at nine of the clock, and she continued in the press until three at afternoon.'

Directions: *The Shambles house (No 35) of Saint Margaret Clitherow, who was canonized in 1970, is now a shrine to her memory and can be visited for daily contemplation and prayer. The house was described by Nicholas Pevsner as '...an object lesson in how not to restore.' Inside the house is a fragment of lace used to wrap up the martyr's severed hand. This relic is preserved in the Bar Convent at the junction of Blossom Street and Nunnery Lane. Margaret Clitherow was incarcerated in a prison that faced Fishergate. The Tollbooth place of execution was near to Skeldergate Bridge. Map Landranger 105 – Grid Ref: 604518.*

125. YORK: MASS SLAUGHTER OF JEWS

In twelfth century England, the Jews were a hated and a persecuted race and it was commonly believed that they were guilty of sorcery. They were the principal bankers of Christendom and frequently charged extortionate interest rates on loans. At the time of the Third Crusade, this particularly incensed the holy recruits who were about to risk their lives for Christ. Mob violence in York, incited by Richard Malebisse, led to murders and attacks on Jewish property and on the night of 16th March 1190 the harassed Jewish community took refuge in Clifford's Tower. After heated negotiations, the governor of the city ordered an attack on the building. Rather than capitulate, the desperate Jewish leaders killed their wives and children, torched the citadel and finally committed suicide. The total death toll, which included traitors to the Jewish faith who escaped from the tower and pleaded unsuccessfully for their lives with the besiegers, was in excess of 150 souls. After the slaughter, Jewish financial records were fired by the mob in the Minster nave.

Directions: *Built between 1250 and 1275 to replace the previous fortification of wood, Clifford's Tower in Tower Street, York is of a quatrefoil plan unique in England. An imposing and a mightily protected building on a steeply battered mound, it had a portcullis and still extant corbelled turrets and arrow-slits. It is open to the public (entrance fee) and is accessed via 55 steps. A plaque records the tragic events of 1190. Other bloodshed has also stained this place. Robert Aske – the leader of the doomed Pilgrimage of Grace – a rising against the Dissolution of the Monasteries in 1536 – was executed here and hung in chains from the battlements. Map Landranger 105 – Grid Ref: 605513.* ☛ ***See also 150 (Aughton)***

East Yorkshire

126 to 165

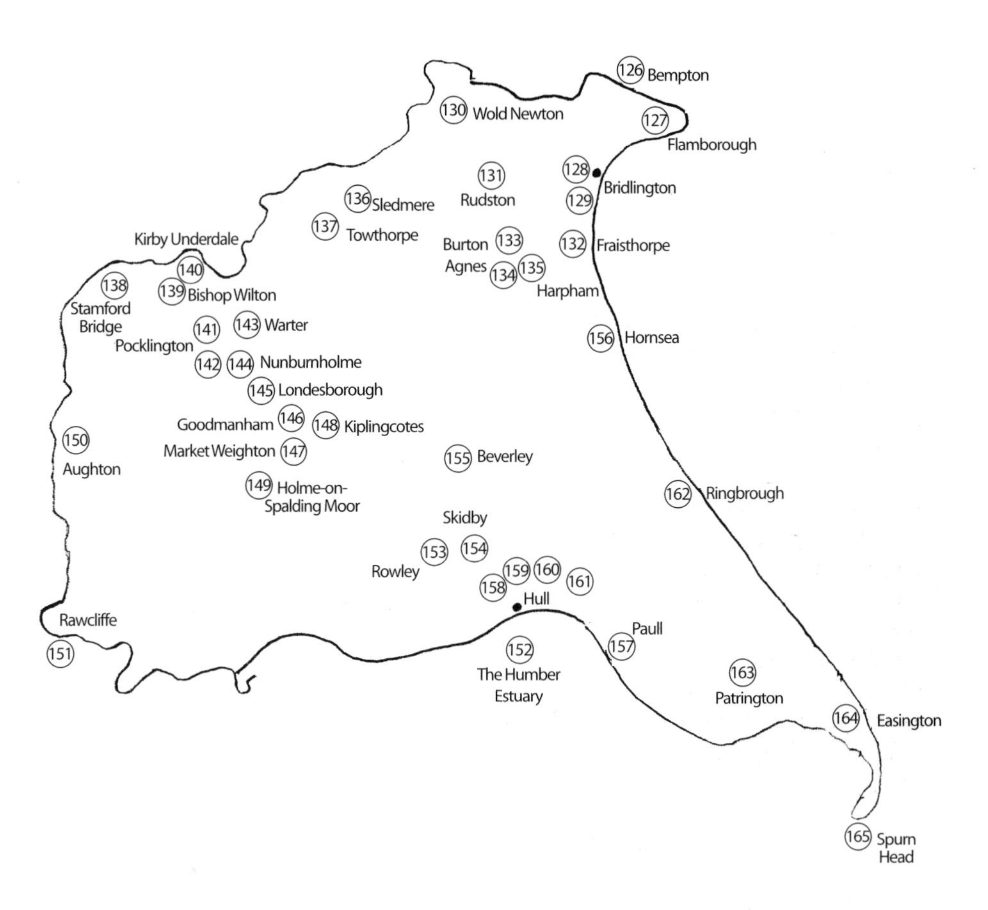

As distinct from the rest of the county as Flamborough Head is to cheese, rolling East Yorkshire with its characteristic chalky wolds and dry valleys, is a beautiful and unspoilt region largely devoid of the industrialisation associated with its western neighbours. A rural area for thousands of years, it has largely been tumult free, agriculture, fishing and shipping being its main occupations. Out on a geographical limb that stretches its shifty finger into the Humber at Spurn Point, Holderness is the remotest part of the county, this underpopulated Yorkshire outback developing a keen sense of identity shared by the rest of East Yorkshire. Characters: great clod-hopping, obstinate, tenacious, eccentric, boundlessly energetic and immensely friendly chaps – are what smack you on the back in this county. Turn over and meet a man who kept his bread in a coffin, a colossus who grew up to be the tallest Englishman that ever lived and a rich country gent who would regularly break up road stone for a hobby.

DERVENTIO MERCURY – 6th AUGUST 193

GARRISON COMMANDER TO UNVEIL TRIBUTE TO MERCURY

Sponsored by this publication, a tribute to Mercury has been carved for permanent display on the summit of the *Derventio* to *Petuaria* road. The carving, which acknowledges continuing peace in the area, will be unveiled next week by Commander Gaius Trebonious. One thousand doves will be released to mark the occasion.

WOLDS WEEKLY – 14th DECEMBER 1795

'PLANET JUST MISSED MY HEAD' SAYS PLOUGHMAN

The unearthly object was still smouldering as our correspondent responded to the frantic cries of ploughman John Shipley, yesterday's dramatic bombardment of earth signalling a premature call to arms. 'It almost parted my hair,' said John pointing to the deep crater left by the object. 'I know what it is now, but all the time I thought it must be a bomb or some such thing, so I lit the beacon fire. You can't be too careful with all these Frenchies hanging about'.

126. BEMPTON: DANGLED EGGS

Eggs are laid at Bempton as thick as pebbles on a beach, in season, vast roosts of guillemots, razorbills, puffins, kittiwakes and gannets occupying its cliffs in a cacophony of sound. Perched precariously on every ledge and shelf, the myriads of eggs were invulnerable to even the most ingenious of predators. But then along came a more determined foe, the death-defying men known as climmers employing their ropes in a prodigious harvest.

For centuries, egg collecting was an important feature of the local economy. Eggs were sold to collectors and to the manufacturers of patent leather and they were also gathered as a supplement to the local diet. The season lasted from May to September, the climmers operating in small gangs between Bempton and Speeton.

Harvesting up to 400 eggs each day – some ledges were completely cleared of eggs but in the interests of conservation some were allowed to remain fallow – teams consisted of just two men, one paying out the rope and another gathering the eggs. The rope passed over a pulley driven into the cliff with a spike, the egg collector using a second rope anchored into the cliff top with an iron crowbar to guide his movements. Pecked at and reeling from the nauseous smell of guano and rotten fish, the climmer dangled hundreds of feet above the waves in the hot sun, twin collecting bags slung either side of his waist restricting his movement, only delicate manoeuvring of his feet ensuring a crack free haul.

Climming was not without its humour, one confused Japanese tourist plunging over the cliffs with a dagger. Assuming that the intention was to kill the birds, he lashed out in a stabbing frenzy, becoming hopelessly ensnared in the ropes.

When food was scarce during World War II, climming underwent a minor rival, only becoming illegal in 1954. Today, the cliffs are part of an RSPB Nature Reserve that forms part of England's largest seabird colony.

Directions: *Bempton Cliffs are at the end of Cliff Lane in Bempton (take the B1229 for two and a half miles north-west from Bridlington and turn right at the White Horse pub). Parking fee payable. If you look carefully on the clifftops, you will discover a number of rusting iron crowbars. Map Landranger 101 – Grid Ref: 198741 (RSPB car park).*

127. FLAMBOROUGH – NORTH LANDING: COBBLES AND GANSEYS

Plainly named to keep the secret, this ruggedly picturesque cove has no better description than that in the pages of R. D. Blackmore's romantic novel *Mary Anerley:*

> *Half a league to the north of bold Flamborough Head the billows have carved for themselves a little cove among the cliffs, which are ragged but not very high. The opening is something like the grain shoot of a mill, or a screen for riddling gravel, so steep is the pitch of the ground, and so narrow the shingly ledge at the bottom. And in truly bad weather and at high tide there is no shingle at all, but the crest of the wave volleys up the incline, and the surf rushes on to the top of it. For the cove, though sheltered from other quarters, receives the full brunt of north-easterly gales and offers no safe anchorage. But the hardy fishermen make the most of its scant convenience, and gratefully call it the 'North Landing'. Albeit both wind and tide must be in good humour, or the only thing sure of any landing is the sea.*

These fishermen, these invaders who made the Yorkshire cliffs their own, would annually launch a symbolic silver-tipped arrow into the sea as a token of fealty to the King of Denmark. Masters of the sea, they came to England in their longships. Adapting the design of their vessels to suit local conditions, they created the Yorkshire cobble, a highly seaworthy craft whose basic lines have remained largely unchanged in centuries.

As ancient a sea-going craft as to be found anywhere in Britain, the streamlined, clinker-built coble has a high prow, curving sides and a steeply raked stern, the absence of a keel making it suitable for beaching in coves like North Landing. Cobbles were always landed stern first and dragged ashore out of reach of the surf, horses, and in more recent times tractors, helping with the work. The cobbles at North Landing had individual names such as *May Morn* and *Two Brothers*, each boat having a distinguishing painted livery of browns and reds.

Long-lining for species such as cod, haddock, ling and skate was the preferred method of fishing, the fishermen, in up to 80 boats operating from North and South Landings, baiting thousands of hooks off Flamborough Head and other favourite deeps. The catch was loaded into pannier baskets, donkeys struggling up the inclines to the gaggles of fishwives who waited on the tops with their filleting knives. Crabbing and salmon netting were pursued at other times of the year.

Despite the inherent stability and ruggedness of the cobbles, fishing was a precarious occupation. Contrary tides and currents, and frequent squalls brought fatalities, six brave fishermen perishing in one great gale on 5th February 1909.

With a suddenness that defied belief, a tempest roared in from the sea, howling winds and churning water causing the little fleet to dig deep for North Landing. In racing for the beach, *The Gleaner*, manned by John Cross and his two sons, took a broadside. Driven onto the West Scar, she capsized and the three men were thrown into the water, the crew of the *Two Brothers* changing course and attempting a frantic rescue. All three men were plucked from the waves, huge seas swamping the second boat and all in her. On shore, just forty yards to the east, a crowd watched helplessly as all six men drowned.

There is a chilling postscript to all too frequent incidents like these. Coble men traditionally wore specially knitted, thick, blue-woollen jerseys, colloquially known as ganseys, each fleet having it own highly individual patterns and designs. As effective as dog-tags, these garments were sometimes the only means of identifying their wearers after long immersions in the sea.

Changing methods of fishing and the decimation of fish stocks have led to a dramatic decline in the numbers of cobbles that operate along the 'Coble Coast' between the Humber and the Tweed. North Landing manages to retain a few ageing craft, local fishermen organising fishing and sight seeing excursions for visitors during the summer months.

Directions: *Flamborough North Landing is around five miles north-east of Bridlington (A165/A166) on the B1255. Cobbles can be seen in their natural setting operating from the beach. A red granite memorial to the six men who lost their lives in the gale of 1909 is in Flamborough village. Map Landranger 101 – Grid Ref: 238722 (North Landing).*

128. BRIDLINGTON: THEY ALL WENT DOWN TOGETHER.

In one foul day in 1871, the German Ocean claimed a harvest of ships that has gone down as one of the worst maritime disasters in Yorkshire history. As barometers dropped like stones on the 10th February, scores of vessels sought refuge in the normally safe haven of Bridlington Bay. But even here, the storm played havoc, winds screaming amongst the yards of ships engulfed in mountainous seas, especially above the treacherous Smethwick Sands. Plucked from the waves, scores of men were rescued that day but the loss of life was huge, more than seventy sailors loosing their lives in just a few hours. Including the Bridlington lifeboat, over thirty ships were smashed to matchwood, successive tides delivering gruesome slicks of pulverised wood and bodies.

Directions: *Bridlington is on the Yorkshire Coast just south of Flamborough Head. The principal access route is the A166. Inland, a mile from the bay, is Bridlington's ancient Priory Church (in the Old Town off High Street). In the north-east corner of its churchyard is the Seamen's Memorial to the men who perished in the Great Gale. Every year until the centenary of the tragedy in 1971, an annual service of commemoration for the dead was held in the priory. In subsequent years, memorial wreaths have been laid on the monument. Map Landranger 101 – Grid Ref: 177680.*

129. BRIDLINGTON: IS ANYBODY IN THERE?

The endurance of pain and self-immolation is intrinsically associated with many cultures and religions. Through suffering, it is taught, comes redemption and a guarantee of eternal happiness, myriads of people over time making the ultimate sacrifice. Christianity has its fair pantheon of martyrs and saints who have died for their religion, the manner of their dying provoking outrage and compassion. There has, however, been one method of meeting the Creator that has aroused only incredulity, death through self-imprisonment in an oubliette amazing even the most zealous of souls.

Oubliettes are best described as cupboard like receptacles in building walls, the French term originally referring to secret dungeons like those in the Bastille. These were accessed through trapdoors, often having pits below where the worse categories of prisoners were kept for months on end.

The early Christian church used incarceration in oubliettes as a cruel pronouncement of death for those convicted of the vilest crimes, but some believers volunteered for this ultimate ordeal. With only a ceremonial jug of

An oubilette at Bridlington Priory.

water and a loaf of bread for sustenance, the victim was walled in during a solemn service of commitment, hundreds of followers chanting and praying for his soul.

Surviving oubliettes are quite rare and not easily recognised but there is a good example set into the north exterior wall of Bridlington's Priory Church. It is not known whether these particular stones hide a macabre secret, but skeletons have been found from time to time in other similar recesses.

Directions: *Bridlington is on the Yorkshire Coast, just south of Flamborough Head. The Priory Church is in the Old Town off High Street. The oubliette is a feature of the north exterior wall. Map Landranger 101 – Grid Ref: 177680.*

130. WOLD NEWTON LIKE NOTHING ON EARTH

Had you been stood 'on this very spot' at 3.30 pm on 13th December 1795, you might have had a close encounter of the blurred kind, a 56lb visitor from outer space changing our views on extraterrestrial rocks forever.

Ploughman John Shipley was busy at his traces, when the meteorite missed his head by just a few yards, mud and soil from the impact leaving him dishevelled and shaking. Smashing through six inches of solid chalk, the object left a crater 19 inches in depth. Alarmed and intensely aware 'that something very singular had happened', Shipley dug up the still smouldering 30 inches by 28 inches rock with the help of two fellow workers and presented it to local magistrate Major Edward Topham. Exhibited in London, the meteorite provoked intense debate. One scientist suggested it had been spewed from some Icelandic volcano, another expert claiming it was an aggregation of stony material from thunderclouds. After seven years discussion and analysis, it was finally concluded that this indeed was an alien substance whose mineral and chemical make – up was like nothing on earth. The science of meteorography was born. In 1999 a leading expert on the planetary sciences said: 'It played a key role in the process by which meteorites were accepted as stones from the sky and indeed as extraterrestrial objects.'

Directions: *Wold Newton is seven miles south-west of Filey. The best access is off the A64 at Saxton Hill. Go south on the B1249 for four miles and turn left on a minor* *road to Wold Newton. The site of the impact, on agricultural land a few hundred yards to the south-west of Wolds Cottage farmhouse, was planted with a commemorative obelisk by Major Topham in 1799. The monument has since been repaired and although it is on private land, the landowner usually gives permission to view. Map Landranger 101– Grid Ref: 038721.*

131. RUDSTON: THE MONOLITH

Tumuli, henges, earthworks and the sites of abandoned villages etched into the landscape for millennia. Whispers from the past, they surround Rudston and its age-old umbilicus – the largest standing stone in Britain.

The famous Rudston Monolith measures 25 feet four inches high by six feet wide. A massive finger of black carboniferous sandstone, it is estimated to weigh 26 tons, geology tracing its origins to an outcrop of similar material in nearby Cayton, some 10 miles to the north. Some old manuscripts suggest that the stone may have been dragged over Saxton Brow on a specially-constructed road. A glance at the map, however, shows that this would have involved a circuitous line of advance. So surely our ancestors would have chosen an easier route? If their technologies embraced the manufacture of ropes, rollers and the conjectured A frames necessary to haul the stone into its final position, could they have employed a barge, bringing their precious rock part of the way be sea? A landfall at Speeton Sands would have reduced the dragging distance by half!

At the intersection of four Neolithic ditches that enter the village from all four compass points, the monolith was the focus of religious ceremonies centuries before the advent of Christianity. Following Pope Gregory I's advice that Christian churches should be built on pagan sites, the monolith was incorporated into the grounds of Rudston's All Saints' Church.

Directions: *Rudston – it is reckoned to be the oldest inhabited village in England – is on the B1253, five miles west of Bridlington. Rudston Monolith is in the churchyard. Map Landranger 101 – Grid Ref: 098678.*

The Rudston Monolith.

132. FRAISTHORPE SANDS: BEACH BUMS

I spied it through my telescope, its extension tube retracting in horror and leaving me with the sorest black-eye. I refocused the other orbit, and, there it was, wallowing naked in the surf; a veritable elephant seal in a bright pink cap, the waves creaming around milk-sacks that bobbed around like buoys. My boots came to a dead stop, burrowing in the sand. I looked along the strand at the other nudists and realised that I was as out of place as a G.I. on Omaha. Hit the beach? I pounded it, retreating faster than a rat up a pipe.

Other casual walkers had similar experiences on discovering Yorkshire's only naturist beach. Drenched by perennial rain rather than the sunshine beloved of *Health and Efficiency* magazine and occupied by a class of mermaids that would have the producers of 'Baywatch' turning to documentaries, bracing Fraisthorpe was once an outpost of pimpledom. But what attracted the stripping classes to this nondescript sandpit by the sea? There are no hiding bluffs or discretely growing palms in this vicinity and there is certainly no need for Piz Buin here. So what was the attraction? Perhaps it was the girding presence of land mines and incendiaries left over from the war that offered just a little privacy. Whatever, the pull, the nudists pulled up their drawers and left, public disquiet (in this day and age!) filling the beaches in Cannes.

Directions: *Fraisthorpe is one mile from the Yorkshire Coast on the A165, three miles south of Bridlington. Fraisthorpe Sands are due east of the village. Take the Auburn Farm road to the picnic spot. The depression in the sand (100 yards south of the picnic spot) was not made by the detonation of the mines and incendiaries that were decommissioned some years ago. It was excavated by that milch-cow who made me blind in one eye. Prominent among the lines of anti-tank blocks is a massive, tilted pill –box. On its landward face, you can just make out the words: 'NATURIST BEACH 1[?] MILES – THE AREA IS CLEARLY DESIGNATED …' The rest of the notice has been obliterated. Map Landranger 101 – Grid Ref: 171628.*

133. BURTON AGNES: NINE MEN APIECE IN GAME OF WITS

Forget the red cards. There are *meant* to be nine men each side in this game. Nine men but no ball, in a contest that pre-dates the national game by centuries.

A mental set-to between two opponents, Nine Men's Morris, or Merrills, is an internationally popular board-type game that has been known in England since at least the Norman Conquest, its simplicity, portability and inherent fascination accounting for its continued popularity.

The game can be played on a purpose made board but any convenient surface can be used. Three concentric squares are drawn onto the surface and three sets of three, equally-spaced holes are drilled on each of the opposing parallels to take the nine black and the nine white pegs.

Improvisation and opportunity have created a wonderful array of playing surfaces over the years, the materials used including all types of wood, stone

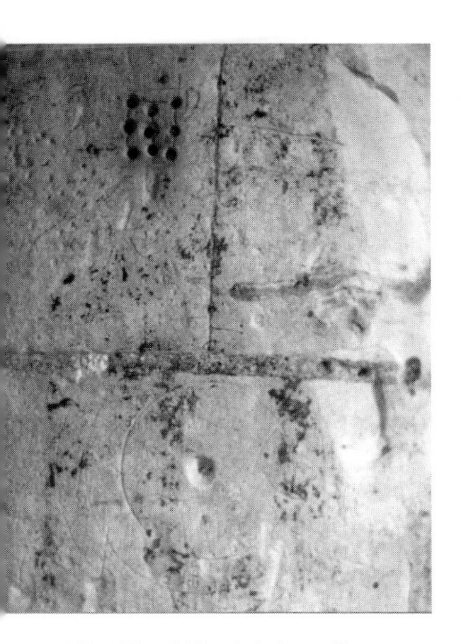

Nine Mens' Morris holes at Burton Agnes Hall.

and turf, Titania lamenting in Shakespeare's *A Midsummer Night's Dream* that: 'The nine men's morris is filled up with mud, and the quaint marks in the wanton green for lack of tread are indistinguishable.'

Nine Men's Morris boards have been found ingeniously incised into barrel tops, corn bid lids and lumps of stone (a fine medieval example was unearthed at Wharram Percy) but perhaps the most intriguing finds have been those carved into the very fabric of monasteries, castles, churches and manor houses. The game was obviously played by the monks in Byland, Kirstall and Whitby Abbeys and by their lords in Scarborough and Helmsley Castles. The evidence though, in Pickering and Kirby Underdale churches, and in the twelfth century manor house at Burton Agnes, points to more opportunistic and clandestine enjoyment by bored choir-boys and workers. Some boards have been discovered in the most seemingly inaccessible and unplayable places. Are these evidence of the meal break diversions of stone – masons and woodcarvers, or should we suspect deliberate concealment by skivers? 'Quick! Pull out the pegs. Here comes the boss!'

Nine Men's Morris was played in the undercroft of the Burton Agnes Manor House built around 1170 by Roger De Stutville. Used for 500 years until 1610, when the family moved into the purpose built hall next door, the Manor House had a large complement of servants. Was it they who drilled the tell-tale holes in the central pier of the undercroft, playing their games by tallow light between servicing their masters? Or, at a time when this dungeon-like place became a laundry for the big house, did the maids have a quick move between scrubs?

Directions: *Burton Agnes is mid-way between Driffield and Bridlington on the A166. Burton Agnes Manor House is immediately west of Burton Agnes Hall. It is owned by English Heritage and is permanently open to the public. Map Landranger 101 – Grid Ref: 103633 (Burton Agnes Manor House).*

134. BURTON AGNES: THE SKULL AND THE EXTREMELY CROSS BONES

Like any young people, the daughters of Sir Henry Griffith were excited at the prospect of moving into their new home. But this was not just any new home. This was a palace 10 years in the making, a spacious and sumptuous light-filled hall where young ladies could twirl their petticoats and dance. The girls would leave the dark and cramped manor house next door and really start to live!

Anne, the youngest of the three sisters, was particularly enchanted with the new house and talked of nothing else. One day in 1620, after praising the virtues of Burton Agnes to her St Quentin family friends in nearby Harpham, she was accosted by thieves near St John's Well. Robbed and battered by the footpads, she limped home in a sorry state, her distraught sisters nursing her considerable wounds and keeping a bedside vigil for three nights. Near death, the delirious Anne made her sisters give a desperate promise. So attached was she to the new house, that she was determined to reside there forever. 'Promise me! Promise me,' she implored, 'that when I am dead you will cut off my head and leave it in our beautiful home as long as it shall last.' The tearful girls gave their word and Anne died.

After conferring with the local parson, it was decided to bury Anne intact in the adjacent churcyard. But soon after she was laid to rest, her angry ghost returned. Her dying wishes had not been complied with and she stalked a stately room. Her family were naturally concerned and arranged for an exhumation. Her head was duly severed and reverentially walled up inside the hall. The hauntings stopped ... but not forever.

A later ancestor thought it very macabre having a skull in the hall and he ordered it removed and put back in the coffin. Because the skull had left the hall, the hauntings re-restarted, only a third disinterment solving the problem. The skull was restored to its niche in the wall and Anne, at last, can rest in peace.

Directions: *Burton Agnes is mid–way between Driffield and Bridlington on the A166. Burton Agnes Hall is 100 yards or so north of the main road. Anne Griffith's skull is said to be walled up in the Great Hall. A portrait of her and her sisters – the* Miss Griffiths *by Geerhardt – is hung in the Inner Hall. Anne haunted the Queen's State Bedroom. Appropriately, a Geerhardt*

Burton Agnes Hall.

portrait is displayed in that apartment. The Griffith family tombs, vaults and memorials are in the nearby church of St Martin's (beyond the Manor House to the west). Map Landranger 101 – Grid Ref: 104633.

135. HARPHAM: MIRACLE CURES

Before the age of science made us all sceptics and we lost our sense of wonder, Harpham was a place of pilgrimage, people flocking to its holy well from all over the country to seek the intercession of St John.

St John was born in the village in the year 640, going on to become Bishop of Hexham and York. In a wilderness of swamp and forest, he founded what was to become Beverley Minster where he was buried in 721. In 934, King Althelstan visited his tomb, craving a blessing in his fight against the Scots. St John is said to have appeared in a vision, promising a victory that surely came. Afterwards, the thankful king endowed the church with grants of land, also bestowing the right of sanctuary. So numerous were the miracles ascribed to St John that, in 1037, he was canonized, his banner flying in the van at the Battle of the Standard in 1138. Edward II, Henry IV and Henry V all paid visits to his shrine, legend suggesting that during the Battle of Agincourt in 1405, the tomb shed tears of holy oil.

Lesser mortals came to the well in Harpham, to pray and to collect the waters, St John becoming the patron saint of the deaf and dumb. The miracle worker is still revered in the village, local children gathering primroses in Harpham Woods every year for display on the saint's tomb. And on the Tuesday evening nearest to 7th May – St John of Beverley's Day – a colourful, choral procession leads from Harpham Church to the decorated well in an annual ceremony of prayer and thanksgiving.

Directions: *Harpham is seven miles south-west of Bridlington (near Burton Agnes), one mile south of the A166. St John's Well is east of the village (500 yards from the crossroads, round the bend) at the side of a country lane. West of St John's Church is the Drummer Boy's Well. Tradition has it that when the sound of a drum rises from the depths, a member of the St Quentin family is about to die. Map Landranger 101 – Grid Ref: 095617.* ☛ ***See also 155 (Beverley)***

St John's Well at Harpham.

136. SLEDMERE: ARCHETYPAL TYKE

In imminent launch mode, the monument leaves Nelson's Column standing. Rearing up from the surrounding countryside like some Mars-bound rocket, it was raised in 1865 by 'friends, tenantry and admirers' to the remarkable Sir Tatton Sykes.

Born into a wealthy family in 1772, this fourth baronet of Sledmere was one of the outstanding characters of his age. A practical, hands – on, no nonsense man who shunned the golden spoon in favour of hard work, agricultural reform and the excitements of the saddle, he became famous for his equestrian feats, going on to breed some of the finest racehorses in turf history.

Modest and unpretentious, Sir Tatton ate and dressed soberly and he always carried a stick. Like that gnarled length of thorn, which is preserved in Sledmere House, he was earthy, stout, robust and honest, if at times not a little prickly.

Blunt, parsimonious and generous in the same breath, he, more than any other man of his age, helped forge the Yorkshire identity. 'There are only three things worth seeing in Yorkshire' went one old saying, 'York Minster, Fountains Abbey and Sir Tatton Sykes.' A man who 'never made an enemy or lost a friend', he was a champion of the poor, not even the meanest beggar leaving his back door without a piece of bread and a pint of his renowned home-brewed ale. When he died in 1863, over 3,000 mourners attended his funeral.

His monument rises 120 feet on the 450 feet high Garton Hill giving views from the top over Holderness to the sea. Built in the Gothic style from banded sandstone, it is simply marked: Erected To The Memory Of Sir Tatton Sykes Baronet – By Those Who Loved Him As A Friend – And Honoured Him As A Landlord – The Memory Of The Just Is Blessed.'

Directions: *The monument is on Garton Hill beside the B1252 road, two and a half miles south east of Sledmere. Sledmere House, which is open to the public, has many other memories of the great man. Map Landranger 101 – Grid Ref: 957618.*

137. TOWTHORPE: MAGIC DEW

Rudyard Kipling contributed to the myth about dewponds:

We have no waters to delight
our broad and brookless vales –
Only the dewpond on the height
unfed, that never fails.

Created on the Wolds, as a consequence of the revolution in agriculture that enclosed remote fields far away from traditional water supplies, dew ponds were, according to the author of the *Rural Economy of Yorkshire* published in

1788, the ingenious creation of 'Francis and Robert Gardiner, well-diggers and fishpond makers of Driffield.' They, and other tight-lipped experts after them, right up to the advent of piped water supplies in the 1930's, fostered a romance and a mystique that surrounds the existence of dewponds to this day.

In purely scientific terms these ponds, many of which survive, saw not a drop of dew, overwhelmingly deriving their water supplies from rainfall and run off. The tricks were in choosing suitable locations for these vital reservoirs and in making linings impervious to seepage and root damage. Closely guarding their methods, the excavators scooped out the chalk to a depth of six feet, ensuring a slope of about one in 10 from the pond centre to its rim. The strict adherence to these dimensions addressed the hallowed hydrographic principle of having a collecting and storage area considerable larger than the area of evaporation. In these excavations, the makers produced dewponds of all sizes up to 100 feet in diameter, using a multi-layered combination of rammed clay and lime, overlaying inverted sods and chalk rubble providing a durable surface. If the ponds were made properly, uncannily, even in drought conditions, they never failed.

Needing the importation of specialist clays, the dewponds were expensive to construct. For this reason, to optimise their usefulness, many were sited at bisecting boundaries to serve a number of fields. The best example of such a pond is at Towthorpe.

The last surviving Wold pondmaker was the eccentric character 'Pondy Welburn' who could be regularly seen walking to work from his home in Fridaythorpe with his barrow of tools. He must have visited Towthorpe and he may have dug its ponds.

Like Kipling, the Reverend Clutterbuck, a well-respected commentator on scientific affairs, invested dewponds with a touch of magic. In 1865, he wrote that '... they presented a phenomenon not easily accounted for by recognised physical causes', old Pondy taking such sentiments to the grave in 1947.

Directions: *Towthorpe is four miles north east of Fridaythorpe. Take the A166 and B1251 through Fimber to the crossroads and left on the B1248 for one mile, then right on a minor road, swinging right and left to Towthorpe Manor Farm. Turn left between the farm buildings (ask permission to use the private road straight ahead – use a four-wheel drive vehicle or walk) and continue on the track, forking right downhill to the bottom. Two hundred yards right of the bend is the first dewpond. Continue uphill to the derelict stock buildings and swing right on a track passing an old quarry on the left, going forward hedgeside for about 500 yards to what is regarded as the best preserved dewpond in the Yorkshire Wolds. This dewpond was constructed at the intersection of four fields on the heights of Towthorpe Wold about one and a half miles travelling distance from the farm. Map Landranger 101 – Grid Refs: 893633 (first dewpond); 894638 (second dewpond).*

138. STAMFORD BRIDGE: 'THOU SHALL NOT PASS!'

Involving thousands of men, pitched battles tend to be anonymous affairs, individual identities becoming lost in the melee and mayhem. Usually, only the generals are remembered, history seldom recalling the yeomanry and the gun fodder. The Battle of Stamford Bridge, fought between King Harold and his Norwegian brother Tostig, aided by his ally Harold Hardrada the King of Norway, resulted in victory for England's Harold. But it's not his exploits that are recalled at the site of his bloody victory on the Derwent, the facts of troop strengths and displacements and all the arguments about allegiances and claims to sovereignty vanishing in the mist. What emerges from the smoke of battle in that September 1066, is the vision of one man, a Norwegian giant who, single handedly kept the forces of Harold at bay for three hours.

After ravaging Scarborough, Hardrada's 300-strong battle fleet sailed into the Humber and assembled off the town of Ravenser. Onward up the Ouse it came for a final confrontation at Stamford Bridge, where one man became a legend.

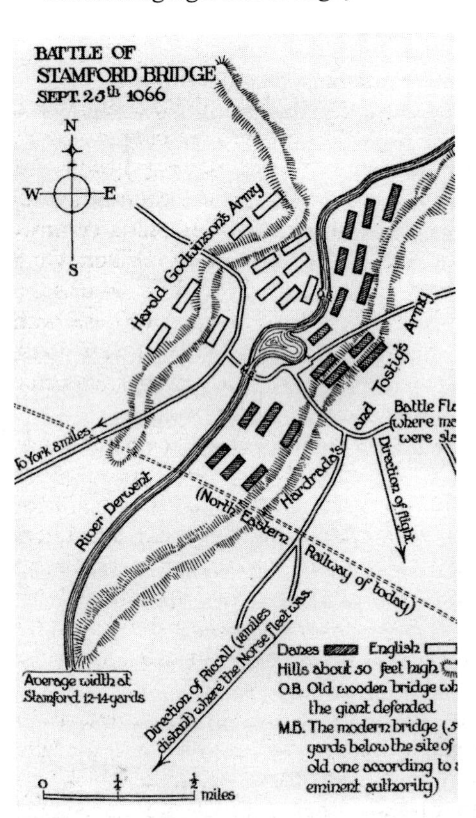

Map of the battle.

With the battle finely poised, this nameless warrior bestrode the Derwent Bridge, slashing and flailing with a mighty battle-axe, resisting all attempts at his removal and thwarting Harold's entire army. As the mound of corpses mounted, desperate measures were proposed, one enterprising soldier commandeering a riverside pig trough and floating down river. When he was underneath the bridge, he thrust a spear through the bridge planks and 'pierced him terribly inwards under the coat of mail' killing the giant. Harold's troops poured over the bridge and won the day.

To commemorate the resistance of the giant, the Spear Pie Feast was held in Stamford Bridge up to 1878 on the first Sunday after 19th September. On this anniversary, boat-shaped pies were made using

This plaque commemorates the battle at Stamford Bridge.

over-ripe pears. Their crusts were impressed with the outline of the fateful spear that won victory for the English.

Directions: *Stamford Bridge is five miles north-east of the York bypass (Grimston Bar) on the A166. The wooden bridge defended by the Norwegian warrior was about 350 yards upstream of what was the Corn Mill. There is a battle plaque near the Old Corn Mill. Map Landranger 105 – Grid Ref: 714556.* ☛ ***See also 165 (Spurn)***

139. BISHOP WILTON: A THIRTEENTH-CENTURY HOLIDAY VILLAGE

The high-living Archbishops of York created Yorkshire's first holiday complex at a time when the 'holy day' thoughts of ordinary people extended only to prayer, penance and cold fish. Such was their eminence's wealth and opportunity for ecclesiastical delegation that they could afford to decamp to the country during the summer months and around the year 1200 one archbishop built a summer palace some 15 miles east of York at a place now known as Bishop Wilton. On a lofty plateau, the palace had panoramic views over the Vale of York towards the Minster. Thirteen archbishops starting with Grey and ending ignominiously with Neville developed their six-acre retreat which was surrounded by a deep moat enclosing some 10 buildings including a large hall, a library, dormitories, kitchens, stables, stores, a dispensary and a chantry chapel.

The archbishops used the palace for spiritual reflection and relaxation, documentary and topographical evidence suggesting the existence of bountiful gardens and an adjacent hunting park. The palace flourished for over two hundred years until the incumbent Archbishop Neville, a political schemer who supported the unpopular Richard II, was forced to escape to Flanders where he finished his days as an impoverished priest. All his possessions, including those at Bishop Wilton, were forfeited to the crown. By the year 1400, the palace was in ruins. One hundred years later, only the present grassy field remained.

The protected palace site and its deep moat can be inspected from Worsendale Road (three entrances over the moat are still intact), from the lane outside the primary school and from the surrounding hillsides, which are accessible by public footpath. At the south-east corner of the site are the remains of ancient fish-ponds. A latinised list of buildings or rooms at the palace was given in the will of Martin Collins, treasurer of York Minster, who died in 1508.

York Minster can still be seen across the vale. A fascinating artefact from the days of the indulgent priests can be found in the nearby church of Kirkby Underdale. Unearthed by a plough, the base stone is all that remains of a large cross set up to mark one of the palace boundaries. Ironically, the ancestors of deer that filled the holy larders still roam on Bishop Wilton Wold.

Directions: *The palace site is in the village of Bishop Wilton, around 14 miles east of York. Turn right off the A 166, at the foot of Garrowby Hill for one mile. Map Landranger 105 – Grid Ref: 800554.* ☛ ***See also 31 (Cawood)***

140. KIRBY UNDERDALE: MERCURY SENDS A MESSAGE

Carved stone is sensual and tactile. It puts you in touch with the time and the place. Run your fingers over its surface and feel the energy of the man and his chisel. Stone: an enigmatic open book, timeless and whispering.

Throughout the county, there are many examples of medieval carved stone to wonder at, although outside of museums, the legacy of Roman fashioned pieces is sparse indeed. So that makes the treasure in Kirby Underdale's church of All Saints' doubly precious.

Dicovered in the rectory garden in 1916, this image of Mercury has been incorporated into an arcade wall. An effigy with winged horns, the figure holds a purse in his right hand. In his left hand, he clutches a wand or a caduceus. This rod was carried by Roman heralds when they went to treat for peace. According to the Roman writer Juvenal, posts with a marble head of Mercury were erected at important crossroads, and it is fascinating to think that this stone might have originally marked part of the legionnaires' route that crossed the top of Garrowby Hill, just a mile or so to the south.

Kirby Underdale's church.

Directions:** Kirby Underdale is around seven miles north-east of Stamford Bridge. Ascend Garrowby Hill on the A166 and go first left and first left again. All Saints' Church is in a delightful dell at the foot of the village. The Roman carving is set into the wall on the left-hand-side of the nave. Map Landranger 106 – Grid Ref: 808586 (All Saints' Church).* ☛ ***See also 36 (Aldborough)

141. POCKLINGTON: GUNS AND LILIES

In these conservation-minded times, the legacy of Major Percy Marlborough Stewart seems strangely contradictory, the largest collection of hardy water lilies in a natural setting in Europe and a trophy roomed crammed with the heads of exotic animals, speaking loudly of crossed purposes. However, this former assistant master at Pocklington School, Cambridge lecturer and major in the Royal Fusiliers was born into the era of the great white hunter, the collection of animal trophies, in an Edwardian world of apparent plenty, being synonymous with bravery and adventure.

Major Stewart returned to Pocklington in 1904, first leasing and then buying the mansion then known as Ivy Hall. Renamed Burnby Hall, the mansion and its extensive grounds were restyled, the major's sporting instincts inspiring him to embark on the construction of two large fishing lakes. Ambitious to explore the world, Stewart and his wife toured Europe, Asia and the American continents, completing a round the world trip in 1906. In later years, Stewart embarked on seven further global journeys, his odysseys with the rod and gun taking him to Norway, Florida, Rhodesia, Canada and elsewhere. This fearless hunter wrote three books. *Round the World with Rod and Rifle* was published in 1924. *Travel and Sport in Many Lands* followed in 1928, the final publication *Tales of Travel and Sport* appearing in 1930. He would have thought it ironic however, that neither these books, nor the expertly preserved and mounted heads of rhinoceros, water buffalo, lion and the rest, brought him lasting fame, the books and the grisly menagerie gathering dust as his lilies bloomed.

When Major Stewart died in 1962, he left his gardens and collection of water lilies to the people of Pocklington. Today there are some 45 varieties of hardy lilies in the Burnby Hall Gardens, which, since they were opened in 1968, have been visited by thousands of people each year.

***Directions:** Pocklington is between York and Market Weighton, off the A1079. Burnby Hall Gardens and the Stewart Collection Museum are a few hundred yards south-east of the church (down Regent Street and The Balk). Major Stewart and his wife are buried under a black marble headstone in Hayton churchyard. Map Landranger 106 – Grid Refs: 805489 (Burnby Hall Gardens); 822461 (Hayton churchyard).*

142. POCKLINGTON: ON A WING AND A PRAYER

In another age, dare-devil Thomas Pelling would have been a sky-diver or a base-jumper. But in the absence of planes and parachutes he had to settle for less altitudinous thrills, throwing himself off church steeples and gliding to earth on a rope.

Pelling, from Burton Stather in Lincolnshire, earned a precarious living by launching himself into space, spectators paying for the privilege of watching him descend to earth on a cable or rope affixed to some prominent high building. After perfecting his act across the North of England, he came to Pocklington with an impressive reputation, handbills, which proclaimed the exploits of the 'Flying Man', drawing crowds for his dicing with death on 10th April 1733.

But this was to prove just one jump too many for the intrepid Thomas Pelling. One of his inattentive assistants forget to tension the cable on the windlass, Pelling committing himself to the slack and falling from the top of All Saints' Church tower. With his theatrical feathers flying, he stuck the battlements of the choir and was killed stone dead. Four days later, he was buried under the sods where he fell.

Directions: *Pocklington is between York and Market Weighton, off the A1079. A plaque on All Saints' exterior chancel wall records Thomas Pelling's last flight. The suspect end of his rope was fixed to the since demolished Star Inn in Market Square – now Market Place. Map Landranger 106 – Grid Ref: 803490 (All Saints' Church).*

143. WARTER: LIFE'S BREAKERS YARD

Like abandoned hulks, the monuments to the Wilson family lie forgotten and rusting, the only memories of a dynasty that once commanded the largest privately owned shipping fleet in the world.

Founded in Hull around 1829 by Thomas Wilson, the famous Wilson Line inaugurated trade routes across the globe, its mercantile empire of almost 100 steamships and tens of thousands of men producing immeasurable power and wealth. Vessels such as the *Bayardo*, *Polo*, *Hero*, *Kovno*, *Borodino* and *Oslo* came down the slipways in quick succession and the champagne flowed, Charles Wilson buying Warter Priory in 1875 and beginning a lavish programme of refurbishment and modernisation. With over thirty bedrooms, extensive kitchens, sumptuously furnished public rooms and

The effigy at St James' Church, Warter.

magnificent gardens, supervised by over sixty members of staff, the mansion was the scene of indulgent living, the Wilson's entertaining the cream of society on a grand scale. On one indulgent day in January 1899, the family hosted a feast for 300 guests, Prince Henry and Princess Daisy of Pless leading the after dinner applause for a tour-de-force in spun sugar, twinkling models of a huge steamship and a lighthouse – both internally lit with electric light bulbs – drawing gasps of delight.

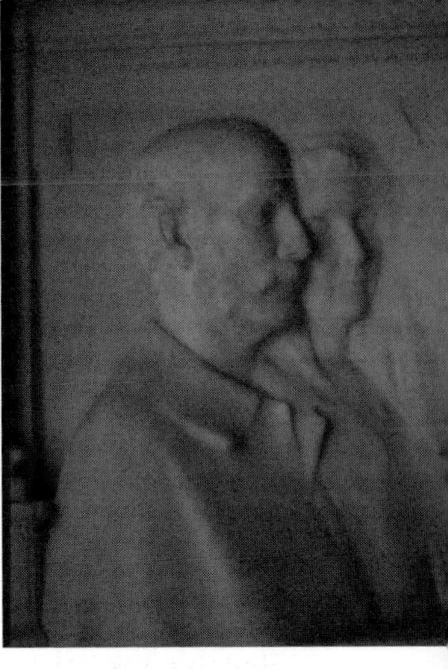

Lord Nunburnholme and wife.

Charles Wilson was created Lord Nunburnholme in 1906, but a combination of increased competition and repeatedly poor investments crippled his business. A year later he was dead, his widow lingering on in the deteriorating Warter Priory for a further 20 years. In 1929, the estate was sold, the mansion finally going to the breakers yard in 1972.

Apart from a few civic monuments and a fleet of stirring model ships in Hull's Town Dock's Museum, very little remains of the Wilson legacy, their ephemeral fame and riches dissolved in a decaying huddle of gravestones and memorials.

Directions: *Warter is five miles east of Pocklinton on the B1246. Nothing remains of Warter Priory which was south-west of the village between the road and Nunburnholme. There is no more poignant mockery to riches than the Wilson monuments in the churchyard. Expensive creations of obvious skill and quality, they lie abandoned to the elements amidst rank weeds, one memorial crying copper tears. Inside the church of St James is a cobwebbed plaque to Lord Nunburnhome and his wife. Nearby is an effigy of rare beauty and presence, the recumbent marble of Isabel, the daughter of the seventh Duke of Roxburgh and wife of Guy Greville Wilson, the only flicker in a once mighty family flame. Map Landranger 106 – Grid Ref: 870504 (St James' Church).*

144. NUNBURNHOLME: THE BIRD MAN OF NUNBURNHOLME

The Reverend Francis Morris had been known to pause in his sermon and listen, some distracting trill from the nearby rectory garden causing confusion in chapter and verse. A pioneering ornithologist and entomologist who set new standards in the study and science of birds and insects, he wrote a defining series of books, *A Natural History of British Birds*, *A Natural History of the Nests and Eggs of British Birds*, *A Natural History of British Butterflies* and *A Natural History of British Moths* bringing him international acclaim.

Morris moved to St James rectory in Nunburnholme in 1854. For 39 years, its garden was his workshop, his studies and field collection trips taking him all over the country. Morris worked prodigiously on his wildlife passions, combining his religious duties with writing and experimentation. He observed bird habitats and behaviour, typically describing a cuckoo: 'Even a canary in whose cage a young cuckoo was lodged, fed it with caterpillars placed there for the purpose....' He also lamented the decimation of the nightingale: 'In Yorkshire I have known them in the neighbourhood of Doncaster but the bird catchers make sad havoc of them.' Hundreds of other species received his attention, his colour illustrated book on British birds running to six lavish volumes.

A pioneer in the movement to establish nature reserves and to protect birds, he petitioned the House of Commons for a tax on guns and a tightening of the laws of trespass.

Morris died in 1893. Re-erected in 1902, the tower of St James was fittingly dedicated to his memory: 'The barn owl is a high churchman of a bird, almost proverbially attached to the church, within whose sacred precincts it finds a sanctuary, as others have done in former ages: and in whose ivy mantled tower it rests it brood.'

Morris was succeeded by his equally talented son, Marmaduke Charles Frederick Morris who wrote a number of books on local dialect.

Directions: *Nunburnholme is between Pocklington and Market Weighton. The easiest access is from the A1079 at Hayton. Go north-east through Burnby for just under three miles. The graves of Francis Orphen Morris and his wife are head to toe by the porch. Inside the church (on the east wall) are portraits of both Morris and his son. The inscribed treble bell in the tower remembers the birdman's work. In Latin, it translates: 'I will always imitate your birds Francis, by singing.' Across the graveyard, the rectory garden has hardly changed. Map Landranger 106 – Grid Ref: 848478.*

145. LONDESBOROUGH: THE SHEPHERD LORD

Set into the chancel floor of All Saints' church in Londesborough, is an enigmatic plaque inscribed in Latin. It is dedicated to the 'most noble of men', John, Lord Clifford, who died on the eve of the Battle of Towton in 1461. Flying the doomed standard of the House of Lancaster, he was struck in the neck by a headless Yorkist arrow as he took off his gorget whilst fleeing a melee at Ferrybridge. Although revered as a man of courage by the champions of the red rose, Clifford has gone down in history as a vicious tyrant. Shakespeare in Henry VI refers to him as 'that cruel child killer,' as 'hard-hearted,' and 'unrelenting', many subsequent writers giving him the sobriquets 'Blackfaced Clifford' and 'Bloody Clifford.' Killed by a single shaft, Clifford might have escaped a more frenzied death. Had he struck his colours on what is referred to in contemporary chronicles as Palm Sunday Field, he may well have been chopped into a hundred pieces.

Many East Riding families lost men folk at Towton, the county of Yorkshire ironically providing most of the troops on both sides. Some of the corpses were saved from the ignominy of mass burial and the body of the disgraced John Lord Clifford was committed to a hidden grave in Londesborough, the village holding a more compelling secret for the next twenty years.

In desperate fear of having her sons killed after the defeat, the widow of Lord Clifford fled to her father's house in Londesborough. Her younger son Richard was promptly despatched for Flanders, and his brother Henry was anonymously placed under the guardianship of a local shepherd and his wife. Unaware of his noble ancestry, for some years the lad remained in Londesborough and led a frugal life, tending sheep without any formal education. Even in this remote place, however, there was danger of exposure and he was sent, along with his foster parents to the wilds of Westmorland where he remained until the dynasty of the House of York was terminated after the Battle of Bosworth. Henry, who was henceforth known as the 'Shepherd Lord', was restored to his estates at the age of 32, spending most of the rest of his life in the study of science and natural history. A quiet and studious man of 60, he was nevertheless sparked to belligerency, holding a command at the Battle of Flodden in 1513. But unlike his father, he died with his spurs off at the grand old age of 72.

Directions: *Londesborough is two miles north of Market Weighton (take a minor road crossing the A163). The church of All Saints' is in the centre of the village. The Cliffords owned the Londesborough estate for almost 200 years, the property passing by marriage into the Burlington family. Richard the third Earl of Burlington designed and erected Londesborough Hall (site immediately adjacent to the church) a lavish mansion surrounded by sumptuous parkland. The estate again passed by marriage, this time into the Devonshire family. In 1819, it was decided to demolish the mansion for use in the new range at Chatsworth. Only the cellars, gate-piers and the orangery remain. Map Landranger 106 – Grid Ref: 868454 (All Saints' Church and site of Londesborough Hall).* ☛ ***See also 33 (Towton)***

146. GOODMANHAM: DRUID TEMPLE TORCHED

This East Riding hamlet can rightfully claim to be the birthplace of Christianity in the North of England. But, once a centre for Druidism, it had a temple dedicated to Woden and a reputation for satanic rites and blood sacrifice. Its shadow of evil spurred the Christian missionary Paulinus to action in the year 627 and he came to Goodmanham with a determination to oust the false God.

Paulinus, who was chaplain to Queen Ethelburga – her husband King Edwin ruled a vast kingdom from his palace in nearby Londesborough – persuaded the king to embrace Christianity with the words: 'There is an eternal purpose in Creation. Mankind has a special value in the sight of the Creator. He is our reconciliation, the truth and our hope of resurrection.'

Fired by the oratory, the followers of Woden turned to their high priest Coifi for guidance, he addressing the assembly with the words: 'I have long known since that there is nothing in this religion we have professed. The more I sought for the truth, the less I found. This can give us life, salvation and eternal happiness. I advise now that we burn down the useless sanctuary. And who better to do it than myself?'

With some trepidation, the multitude rode to Goodmanham, Coifi braving desecration and the ire of Woden by flinging his axe into the ring. No lightning flashes answered this challenge and, emboldened, the assembly fell on the temple with torches and burned it to the ground.

King Edwin and many of his followers were baptised soon afterwards, the royal entourage making its solemn way to York, where they laid the foundations of a great church – York Minster.

Directions: *On a minor road, Goodmanham is one and a half miles north-west of Market Weighton (A1079). The ashes of the heathen temple lie under the largely Norman Church of All Hallows'. In 1927 a service in the church marked 1,300 years of Christianity in the north. The event was commemorated by the erection of a wooden cross set on a bed of stones from Londesborough Hall where Edwin's palace had once stood. Inside the church is a font reputed to have been use by Paulinus to baptise Coifi. Map Landranger 106 – Grid Ref: 890432 (All Hallows' Church).* ☛ ***See also 121 (York)***

147. MARKET WEIGHTON: 'HE'S A BIG LAD FOR HIS AGE'

Born in 1787, William Bradley wore nappies the size of sails and by the age of 11 weighed an impressive 11 stones. But it was his height that caused him to stand out, his eventual 7'9" inches making him the tallest ever Yorkshireman. One of thirteen children, Bradley worked in local fields as a young man, but he went on to make his fortune, exhibiting himself at fairs and circuses. On one occasion, he met King George IV, receiving the gift of a gold souvenir on a chain.

Although he was a teetotaller and a sparse eater, everything about Bradley was mansize. He weighed 27 stones and wore shoes measuring 15 inches long and five

Market Weighton church.

and a half inches broad. His stockings were three feet nine inches from top to toe and he carried a walking stick over four feet in length. A man of some charm, he was well-proportioned, although in later life he developed arthritis and was compelled to use a crutch. He died in 1820 and was buried in a coffin measuring nine feet by three feet under a marble slab in Market Weighton's All Saints' Church.

Directions: *Market Weighton is off the A1079 by-pass between Pocklington and Beverley. Our Yorkshire giant was born in a specially adapted home – No 89 York Road – two hundred yards north-west of the church. The house is sometimes open for visitors on Giant Bradley Day, usually held in the town in late May. A wall plaque shows the size of his enormous shoes. In the Londesborough Arms (next to the church) is one of Bradley's oversized chairs. Map Landranger 106 – Grid Ref: 877418 (No 89 York Road).*

148. KIPLINGCOTES: THE FIRST SHALL BE SECOND

Founded in 1619, the Kiplingcotes Derby is the oldest endowed horse race in England. Perversely, and this could only happen in Yorkshire, it's the only such contest in the world, where the jockeys strive to come second.

The race was conceived as a test for foxhunters, the course extending for some four miles, starting near the former railway station at Kiplingcotes and following part of the line of the old Roman road across the western escarpment of the Wolds, to a finishing post in the parish of Middleton-on-the-Wolds. The race rules are these:

> *A horse race to be observed and ridd yearly on the third Thursday in March; open to horses of all ages, to carry horseman's weight, 10 stones, exclusive of saddle, to enter at ye post, before eleven o'clock on the morning of ye race. The race to be run before two.*

A prize is offered to the winner (I thought your ears would prick up at that) several bigwigs such as the Earl of Burlington, Sir John Legard and Sir William Strickland getting together around 1665 and contributing to a fund. Until 1822, the fund was held by private individuals, but in that year, the entire sum of £468 11s 10d was invested at three per cent in Consolidated Bank annuities. And this is where it gets interesting.

Kiplingcotes racecourse.

The winner of the race creams off all the interest, returning enough profit to have his horse re-shoed – one hoof only. The second past the post, though, gets the majority of the entry fees, so if there are more than four competing horses the second comes a definite first.

Yorshiremen are all for tradition and the race continues into its fifth century. But can't we get a better return than three per cent?

Directions: *Kiplingcotes is three miles north-east of Market Weighton on a minor road. The course extends for four miles (a very pleasant walk at any time of the year) between a point near Kiplingcotes Station (defunct but used for other purposes) and the winning post to the east of Londsborough Wold, 400 yards north west of the A163 junction with the road signposted to Warter. Map Landranger 106 – Grid Refs: 929439 (Kiplingcotes Station); 896476 (winning post).*

149. HOLME-ON-SPALDING MOOR: BOGS AND BOATS

Aloof from its village on a commanding hill, All Saints' Church surveys a vast landscape, this spiritual Camelot looking out over a once treacherous land strangled by creeks, streams, woods and swamps. Fertile and perennially water-logged, the land hereabouts supported vast numbers of oak trees, regular excavations on local farms revealing the remains of age-blackened bog-oaks and, just occasionally, something else.

Thousands of years ago, the land south of All Saints' hill was a vast and teeming larder, our enterprising ancestors accessing the area by boat from the Humber, to fish and to hunt and to deliver cargo. Preserved in the clay, a number of their hollowed-out craft have been unearthed locally in recent times, one astounding discovery at Hasholme Carr in 1984 shedding new light on Iron Age man.

The biggest surviving prehistoric log boat in Britain, the Hasholme Boat, was made from a single gigantic oak tree. It measures 42 feet in length and weighs some six tonnes, remarkable ground conditions preserving constructional tool marks and mysterious carvings. What other secrets, what bodies from more recent times lay on undisturbed? Only in the last few centuries has the land been drained and accessed by modern roads. Prior to then, travellers risked a crossing to Holme's hill at their peril, although at both edges of the mire, monks tolled their nightly curfew bells to warn of the dangers.

Directions: *Holme – on – Spalding Moor is on the A164, four miles south-west of Market Weighton. Raised on the site of the monks' citadel, All Saints' Church dates from the thirteenth century. The Hasholme Boat was unearthed three miles south-east of the church on Hasholme Carr Farm (south on the A614 and turn left down Drain Lane). The boat is on permanent display in Hull's Hull and East Riding Museum. Map Landranger 106 – Grid Ref: 822390.*

150. AUGHTON TWO FINGERS TO HENRY VIII

Scratched deep into the buttress wall is an image that has intrigued me for years, the carved figure of a newt radiating a silent message across the years. There is no reference to this elemental graffiti in any published tomes, the guidebooks on All Saints' Church referring only dryly to scalloped capitals, beakhead mouldings and a Norman chancel arch. So I pondered on the creature, finally hearing an echo of defiance from beyond the grave.

In 1532, Yorkshire was a hotbed of insurrection, Robert Aske of Aughton Hall organising opposition to the closure of the smaller monasteries by Henry VIII. Aske's so-called 'Pilgrimage of Grace' recruited a passionate following of 30,000 men, monks in the vanguard bearing images of the Crucifixion and the Host. This peaceful revolt was suppressed, however, the king making false promises to Aske who was eventually arrested and hanged in 1537 from the top of Clifford's Tower in York. There followed a tide of brutality unsurpassed in England, Henry's henchmen executing the rising's leaders and hanging hundreds of other supporters in country lanes.

If Adolf Hitler's armies had invaded these shores, his opponents, like those against Henry VIII, would have got short shrift. Like that in occupied France, opposition in this country would have been an underground affair, a derailment here and a daubed slogan there. And after the execution of Winston Churchill, defiant images of cigar smoking bulldogs would have appeared everywhere. In 1537, did a similar act of defiance take place in Aughton?

Wander through Aughton churchyard and let your eyes alight on that fascinating carving. As plain as the day it was cut, you can see the image of a newt. The significance? The word for newt in Old English is aske.

Directions: *All Saints' Church is in the village of Aughton (at the very end of the access road) between Sutton-on-Derwent and Bubwith, east of the River Derwent. Take the minor road west off the B1228, one and a half miles north of the B1228/A163 crossroads. The carving is on the south-west buttress to the tower. Next to the church is the moated site of the Aske's manor house. In the churchyard are some fascinating gravestones. Map Landranger 106 – Grid Ref: 702387.* ☛ ***See also 125 (York)***

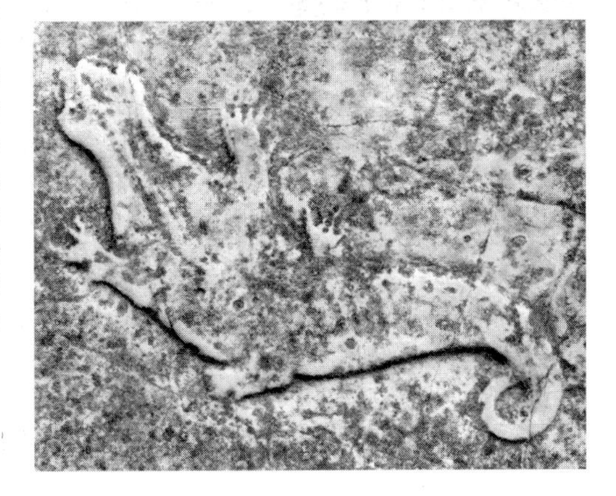

The aske at Aughton.

Rawcliffe's most eccentric inhabitant.

151. RAWCLIFFE: 'AT THE RIVER BANK AT RAWCLIFFE I PROMISED TO SAY FIVE FARTHINGS'

Rawcliffe is a pleasant but largely anonymous riverside town on the Ouse. To quote an old guide book: 'It does not appear to have been particularly famous for anything but Jimmy Hirst; but Jimmy left a sufficient amount of history behind him to have made the reputation of any place.'

Unlike the dour and colourless river that flowed at his door, James or Jemmy Hirst was as bubbly as a spring. An eccentric of the first water, he was born in 1738, becoming a celebrated Yorkshireman whose rare antics brought him astonishing fame.

As a schoolboy, Jemmy was destined for the church, a spurned infatuation with the local tanner's daughter diverting his ambitions to more secular ways. Upset by the rejection, he fell ill, a fever affecting his brain. Some of his neighbours thought he had gone mad, but madness is not made of this! Refusing to work for a living, Jemmy invested in a number of speculative enterprises using a £1,000 endowment left to him by his father. He harvested a five-fold return on his capital and set out to enjoy himself.

I have referred elsewhere in these pages to Sir George Cayley, the 'Father of Aerial Navigation.' In attempting to emulate the birds, the feathered Jemmy beat Sir George by several decades. He climbed to the mast-head of a vessel anchored in the river and took the plunge. And he did a host of other daft things.

Fond of sport and all animals, he broke his bull Jupiter to the saddle, riding him to hounds. Not content with a crimson hunting jacket, he wore an ensemble as loud as a hunting horn, the sight of his 'yellow top, harlequin breeches, waistcoat, and red coat with blue sleeves, and his habitual huge lambskin hat, which was three yards in circumference,' sending any self respecting fox bolting into the next county. He trained a pet pig as a pointer and used it on partridge shoots and in his cottage, which was described as a cross between a saddler's shop and a menagerie, housing a bear, a monkey, foxes, otters, badgers and assorted vermin. But his most outlandish eccentricity was in his mode of transport.

Most villagers of the time were content with equestrian modes of travel. Not so Jemmy. He built himself a famous wickerwork carriage, old Jupiter himself providing the motive power. Invited to London by an intrigued King George III, Jemmy harnessed four mules to his carriage, also using the animals for his frequent excursions to Doncaster racecourse.

Jemmy had a reputation for hospitality. Children and old ladies were invited to his cottage for tea on separate days each week, when the leaves were brewed, their host dispensing with formal invitations in favour of blasts on a hunting horn.

The clearly deranged Jemmy made tidy sums of money to keep him in pigeon corn. He sold thousands of flash currency notes bearing the inscription: 'At the River Bank at Rawcliffe I promised to say Five Farthings.' He also charged people for seeing his coffins. He kept two in the cottage – one was used as a larder and the other was fitted out with a bell, 'so that I can ring for anything I want from the grave.'

When Jemmy died in 1839, he left a will, bequeathing 'half a Guinea' each to eight old maids who were to act as his pall-bearers. But there was one rather awkward stipulation. Each of the old maids was to swear on oath to being a virgin. When only two pure ladies could be found, the vicar had to compromise by allowing eight much younger and less sullied women to take the box, although he did put his foot down in regard to another of the deceased's requests, Jemmy having insisted that a fiddler and a Scotch piper play at the head of his funeral.

Directions: *Rawcliffe is four miles west of Goole (exit at junction 36 of the M62 and go west on the A614). James Hirst's cottage was at the bottom of Chapel Lane (on the right as you walk down the lane towards the river from St James Church). There is a memorial to his parents in the church. Nearly opposite the site of Hirst's cottage is a modern development known as Hirst Gardens. A specimen currency note issued by Hirst is in Goole Museum. In recent years, Rawcliffe Women's Institute re-enacted Jemmy's funeral in a float as part of the Rawcliffe Festival. A coffin installed with a corpse and a bell was trundled through the village streets by institute members, 'who wouldn't swear on oath either!.' Map Landranger 106 – Grid Ref: 685232 (Chapel Lane).*

152. THE HUMBER ESTUARY: ZEPPELIN'S BUBBLE BURSTS

It's amazing to think, that a glorified bag of wind with the delicacy and manoeuvrability of a soap bubble, was the Domesday machine of its day. The Zeppelins were designed as 'height climbers' to avoid air defences and were a formidable weapon of war. But in the era before the widespread use of winged aircraft, they were also employed as passenger vehicles, regular excursions linking Germany with Brazil and the United States. Invented by Count Ferdinand von Zeppelin, LZ1 the first of the duralumin, internal-framed dirigibles, made its maiden flight on Lake Constance, near Friedrichshafen in

Southern Germany on 2nd July 1900. In subsequent years, such aircraft logged over a million miles of passenger travel without loss of life. Two spectacular crashes, however, helped end the Zeppelin era. The most dramatic was the destruction of the Hindenburg on 6th May 1937, an earlier accident in Yorkshire underlining the inherent flaws in these spectacular machines.

In July 1921, the newly sold R 38 flew into the Howden Airship Station for trials and crew testing. Bought by the United States Navy and re-designated ZR2, the world's largest airship was 699 feet long and 85 and a half feet in diameter. Covered in an outer skin of linen canvas, it was constructed from an intricate scaffold of girders braced by miles of steel wire, fourteen cotton gas cells lined with goldbeater's skin and filled with 2,724,000 cubic feet of hydrogen gas, which provided the lift. Propulsion came from six externally mounted Sunbeam Cossack engines delivering 2,100-horse power and a maximum speed of 71 miles per hour. A control cabin was located below the airship's nose.

Officers and crew of the United States Navy Howden Detachment had been in Yorkshire since April 1920. They had integrated well, 10 of their number marrying local girls and settling in Hull and nearby villages. On the 23rd August, 17 of these men, assisted by 27 RAF personnel and hundreds of ground crew prepared the giant craft for its proving flight. Also on board were the craft's designer – Constructor Commander Campbell – and three scientists from the National Physical Laboratory. ZR2 took off for its final flight under RAF command, heading out into the North Sea. Its destination was Pulham in Norfolk where it was to be handed over to its new owners.

At the end of a day of successful testing, fog hampered the final flight to Pulham and it was decided to keep the airship over the sea ready to resume tests on the following day. Again, the routines went well, although persistently foggy skies thwarted a second attempt at landing in Pulham. The airship was turned into the wind for a return to its Howden base, its distinctive engine noise above the city of Hull alerting thousands of people who were clocking off from work. At around 5.35 pm on the balmy summer evening of 24th August, crowds of excited spectators craned their necks for a sight of the most impressive aircraft ever built, watching in awe as she appeared from the cloud cover above Alexandra Dock. There was a carnival atmosphere on the promenade of Victoria Pier, elation turning to despair and horror in a split second. Approaching from the left, the airship shuddered and moved erratically at an estimated height of 2,500 feet, a tear appearing in her outer cover. In moments, the network of girders cracked 'like an egg', fuel tanks, equipment and men, some wearing burning parachutes, spilling into the river. Doomed, the stricken craft was wreathed in flame, children with lollipops frozen to their lips looking on in horror as the great ship split asunder in a terrific explosion, burning fuel showering the Humber and a shock wave breaking windows in nearby buildings. With the front half of ZR2 falling in the direction of the Victoria Pier, frightened onlookers beat a hasty retreat, a second explosion timed at 5.38 pm erupting when debris hit the water. Like a piece of gossamer, the detached tail section floated eerily to the ground, coming to rest about 300 yards from the pier on the sand bar known as Middle Sand. In just three minutes, ZR2 had been ripped to pieces and 44 people were dead. Only one U.S. crewman and four RAF personnel survived the disaster.

All the dead Americans were repatriated, nine of the British casualties being buried in Hull Western Cemetery. The cause of the tragedy? According to the court of inquiry, this was put down to 'insufficient attention to aerodynamic force' – a euphemism for a catastrophic design fault.

Directions: *Hull and the Humber estuary, where the fateful accident occurred, can be reached via the M62 and A63. The re-modelled Victoria Pier is between Hull Marina and the outlet of the River Hull (off Castle Street via Humber Dock Street and Minerva Terrace). Hull Western Cemetery is on Spring Bank West immediately west of the city centre. In Elloughton Church (about 10 miles west of Hull along the A63) is a plaque to four of the dead U.S. personnel who are thought to have resided in the village during their posting to Howden. Map Landranger 107/106 – Grid Refs: 107/100281 (Victoria Pier); 107/075296 (Hull Western Cemetery); 106/944283 (Elloughton Church).*

153. ROWLEY: THE WHITE ROSE BLOOMS IN NEW ENGLAND

Forlorn, St Peter's Church sits alone without a village, only a nearby hotel, a former vicarage, keeping it company in centuries. Large and accommodating, the church was designed for a sizeable congregation of farmers and their families who once occupied local homesteads. But in 1638, they upped sticks and left for America.

Stained glass in Rowley church.

The zealous people of Rowley and its surrounding parishes were Puritans who observed a strict code of moral conduct and behaviour. They would neither work nor indulge in any form of sport or amusement on the Sabbath, their insistence on keeping Sundays holy bringing them into conflict with an edict of the king. James I died in 1625 but he had decreed that the *Book of Sports* should be read in churches throughout the land. This book instructed church – goers to indulge in dancing, archery and games after Divine Service each week, desisting parishioners risking a fine and imprisonment. In Yorkshire, the Archbishop of York had refused to sanction the weekly readings, but when he died, shortly after Charles I assumed the crown, the new appointee was determine to uphold the law.

He wrote to all parishes in the county insisting that the *Book of Sports* be read, one of his missives arriving on the desk of Rowley's Reverend Ezekiel Rogers. Under a barrage of threats, the vicar refused to comply with the instruction and called his congregation together for a crisis meeting. Resolutely, thirty local farmers supported Rogers, and all, to a man, resolved to quit England and its religiously intolerant state. Rather than compromise their beliefs or risk imprisonment, they stripped their homes of all they could carry and set out for America by ship, leaving only a handful of labourers and their 1,000-year old church behind.

Currently, the inhabitants of Rowley in Massachusetts are several thousands strong and in recent years a strong bond has developed between the two communities. In memory of their founding father, the New England brethren donated a stained glass window to St Peter's in 1994. The 'Ezekiel Rogers Window', designed and manufactured by Sep Waugh of York, graces the Ellerker chapel. With a galleon at its centre, the window tells the story of the quest for religious freedom.

Directions: *Rowley is about five miles north-east of South Cave (A63). Keep right, heading towards Hull on the minor road, and turn left about 500 yards after the Riplingham Crossroads. St Peter's Visitors' Book shows that the ancestors of Rogers determined band frequently return to Rowley to trace their roots. See several typical entries in the Visitors' Book – 29/5/89, 14/8/89 and 29/08/01. In the past, they have taken cuttings from the guelder roses that grow wild in these parts. The American Rowley is less than thirty miles north-east of Boston. Map Landranger 106 – Grid Ref: 976328 (St Peter's Church).*

154. SKIDBY: WIND SOME

Food production and processing are the engine rooms of life, cereal-grinding mills having a uniquely practical and profoundly psychological place in human existence. For hundreds of years, the English mill, particularly the windmill, was the hub of community living. Along with the village church, sails gently turning, it set the rhythm of life, the sustenance of body and soul linked in a wholesome vision of old England feted in song and verse:

Behold! A giant am I!
Aloft here in my tower,
With my granite jaws I devour,
The maize, the wheat, and the rye,

And grind them into flour'
On Sundays I take my rest
Church-going bells begin
Their low melodious din;
I cross my arms on my breast,
And all is peace within.
H.W. Longfellow

Across the East Riding there were once 200 such windmills. Now, just a handful remain, the rare survivor at Skidby being the only such mill complete with sails. Built in 1821, and a structure of special architectural and historic interest, it is claimed by many experts to be the best example of its type in the country. With the aid of electricity, it continued to function until 1966. Since then, it has been thoughtfully and thoroughly restored to its original condition.

Reaching a height of 72 feet, with a distinctive 'ogee' onion shaped cap, the mill was originally erected by Garton's of Beverley to a Dutch design. Its well-greased innards are linked to four massive sails covered in ship's canvas, each sail weighing over one and a quarter tonnes. A fantail on the opposite side of the sails, employs an arrangement of bevelled gears to ensure that the sails are always in the optimum position for exploiting the wind.

Unlike Longfellow's miller, Skidby's flour-dusted chap grinds on Sundays.

Directions: *Skidby is about eight miles north-west of Hull (A63 and A164 north). Skidby Mill is open to the public. Displays, graphic panels, scale models and historic agricultural implements explain the process of milling. Stone ground flour is available for purchase. Map Landranger 107 – Grid Ref: 020334.*

155. BEVERLEY: 'SANCTUARY! SANCTUARY!'

Alongside the image of Charles Laughton's memorable portrayal of Quasimodo in the film 'The Hunchback of Notre Dame', is the echo of one resounding word that signified blessed refuge. 'Sanctuary!' was the cry, the ogre winking with his one good eye as he snatched Esmeralda to safety.

The right of sanctuary was a medieval law conferring immunity from arrest on fugitives who took refuge within church precincts. The protection usually lasted 40 days. Sanctuary status was conferred on Beverley in 938 by King Athelstan as a reward for St John's divine intervention in his struggles against the Scots, the right lasting for over 600 years until 1540.

The sanctuarial cordon radiated from Beverley Minster for a mile in every direction, three upright stones marking the sanctuary boundaries on the main approach roads. Many a fugitive and escapee arrived breathless at these stones, praising God for their deliverance. But they were not safe yet, the level of safety depending on how fast they could run!

If they were apprehended just inside the cordon, the pursuers had to pay a fine of £8, the fine increasing to a staggering £96 if the fugitives were captured frantically rattling the sanctuary knocker at the Minster door. And the pursuer had to be a rich and desperate man indeed if he ran his quarry to ground at the sacred altar, the risk of excommunication and a fine of £144 really focusing the mind.

Once inside the Minster, the fugitive would be cared for by the canons for 30 days. As part of the compact, he would have to take an oath, promising not to 'bere no pointed wepen, dagger, knyfe, ne none other wepen ...', to assist in the mass, to help extinguish fires in the town and to help suppress riotous behaviour. During the period of his protection the canons would evaluate the evidence against the accused. If he was found guilty, he would be taken under escort to the coast and effectively banished from the land. By law, he was not allowed to return '... without the special grace of our lord the King.' A verdict of innocence conferred a lifting of sanctuary and freedom.

Directions: *Beverley is nine miles north-west of Hull (A1079/A1174). Beverley Minster is south-east of the town centre down Minster Moorgate. At the far-eastern end of the Minster, to the left just beyond the east transept, is the Frith Stool. This simple Anglo Saxon stone chair was the ultimate goal of sanctuary seekers. If they managed to sit here, they had truly made it! Resting here conferred absolute safety on the fugitive, not even the King daring to 'violate its sacred peace.' The seat is devoid of any decoration or inscription, but it was once engraved with a Latin inscription whose English translation ran thus:*

> This stone seat is called FREEDSTOLL, that is, chair of peace, on reaching which a fugitive criminal enjoys complete safety.

Directions: *In the south transept is a fifteenth-century painting of King Athelstan and St John. The sanctuary stones are located on the B1230 road to Walkington, the A164 road to Skidby and the A1035 road to York. Map Landranger 107 – Grid Refs: 038393 (Beverley Minster); 003373 (sanctuary stone B1230); 028366 (sanctuary stone A164); 005397 (sanctuary stone A1035).* ☛ ***See also 135 (Harpham)***

156. HORNSEA: A PISCATORIAL PUNCH-UP

The largest freshwater lake in Yorkshire is full of fish, anglers from all over the county travelling to Hornsea Mere to do battle with its roach and legendary pike. Fishing is, of course, a contemplative and restful sport seldom associated with the rousing of passions. Unless that is you happened to be a monk involved in an unholy clash of arms that preceded the Cod Wars by seven centuries.

Hornsea Mere.

In the year 1260, the fishing rights in Hornsea Mere were hotly contested by William, the 11th abbot of Meaux Abbey and his holy counterpart from St Mary's Abbey in York. The pair both claimed sovereignty over the fish in the southern half of the mere, protracted negotiations only serving to furrow the anointed brows even further. So, unable to settle the argument by diplomacy they opted for arbitration, each selecting a troupe of monastic champions for a trial by combat, the last man standing winning the right to sling his abbey's hook.

Properly accoutred by the abbots, the champions were said to have knocked seven monastic bells out of each other from dawn until dusk, the lads of Meaux finally eating dirt as darkness fell. From that day forth, the Abbot of York had rights over the whole mere.

Directions: *Hornsea is on the east coast around 15 miles from Beverley. Take the A1035 and turn right at the B1244 junction in Leven. Hornsea Mere is directly west of the town. The combatants are thought to have fought on the southern shore. The site of the Cistercian Meaux Abbey which was founded as a Fountains' offshoot in 1150, is along a minor lane, two miles south of Routh and the A1035. Map Landranger 107 – Grid Ref: 190470.*

157. PAULL: EYE ON THE HUMBER

Lurking and hidden, Paull's forts have cast their menacing eyes over the Humber since the sixteenth century, successive threats of invasion seeing the construction of a pentagonal Napoleonic stronghold that continued its operational role until World War II when, as an anti aircraft battery, it saw nightly action against the Luftwaffe. Abandoned to the elements thereafter, this highly secret and reclusive establishment mouldered on, attracting only the interest of passing walkers like some overgrown Mayan temple. In recent years, however, it has been opened as a visitor attraction.

In Napoleonic times, the fort was massively reconstructed, its thick walls and large calibre cannons overlooking the estuary. In the Victorian era, it was served by a railway and a long jetty, later years seeing the construction of an intricate Maginot line type network of underground labyrinths leading to a complex of vaults, gun and bomb stores, an underground hospital and massive caponieres.

***Directions:** Paull is on the Humber estuary just beyond the eastern boundary of Hull near the Saltend chemical works. (Take the A1033 to the chemical works roundabout and go right on the minor road, following the signpost to Fort Paull). Map Landranger 107 – Grid Ref: 170256.*

158. HULL: 'SLING YOUR HOOK ... YOUR MAJESTY'

The Governor of Hull, Sir John Hotham, is credited with firing the first verbal shot in the English Civil War. After a breakdown in relations with Parliament and a failure to impeach five of its members, King Charles I rode north for Hull. Coveting a citadel town that bristled with the second largest arsenal in the country, he approached its Beverley Gate with 300 men on the morning of the 23rd April 1642. Sir John refused him entry.

Such an affront to a man who professed the 'Divine Right of Kings' rankled deep, a subsequent five-hour tarry in the pouring rain doing nothing for his royal temper. Proclaiming Sir John a traitor, the King retired to Beverley and primed his guns.

***Directions:** Beverley Gate near the junction of Whitefriargate and Alfred Gelder Street (opposite the Princes Quay Shoppng Centre) has since been demolished but its foundations remain and the site has been conserved as a public amenity area. A plaque explains the significance of Sir John Hotham's action. During the stand-off, Sir John had his headquarters in the Ye Olde White Harte inn (pedestrian access off Bowlalley Lane and Silver Street). Its 'Plotting Parlour' is preserved in an upstairs room. Map Landranger107 – Grid Ref: 096287 (Beverley Gate).*

159. HULL: '... THAT ODIOUS TRAFFIC IN HUMAN FLESH.'

William Wilberforce wrote his first letter complaining about the horrors of slavery as a Pocklington schoolboy. Gallons of ink and thousands of quills later, he saw his beloved dream of abolition come true, 30 years of correspondence, discussion, oratory, persuasion and monumental determination resulting in the historic vote in the House of Commons on 23rd February 1807, the decision leaving him with tears streaming down his face.

***Directions:** The local MP from 1780, William Wilberforce was born in High Street, Hull (access off M 62/A63 and Castle Street). His home – Wilberforce House – is now a museum, charting the history of abolition.*

A tribute to Wilberforce at Pocklington School.

Nearby, on Wilberforce Drive, fronting Queens Gardens, is a 90 feet high Doric column commemorating the great man. But the most moving tribute to his work is of more recent origin, a sculpture created by a former pupil at Pocklington School, adorning St Nicholas's Quadrangle. A fine bronze of a Negro slave, it casts a compelling spell of power and dignity. 'I wanted to show a man with self worth and dignity,' says the sculptor. 'The shackles have come off but rather than an upsurge in hatred and violence, my figure displays a deep contemplation of past events.' Map Landranger 107 – Grid Ref: 103288 (Wilberforce House).

160. HULL: 'THE CHIMNEY'S GONE AFIRE!'

In 1754, a whole new lexicon of nautical terms reverberated round the port of Hull, the introduction of new words such as flensing, baleen, crang, closh, milldolling, skeeman, specksioneer and scrimshaw marking the start of nearly a century of whale fishing.

At the height of the slaughter in 1805, Hull was the premier whaling port in the land producing half of Britain's whale products, its 60 ships landing 4,018 tons of oil and 360 tons of bone or baleen for use in brush and chair seat and ladies corset manufacture, together with other products like wax and ambergris. The trade prospered for another 25 years, the fleet setting out every February and March, its captains hoping to return with full holds by the time of the Hull Fair in October.

Plying the Arctic wastes to the east of Greenland and the seas between Jan Mayen and Spitzbergen, specially ice- reinforced ships such as the *Brunswick*, the *Cumbrian*, the *Swan* and the famous *Truelove*, killed tens of thousands of seals, polar bears, walruses, narwhals and whales, every harpooner becoming familiar with the expression: 'The chimney's on afire!' the ecstatic shout describing a whale blowing a column of blood. One ton of blubber yielded 200 gallons of oil but much of the carcase was abandoned, the 1823 log of the *Cumbrian* graphically recording the devastation: '… along the floe edge lay the dead bodies of hundreds of flensed whales, and the air for miles around was tainted with the foetor which arose from such masses of putridity.'

Over fishing, and the introduction of alternative fuels and pharmaceuticals sounded the death knell for the whale industry and by 1850 the Hull fleet had dwindled to just a few ships. The privations of the Crimean War, however, inflated whale product prices and in great optimism, the *Diana* left the Humber for the Arctic grounds. Tragically, she became a victim of the pack ice in the Davis Straits, drifting hopelessly for months before limping home with the body of her dead skipper, John Gravill, wrapped in a tarpaulin. A contemporary newspaper report records the scene: 'Coleridge's Ancient Mariner might have sailed in such a ghastly ship-battered and ice-crushed sails and cordage blown away, boats and spars cut up for fuel in the awful Arctic winter, the main deck a charnel house not to be described. The miserable scurvy-stricken, dysentery-worn men who looked over her bulwarks were a spectacle once seen, never to be forgotten ... Most pitiable of all were the ship's boys, their young faces wearing a strange aged look ...' After just one more cruise – she caught one solitary whale in the endeavour – the *Diana* was smashed to pieces on Donna Nook Sands. Her loss effectively marked the end of whale fishing in Hull.

Directions: *The trade was centred around the River Hull (access off M 62/A63 and Castle Street). The 'Greenland Yards', where most of the processing and manufacturing was carried out, were in the Cleveland Street area of the city, upstream from the wharves on High Street. Visit the Town Docks Museum on Queen Victoria Square to enjoy a treasure trove of Hull's whaling history. The tombstone of John Gravill is in Spring Bank Cemetery, Hull. Map Landranger 107 – Grid Ref: 097288.*

161. HULL: WHAT PRICE FISH?

A seemingly endless tide of fish once flooded through Hull, seasonal gluts of some species so reducing the price, that, on occasions, ship loads were sold as fertiliser. Hundreds of trawlers once brought in a harvest that fed the nation, our highly efficient railways delivering cargoes to all parts of the country, whole trainloads of nutritious, luxury food, whose cheapness and availability we can only dream about today, going to the now almost extinct fishmonger trade and the fast disappearing institutions that are our fried fish shops.

The rise of the Yorkshire trawler industry can be traced to 1843 when fishermen from the Devon port of Brixham sailed out of Hull to try their luck. Sixty miles out, they netted a miraculously heavy catch, the fame of the so-called Silver Pit fishing grounds soon attracting other vessels. In the twenty years between 1845 and 1865, Hull experienced a tremendous growth in its fishing industry. In 1863, 270 fishing smacks were registered to the trade, the gradual introduction of steam power increasing efficiency and the opportunities to fish long distance waters.

Over the years, the size and the sophistication of the vessels increased, crews making longer and more hazardous voyages to the inhospitable waters of the Barents Sea, and the grounds off Bear Island, Iceland and Greenland. Despite all the advances in propulsion and navigation and despite the availability of echo-sounders and radar, fatalities were a terrifying consequence of operating so far north, the sobering words of Herman Melville in *Moby Dick* chilling every Ahab's soul:

> *... however bravely man may brag of his science and skill, and however much, in a flattering future, that science and skill may augment; yet for ever and for ever, to the crack of doom, the sea will insult and murder him, and pulverise the stateliest, stiffest frigate he can make ...*

The most dangerous occupation in Britain claimed hundreds of lives. In October 1952, the Hull trawler *Norman* ran aground on the shores of Greenland. Twenty-one men abandoned ship and plunged into the icy water heading for a nearby rock that was just visible through the thick fog. Only one exceptionally good swimmer, a young deckie-learner, made it. In January 1955, the *Lorella* and the *Roderigo* succumbed to heavy icing and hurricane force winds, 40 Hull fishermen going down with their vessels. The most controversial tragedy in the port's trawling history, was the loss of the *Gaul* in February 1974. Some experts and relatives maintain to this day that she was secretly involved in surveillance work for the Royal Navy, spying on naval movements from the Russian port of Murmansk. What fate befell her is still the subject of fierce debate, but the reality was that she sank with all 34 hands off the coast of Norway.

Despite the heavy losses and successive reductions in catches that forced trawler owners to widen the geographical search for fish, trawling continued, only the devastating and progressively more violent consequences of the Cod Wars with the Icelandic fleet during the 1950s, 1960s and 1970s, effectively ending the industry. Before the dispute with the Icelanders began, over 430,000 tons of cod was consumed each year in Britain. With the gradual extension of fishing limits from two to 200 miles, fishing was severely curtailed, the end of the deep sea fishing industry effectively coming in June 1976 when a formal agreement was signed preventing British ships entering Icelandic territorial waters.

At a stroke of the pen, over 100 ships were tied up, and thousands of fishermen, bobbers, filleters, curers, fish merchants, fish product workers, ship repairers and dockers were laid idle, housewives and mothers in the fishing communities around Hessle Road, wringing their hands in despair.

Twenty-five years on, almost the entire trawler fleet has gone the way of the dodo, only one vessel, the *Arctic Corsair* (believed to be the last distant- water side trawler remaining in its original condition) surviving as a testament to the price of fish.

Directions: *The old docks area in Hull is accessed from the east from the M62 and the A63/Clive Sullivan Way. The docks have largely been converted, very imaginatively so, to commercial and landscape purposes. The history of the fishing industry is told in the Town Docks Museum in Queen Victoria Square (superb models including a 15 feet long model of the Boston Seafire). A former 'sidewinder' the* Arctic Corsair *has been preserved as the last of her line. She is anchored in the River Hull (behind Wilberforce House on High Street) and may be visited between April and October (see www.arctic-corsair.co.uk). Map Landranger 107 – Grid Refs: 095286 (Town Docks Museum); 103286 (berthed* Arctic Corsair*).*

162. RINGBROUGH: 'WE WILL FIGHT THEM ON THE BEACHES'

Examine Adolf Hitler's secret plans for his 'Operation Sealion' and you will see part of the Yorkshire coastline circled in red, all the low-cliffed beaches from Flamborough Head to Spurn Point coming within the purview of the Third Reich. Highly accessible to landing craft, these beaches would have been the springboard for an assault inland and they had to be protected, a feverish programme of anti-tank block and pill box building commencing at all the vulnerable points. Massively built in yards-thick concrete to withstand the German shells, many of these fortifications have succumbed to an even older enemy over the years, erosion by the sea, seeing many of the emplacements tumbling.

It is thought provoking indeed to look out as a raw recruit from one of the gun slits and try to imagine being a lookout here on a D-Day in reverse, witnessing the convergence of 1,000 ships. 'Sarge! Sarge! I know you told me not to wake you. But look at this!'

Part of our national heritage, these untried and unused war veterans have been largely forgotten and abandoned since the war years, although at Ringbrough, as a hopeful prelude to more substantial efforts elsewhere, some long overdue evaluation and conservation work is taking place.

Directions: *Ringbrough is between Withernsea and Hornsea. The access road goes east through Aldbrough (off the B1242) to East Newton and Ringbrough. The prominent look-out tower and battery is on Beacon Hill. Map Landranger 107 – Grid Ref: 277366.*

163. PATRINGTON: THE 'QUEEN OF HOLDERNESS'

One of the great granaries of England, prosperous Holderness once produced some of the finest ecclesiastical architecture in England, town and villagers in this land of sweeping corn, vying to build the tallest and grandest churches. Hedon, east of Hull erected its own contender for the crown in the shape of St Augustine's, which became known as the 'King of Holderness.' For unsurpassed beauty, however, it had to forfeit the majestic crown to Patrington, its church of St Patrick's – the 'Queen of Holderness' – being regarded by many as the best parish church in England.

This magnificent building took shape between the late thirteenth and early fourteenth centuries, at a time when many of the local inhabitants lived in simple cottages made of mud walls and thatch. A testimony to the productivity of the land, the wealth of the church and the faith and generosity of local people, particularly of the gentry, St Patrick's rises in serene perfection to culminate in a glorious spire, whose slender lines have been used as an aid to navigation on the Humber for centuries.

In addition to its spire, St Patrick's has some notable gargoyles, an exquisite reredos and an Easter Sepulchre.

Directions: *Patrington is about 15 miles south-east of Hull on the A1033/B1445. St Patrick's is set back a little from the main street, on the south-western side of the B1445. Map Landranger 107 – Grid Ref: 315226.*

164. EASINGTON: A RUSTIC CATHEDRAL

In its own way, the thatched barn at Easington is just as inspiring as York Minster. A massive upturned ark of a building ribbed with stout timbers, it has served the rural communities of Holderness for countless decades, this repository of life-giving corn and seed dating from the fourteenth century.

The barn's position next to the 800 year-old church of All Saints' is no coincidence. Erected for the donation of tithes – one tenth of local produce had to be given for the benefit of the church – it was a focal point of the local community, bulging and empty, reflecting good times and bad. Regularly damaged by storms, it has been progressively repaired by generations of villagers.

Directions: *Easington is near Spurn Head. About 25 miles south-east of Hull, it can be reached via the A1033 and the B1445. The barn is adjacent to the church in the centre of the village. Map Landranger 113 – Grid Ref: 399193.*

165. SPURN HEAD: WIPED FROM THE MAP

Attrition and aggregation make this lonesome peninsula one of the most changeable on earth, the constant attention of the waves and the scouring action of the Humber altering the shape of the promontory with every tide. Coastal erosion along the Yorkshire coast is amongst the worst in Europe, a strip of land some three-miles wide having disappeared since the time of the Romans. Gone are romantically named villages such as Auburn, Waxholme and Ravenser, a once busy port which existed on an island at the Humber mouth.

The Danes are said to have planted their raven standard here in 867, its unique trading position leading to rapid expansion into a prosperous port. It once returned two Members of Parliament, assisted in equipping the navy and had an annual 30-days fair. A thriving community of fishermen, ship builders and traders of all descriptions, it had two weekly markets, its reputation and prestige even coming to the notice of a young playwright, William Shakespeare referring to the port in King Henry VI and Richard II.

The port's strategic position was underlined when the Norwegian fleet assembled here prior to the Battle of Stamford Bridge in 1066, invasion forces also congregating in its harbour before Baliol's embarkation for Scotland in 1332. Ravenser twice more reached national prominence. In 1399, Bolingbroke, the future King Henry IV, landed in the port, Edward IV following suit in 1471. Soon afterwards, it was entirely swept away, 145 buildings disappearing during just one storm.

Directions: *The maritime outback of Spurn Head (a nature reserve) is reached by via Hull and Hedon going south-east along the A1033 and B1445.*

From the low lying dunes, you can look out to sea and wonder, but the whole peninsula has changed shape and position many times over the centuries and there is no certainty as to Ravenser's exact location. Other neighbouring villages within the arms of the protective beak, have also disappeared, the bones of Tharlsthorp, Frismersk, East Somert, Penisthorp, Orwithfleet, Sunthorp, Ald Ravenser, Ravenser Odd and Kilnsea, joining the rest in a littoral charnel house.

It would seem that the inhabitants of the old port managed to salvage some of their treasures. Two church bells are reputed to have gone to Easington and Aldbrough near Hornsea. The best link to Ravenser is the so-called Kilnsea Cross, recovered from the sea in 1818. Originally erected to commemorate Bolingbroke's landing, it was first re-erected in Kilnsea. From there it went to Burton Constable, finally ending up in the garden of Holyrood House in Baxtergate, Hedon. Map Landranger 113 – Grid Ref: 400110. ☛ ***See also 101 (Whitkirk) and 138 (Stamford Bridge)***